BAD GIRLS OF ANCIENT GREECE

LIZZY TIFFIN

MYTHS & LEGENDS
FROM THE BADDIES THAT STARTED IT ALL

BAD GIRLS OF ANCIENT GREECE

LIZZY TIFFIN

MYTHS & LEGENDS
FROM THE BADDIES THAT STARTED IT ALL

Harper North

HarperNorth
Windmill Green
24 Mount Street
Manchester M2 3NX

A division of
HarperCollins*Publishers*
1 London Bridge Street
London SE1 9GF

www.harpercollins.co.uk

HarperCollins*Publishers*
Macken House
39/40 Mayor Street Upper
Dublin 1
D01 C9W8, Ireland

First published by HarperNorth in 2024

1 3 5 7 9 10 8 6 4 2

This book is contains FSC™ certified paper and other controlled
sources to ensure responsible forest management.

For more information visit: www.harpercollins.co.uk/green

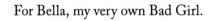

For Bella, my very own Bad Girl.

Contents

Contents

Contents

Contents

Contents

Introduction

I declare
That later on,
Even in an age unlike our own,
Someone will remember who we are.
—**Sappho**

Stories of the mythological heroes are well known and plentiful. Who hasn't heard the legends of Heracles and the labours that made him famous? Who wouldn't recognise the iconic image of Zeus, king of the gods, wielding his mighty thunderbolt? But what about the women who stood beside (or more often than not, behind) these men?

As the patriarchy often dictates, wives, mothers, and daughters are the secondary characters in tales of adventure and heroism. But the ladies of lore were frequently the spearheads or puppet mistresses behind some of the most well-known tales. Often just as badass and interesting as their male counterparts, their accounts can often be overlooked.

Bad Girls of Ancient Greece is a deep dive into the lives of these wild, weird, and wonderful women. You'll find the 'better-known' characters here, like the snake-haired Gorgon, Medusa, but also the more obscure, like Arachne, who bravely stood up for what she believed in, even if it meant going against a powerful deity.

Woven with tales of drama, betrayal, and revenge, there are also sparkling gems of happy endings, true love, and perpetual horniness. Just like the men in their lives, these women are complicated and sometimes flawed, but tend to face much harsher punishments for their mistakes and indiscretions because of their gender.

Despite accounts of Greek mythology dating back more than 2,000 years, the stories are still being shared and enjoyed today, and the recent rise of retellings has proved they are just as popular as ever. When it comes to the initial narratives, though, the tales of antiquity can seem a little daunting. Classical history shouldn't feel like a closed club where the password is a Latin phrase that you can barely pronounce – it's an interesting, exciting, and colourful world we should all be able to engage in and enjoy.

This guide hopes to make the stories of the bad girls more accessible. By discussing these women through a modern lens, we can better understand and appreciate the creative writings they emerged from.

These chronicles have been passed down over thousands of years, often expanding, and sometimes veering off into alternative endings. This book tries to follow the narratives that best complement the stories beside one another. Or, honestly, whichever version is most interesting. These tales are so rich, so bloated with titbits, so intricate in their very roots that they sometimes shoot off into different stories and come back again. Because of this, mythology doesn't always iron out into a neat timeline, and one story may contradict another. You do not need any prior knowledge of mythology to read this; as long as you've got an interest in the eccentric and exciting, you'll get on just fine. Pronunciations have been added to the start of each chapter – these have been given as a guide (as with everything else in myth, pronunciations can depend on the source!)

These women had to face the patriarchal abuse of power relentlessly, including sexual assault, objectification and general sexism in every form imaginable. Despite their experiences and the dangers they faced simply for being female, they demonstrated cunning, wit, strength and far outdid others' expectations. These tales highlight their complexities, brilliance, and ability to just be 'human'.

So, hear the stories and learn the lessons of these bad girls, and see how, even before time itself, we women were causing our own chaos.

1

Wayward Wives

Happy wife, happy life?
Not if you're married to
these ladies . . .

GAIA (*guy-a*)

Gaia was the mother of the world, and was born spontaneously from nothingness. Her name means 'earth', and that's what she was thought to be.

At some point, living alone became tiresome, so she decided to create herself a beau. Gaia made Uranus, personification of the sky, and the new power-couple got straight down to producing offspring. To begin, she gave birth to the first generation of gods. These were the Titans: Oceanus, Coeus, Crius, Hyperion, Iapetos, Theia, Rhea, Themis, Mnemosyne, Phoebe, Tethys, and Cronus. Then, she had the Ourea (mountains), Pontus (sea), a trio of one-eyed Cyclopes, and the Hecatoncheires (giants with fifty heads and one hundred hands each).

Where Gaia was literally the world, it would be Uranus who ruled upon it, commencing an eternity of men staking their claim to Gaia. Uranus hated his children and was terrified that they would eventually overpower him, so he pushed them back into Gaia's womb (which isn't as snug as you'd assume, when you consider she's 'the world'). However, ample space or not, Gaia eventually tired of her partner's lunacy. She forged a silver sickle, the blade so sharp that it could cut through stone as if it were butter, if butter had been invented yet. Sickle in hand, Gaia asked her womb-dwelling children to stand with her to take down their father. The thing is, though, Uranus was pretty intimidating, and they weren't super keen to get on his bad side. Only one agreed: Cronus, the youngest of the Titans, who hid in wait for Uranus to put the moves on Gaia. When he did, Cronus used the sickle to slice his dad's manhood clean off. While Uranus (probably) ran around screaming in agony, Cronus freed his siblings. Last out were the Cyclopes and Hecatoncheires, but Cronus took one look at them and thought, *nope, don't fancy ever going head-to-head with them*, and banished them to Tartarus, a dark abyss in the Underworld.

From the gaping wound, Uranus' blood fell onto Gaia and impregnated her again. This time, she birthed the Fates (responsible for spinning the threads of mortal life), the Giants, and numerous Meliads (the first nymphs of the world).

With his father otherwise indisposed, Cronus became the new king of the gods. Unfortunately for everyone, the apple didn't fall far from the tree – Cronus inherited Uranus' erratic temperament and paranoia. Fearing rebellion, he imprisoned all of his Titan brethren and took to swallowing his own children whole, lest they attempt to usurp him. These consumed kiddies were the Olympians.

Rhea, Cronus' wife, went to Gaia for help, and together they came up with a genius plan to save her children. Next time Cronus demanded Rhea hand over the latest newborn, she would instead present him with a stone, swaddled as if it were a baby. The plan worked like a charm, and the unswallowed baby (Zeus) would grow up to free his siblings by tricking Cronus into drinking a potion that made him vomit them back up. And so, a battle began that would be known as the Titanomachy, a legendary war between the Titans and the Olympians. The battle raged for ten years, and was earth-shaking. Literally – the power of it moved earth as they knew it, and from the cracks and crevices came new life in the form of personifications (hundreds of minor gods and goddesses representing things like certain types of wind, plants etc). As both camps were immortal, it was starting to look like an eternal war. Once again, wise Gaia would be the one with the answers. She advised Zeus to free the Cyclopes and Hecatoncheires from Tartarus and form an alliance with them. With these beasties on their side, the Olympians were quickly able to gain the upper hand, and they were victorious. Now, Zeus became the third and final ruler of the gods. He split the kingdom into three realms, sharing them out between himself and his two brothers: Zeus would rule the heavens and earth, Poseidon could have the sea, and Hades would govern the Underworld.

Although she supported his rise, Gaia didn't just blindly go along with everything Zeus said. She challenged him often, even going against him in the Gigantomachy, a war between the Giants and the Olympians. The Giants (and Gaia) lost this battle, and as revenge, she mated with Tartarus (who, like her, was both a god *and* a place) to create Typhon, a fire-breathing dragon that caused all kinds of issues for the king of the gods.

By this point, she was ready to accept Zeus as her king, and stop actively making his life difficult. Many years later, she'd attend his wedding to Hera, bringing the couple a gift that would inadvertently set another anarchic event in motion . . .

APHRODITE (*aff-ro-die-tee*)

Arguably one of the best-known goddesses, Aphrodite was born when the blood of Uranus' castrated genitals fell upon the sea. She emerged from the waters on the coast of Cythera, fully grown, stark naked and drop-dead gorgeous.

Aphrodite was the goddess of love, beauty, sexuality, and fertility. Insatiable but unattainable, she enamoured gods and mortals alike. When she arrived on Mount Olympus, the inhabitants began drooling and their eyes pulsated with cartoon hearts. This worried Zeus greatly – he knew the trouble such desire could cause. In order to dampen the fires of his comrades' passions, he immediately decreed Aphrodite be married to Hephaestus, the god of fire and metalworking, and blacksmith to the gods.

Now, beauty may very well be in the eye of the beholder, but Aphrodite was truly disgusted by Hephaestus, with his unkempt hair, limping gait, and hunched shoulders from hours stooping over his workbench. Initially, Hephaestus was ecstatic at the match, crafting Aphrodite exquisite jewellery and other trinkets as gifts. In comparison, Aphrodite was resentful to be paired with such an unsightly specimen and fought the god constantly. It wasn't long before poor Hephaestus got the hint and realised this wasn't going to be the happy marriage he'd hoped for.

A bad match from the beginning, their union was filled with scandal. Aphrodite spent a lot of time having various affairs, most notably with the god of war, Ares. Not many people liked Ares because of his, well, *personality*, but Aphrodite thought him the ultimate brooding babe. Luckily for them, they had plenty of time to canoodle, as Hephaestus spent most of his time working in the forge, creating weaponry, armour, and general godly knick-knacks.

The affair would come to be revealed, though, when the sun god Helios spied the couple while completing his daily ride carrying the sun across the skies. Helios spilled the tea to Hephaestus, who hatched a plan to catch them in the act. He fashioned a fine, bronzed net and set it above their marital bed, rigging it to fall down on the sneaky pair once they were in place. Safe to say, Aphrodite and Ares were trapped in a *very* compromising position. Hephaestus then invited all the gods into their bedchamber to point and laugh, which they did with gusto.

Despite her public shaming, Aphrodite wasn't particularly put off, as she went on to have eight children with Ares, including the Erotes (gods representing different aspects of love and sex). In fact, she bedded and bred with most of her Olympian buddies over time, so maybe Hephaestus recognised that she just couldn't be tamed.

Although happy to come and go with Ares (and many, *many* others), Aphrodite was not as accepting when the golden sandal was on the other foot. When Eos, goddess of the dawn, slept with Ares, Aphrodite cursed her with an insatiable horniness for mortals, and wiped her lover's memory of anything to do with the minor deity.

At some point, Aphrodite found herself pregnant after a whirlwind romance with Dionysus, the god of wine. Queen Hera, who was jealous of Aphrodite's beauty, applied a potion to her pregnant stomach to ensure that the child would be born hideous. The baby was called Priapus, and as well as being rather displeasing to look at, he had a constant erection, a potbelly, and a lolling, bulbous tongue.

Disgusted by her unsightly offspring, Aphrodite abandoned the child on earth and returned to Mount Olympus.

She didn't keep her extramarital affairs to the divine, either – Aphrodite bedded at least two mortals – one of them a Trojan man named Anchises. Before him, Aphrodite was quick to laugh at her fellow divinities over the knots they tied themselves in with their pursuits of measly mortals, but she was laughing on the other side of her face when Zeus used his own power to cause her to fall in love with Anchises. Aphrodite appeared to him as a mortal, hoping her feelings would be reciprocated. Of course, he was overwhelmed with desire at the mere sight of her, and the couple made love. With that itch scratched, the goddess revealed her divinity, telling him she'd bear him a noble son if he kept their liaison a secret. Unfortunately, Anchises couldn't hold his own water and immediately blabbed. Zeus, despite being the cause of this mess, wasn't happy with Aphrodite being disrespected, so he struck her lover with a thunderbolt that blinded him. Anchises was never able to see their son, Aeneas, who would grow up to be a great hero.

Despite Aphrodite being a less than enthusiastic mother, she did go out of her way to protect her children. During the Trojan War, she constantly protected Aeneas from harm, even going as far as using her own body to shield him from blows.

Her other mortal beau is perhaps more well-known: Adonis. In not exactly the typical start to an epic romance, Aphrodite found him abandoned as a baby boy, swaddled under a myrrh tree. She took him to the Underworld and asked the queen, Persephone, to raise him. It's worth mentioning that most of the Underworld wasn't the dark pit of hell we may assume it was. While there were certainly places dedicated to eternal punishment (Tartarus), there was also the Elysian Fields (a utopia for extraordinary souls to 'live' in bliss), and the Asphodel Meadows (where the more ordinary but still deserving individuals came to rest). Add in the kingdom where Persephone and Hades lived and ruled, and the Underworld would be as good a place as any to raise a child. When Aphrodite returned to visit Adonis years later, she found he'd grown into a fine specimen of a man (clue's in the name) and promptly fell in love with him. Persephone, who'd also fallen for Adonis over the years, was absolutely not down for sharing, and Zeus himself had to step in to harmonise the situation. He decreed that Adonis would divide his time into thirds – one third with Aphrodite on Mount Olympus, another in the Underworld with Persephone, and the final doing whatever he liked. He chose to spend the portion of his 'free' time with Aphrodite, and preferred her company so much that eventually he was loath to return to the Underworld with Persephone.

It's said that Aphrodite loved Adonis more tenderly and passionately than she loved anyone. After a few blissful years together, Adonis was attacked by a wild boar sent by the jealous Ares while on a hunt. As Adonis lay dying in Aphrodite's arms, anemone flowers sprung from the ground where her tears spilled. These beautiful flowers bloom for only a brief time, much like Adonis' short life, before they're blown away by the wind.

It's well known that Aphrodite gave generously to those who favoured her, but she punished with the same fervour. Spare a thought for the women of Lemnos who, in the goddess's eyes, hadn't paid her sufficient tribute. She cursed them to smell so bad that their husbands wouldn't go near them, and instead the men found their jollies with imported Thracian slave girls. In retaliation, the women murdered the entire male population (fair), as well as the slaves (unfair).

HERA (*hee-ra*)

As the seventh and final wife of Zeus, Hera was the ruling queen of Olympus and presided over marriage, childbirth, and family.

She may be best remembered for her extreme jealousy and epic vengeance, but she wasn't always like that. Hera actually wasn't keen on Zeus in the beginning, even going as far as rejecting him – quite a ballsy move against the ruler of everything. She was well aware of his playboy tendencies, and he proposed to her many times over hundreds of years to no avail. In fact, he only got her to agree to marriage in the end by tricking her. Hera loved animals, so when Zeus appeared to her as a distressed cuckoo, she didn't think twice about comforting him. As she snuggled the bird-Zeus to her breast, he shifted into his true form and raped her. Ashamed, she agreed to marry him to save the scandal. That said, Hera would annually bathe in the spring of Kanathos, which supposedly restored her virginity.

Their wedding was the first 'formal' union in existence and was a huge occasion. It was held in the garden of the Hesperides, and all the gods attended and brought lavish gifts. It's said that the celebrations lasted around three thousand years (imagine the hangover), and it seems attendance was non-negotiable as when the nymph Chelone refused the invitation, the couple transformed her into a tortoise.

Once the festivities were over, however, Zeus resumed business as usual, immediately on the lookout for his next consort. Hera spent a lot of time stewing over her husband's whereabouts and spying on him, and before long she was completely miserable in her marriage. She noticed that the other Olympians were growing tired of Zeus, too. She encouraged the others to join her in a revolt, and Apollo, Athena, and Poseidon agreed to spearhead it with her.

They drugged Zeus and bound him tightly to his bed. Once he was out of the way, the rest of the Olympians argued fiercely over who would now rule the heavens. Unfortunately for them, one of the Hecatoncheires overheard the dispute. The hundred-handers still felt indebted to him after he freed them from Tartarus, so they sneaked into Zeus' bedchamber to undo the knots that bound him. The Olympians fell on their knees and begged for his forgiveness, but the worst of his rage was directed at Hera. Hanging her from the heavens by golden chains, he left her to think long and hard about what she'd done.

The next morning, Zeus agreed to release her, as long as she swore that she would never rebel against him again. Desperate for the agony to be over, she agreed, and from then on turned her sadness and frustrations towards his consorts, instead. Hera became notorious for her vengeance against any woman who dared to even look at her husband.

She was a faithful wife to Zeus, but didn't really have a choice – most gods and mortals wouldn't touch her with a ten-foot bargepole, for fear of repercussions from her spouse. For the one who did dare, he met a very sticky end.

Ixion, a king of the Lapiths (a tribe of Thessaly), was invited up to Mount Olympus by Zeus to meet the gods. To be invited was a huge honour, but Ixion was an idiot, and repaid Zeus by making eyes at his wife. Despite her unhappiness in her marriage, Hera would not be wooed by him. When Zeus got wind of the shifty desires of his guest, he decided to fashion a cloud in Hera's image, leaving it to be found by Ixion to prove his suspicions. The foolish human made sweet, sweet love to his cloudy consort, and was immediately and ruthlessly expelled from Mount Olympus. Zeus ordered for him to be bound to a flying wheel of fire, leaving him to spin for all eternity.

For his part, Zeus wasn't concerned by the marital rules and regs applying to himself. He had many (MANY) affairs, and Hera made sure that the women and their offspring always paid for it. As a rule, Hera hated all of Zeus' illegitimate children, but she held a special kind of loathing for the hero Heracles. To rub salt into the wound that was her husband constantly impregnating other women, the name Heracles literally translates to 'glory of Hera'. When Heracles' mother, Alcmene, went into labour, Zeus announced that a child born on that particular day would become a high king. Hera was displeased to say the least; it certainly wasn't one of *her* children due to be born. She made Zeus swear an oath that this pronouncement was true, then she floated down to earth and delayed the birth of Heracles, generally inconveniencing his mother and casting doubt on Herc's destiny.

When Heracles was still a baby, Zeus managed to trick Hera into feeding the child from her own breast. When she realised it was her mini-nemesis suckling, she wrenched him away – the movement caused the flow of her breastmilk to shoot across the sky, creating the Milky Way.

When he reached adulthood, Hera inflicted a madness on Heracles that would drive him to kill his own family. On top of this, she was also on hand to make sure his labours (twelve of them, assigned to him to atone for said killings) were as difficult as possible. She varied between small acts of annoyance, such as sending crabs to nibble at his feet while he fought the Lernaean Hydra, and larger ones, like sending a whole flood to stop him herding the cattle of Geryon. Some say the adversaries made their peace at some point, when Heracles saved the goddess from a giant that wanted to have his way with her. She's even thought to have grown so fond of him in the end that she offered her daughter, Hebe, as his bride.

Another particularly hated love child of her husband's was Dionysus, the god of wine. We'll find out how Hera punished his mother later, but even after her vengeance, she never warmed to him. It's said that she wouldn't even let herself try the vino that he brought to the world, despite her fellow deities embracing it heartily.

Hera wasn't afraid to challenge her husband, and their disagreements were often renowned. On one occasion, the couple were arguing fiercely over which gender experienced more sexual pleasure when doing the deed, with Zeus being adamant that women got the most out of it, and Hera convinced it was the men. They decided to consult the mortal Tiresias on the matter, who had spent some time as a woman as punishment for aggravating Hera (as a young man, he hit a pair of mating snakes with a stick, and Hera had decided this act was wicked enough to warrant such a punishment). Tiresias confirmed Zeus was correct and that a woman's pleasure was far greater. Annoyed at losing the argument, Hera blinded Tiresias. Zeus, to thank him for siding with him, gave him the gift of prophecy, and from then he became a prominent seer.

PROCRIS (*pro-criss*)

Thanks to the lustful curse of Aphrodite, dawn goddess Eos fancied herself a piece of the mortal Cephalus. Eos abducted him from his home and carried him off to hers, but Cephalus had no desire to be a sexual plaything for Eos and spent most of his time mooning over his wife, Procris. His constant whining became rather tedious, so Eos agreed to release him, but not before planting some seeds of doubt in his head, hinting that Procris had been unfaithful in his absence.

Cephalus' jealousy was piqued, so he disguised himself for his return and put the moves on Procris. She'd actually been faithful to him the whole time, but this new man was tempting (perhaps he reminded her of her missing husband) and she almost gave in.

This brief hesitation was all that Cephalus needed, who shed his costume and went ballistic. Scared and ashamed, Procris fled to the woods, joining the gang of the hunting goddess Artemis. She would come to miss her husband, so decided to return home and take her chances. She brought with her two gifts as peace offerings, given to her by Artemis, who wanted to help. The first was a spear that always found its target. The second, a dog that always caught its prey, named Laelaps.

Cephalus loved his presents and immediately forgave his wife. They lived happily for a while, until another test of faith came along – a local gossip told Procris that Cephalus was having an affair, as she'd heard him calling another woman's name in the woods.

Procris couldn't believe this – after the scene he made upon her hesitation, he had the gall to cheat on *her*? She followed him into the woods during a hunting trip and hid in a bush, waiting for him to slip up. Mid-hunt, Cephalus was feeling a little sweaty, so he called on Aura, goddess of the breeze, to send some of the good stuff to cool him down. Realising the gossip had probably heard this and mistaken it for the name of a lover, the relieved Procris emerged from the bushes to join her husband, thinking he'd laugh at the mix-up.

Cephalus mistook the rustling noise for prey, throwing his spear in the sound's general direction. Being the spear that never misses, it found its target in Procris' stomach. She bled out in his arms, as Eos likely watched on with a triumphant smile.

MEDEA (*med-ee-a*)

Medea was a powerful sorcerer princess, born to King Aeëtes of Colchis. Located on the coast of the Black Sea, Colchis was rich in resources, but considered rather barbaric under the king's reign.

Prince Jason (and his rag-tag group of friends and comrades, known as 'the Argonauts') came to Colchis to take Aeëtes' Golden Fleece, so he could claim his own throne in Iolcus. Medea's father was seemingly happy to hand it over, if only their leader completed a series of tasks first.

Medea, who was a practicing priestess of the witch Hecate, fell in love with the handsome Jason as soon as she saw him. Knowing how sneaky her father could be, she warned Jason not to trust Aeëtes and offered to help him. She had a condition of her own, though: Jason must agree to marry her, and take her away from Colchis. He agreed to her conditions, recognising that her magics would benefit him greatly.

Aeëtes set Jason three tasks – the first, to plough a field using fire-breathing oxen. Medea gave Jason an ointment to apply to himself and his weapons, so the fire would have no effect on him.

Next, Jason was told to take a bag of dragon teeth and sow them into the field he'd ploughed. Medea knew that from the teeth an army would spring up, immediately attacking whoever they encountered. She advised Jason to throw a stone amongst them. He did so, which alerted them to each other's presence, and they began fighting between themselves, ultimately killing one another.

Enraged that the pesky youth seemed to be sailing through his impossible tasks (and suspecting he had some inside help), Aeëtes now plotted to kill Jason. Their time running out, Medea led her fancy-man to the sacred tree where the fleece hung, protected by a sleepless dragon. She crafted a potion that induced deep slumber – Jason was able to sneak into the dragon's lair and kill it. With the Argonauts assembled, the pair fled Colchis.

Aeëtes was hot on their tail though, unwilling to let his daughter and the fleece go. To slow him down, Medea killed and dismembered her brother, Absyrtus, flinging pieces of him into the sea. She knew that her father would have to stop, collect the parts of his son, and give him a proper burial, allowing them sufficient time to flee.

Medea and the Argonauts would stop off to visit her aunt, the witch Circe, on their way home – she was a powerful witch herself and could purify the couple of their sins. Circe agreed, without actually knowing what they wanted to be purified for. Afterwards, Medea cherry-picked parts of her tale, but left the really nasty stuff out so that Circe wouldn't judge her too harshly. Her aunt wasn't fooled – she read between the lines, and although she promised to not get in their way, she demanded that they leave her island immediately.

No matter! They were on the home stretch, briefly stopping off in Scheria to get married. Sailing near to Iolcus, they were blocked by Talos, a giant, bronzed guardian of Crete, who began hurling rocks at the ship. Talos had one vein through his entire body that was stoppered by a single nail – Medea got his attention and convinced him that she'd make him immortal, if he would first remove the nail. He took it out willingly, but quickly bled to death.

Now home, they learned that Jason's father was very ill and likely to die soon. Medea couldn't bear the thought of her love losing someone so dear to him, so offered her magics to help. She drained her father-in-law's body of all its blood, then mixed it together with herbs. Once she returned the blood back to him, he was completely reinvigorated.

King Pelias, Jason's uncle and the current usurping king of Iolcus, had now gone back on his promise to give Jason the throne should he secure the Golden Fleece. Unfortunately for him, he was also in very bad health. His daughters, who loved him dearly, begged Medea to do for him what she had done for Jason's father.

Medea wasn't one to offer help for the sake of it, especially to someone who'd double-crossed her beau. Rather than outright refuse, though, Medea had a much nastier comeback. She told the daughters that for her magic to work, they had to chop their father into little pieces. Once these pieces were placed into a pot, she could make a potion that would allow him to spring up, good as new. The girls excitedly got to chopping, and Medea got to running before anyone realised what she'd done. The girls were left with nothing but dad stew.

Now exiled for killing the king, Jason and Medea fled to Corinth, where they ruled and lived for a further ten years, having many children. Over time, though, it seems that Medea's barbarism and her penchant for dark magic had become quite the issue for her husband. What's more, where the Corinthians loved their hero king, the same couldn't be said for Medea, who scared them and creeped them out in equal measure. And so, with his new power and riches, thanks in large part to Medea, Jason got to thinking he deserved someone a bit more palatable to rule by his side.

Jason unceremoniously dumped and banished the enchantress in order to marry Glauce, a former princess of Corinth. Medea was heartbroken, but, refusing to suck it up – as was expected of women at the time – she vowed revenge. Medea decided to send Glauce a wedding present. She boxed up a beautiful dress that she had steeped in poison and signed it with no hard feelings. On touching the material, Glauce was set on fire. For good measure, Medea also killed two of her own children to Jason. Her broken heart temporarily salved by this act of retribution, Medea fled to Athens. There, she married once again with Aegeus, the ruler of the city. They had one son together, who they named Medus.

At some point, Aegeus' long-lost son, the hero Theseus, came to the city. Aegeus had never met him, but Medea knew exactly who he was and she couldn't risk him claiming the throne that was her own son's birthright. Medea planned to poison Theseus, but Aegeus recognised his son by the coat of arms on his weapon, and at the very last second knocked the toxic tipple from his hand.

Medea fled once again, with Medus in tow, this time back to Colchis. The pair would end up separated en route, with Medus arriving first and being immediately imprisoned by the current usurping king (who had no idea of his true identity). A famine then hit Colchis, and while the people were in the throes of sickness, Medea arrived and approached the king under the guise of being a priestess of Artemis. She told him that she could help lift this plague, but she'd need to make a sacrifice of his prisoner to do so. The king didn't see the harm, so allowed it. Secretly, she slipped Medus a sword and filled him in on what had become of his grandfather at the hands of the king, urging him to take revenge. Depending on accounts, either Medea or Medus stabbed the monarch to death, and restored Aeëtes to the throne, apparently all antics forgiven on both sides.

PASIPHAË (*pa-sif-ay-ee*)

Queen Pasiphaë of Crete had powerful magic in her blood, so when she discovered that her husband was being unfaithful, she cast a spell that had him ejaculating snakes, scorpions, and centipedes into the lady-gardens of his consorts. It killed the women, and it can't have been much fun for Minos, either.

As well as not being able to keep the promise of fidelity to his wife, Minos struggled with keeping his word to the gods, too. He had agreed to sacrifice his best bull every year to honour Poseidon, which he did until it was no longer convenient – this particular year, the herd produced a spectacular bull with a beautiful white coat. Minos wanted the beast for himself, so sneakily swapped it out for his second-best bull. Poseidon immediately knew he'd been short-changed, punishing Minos by inflicting a burning desire for the white bull on his wife.

Pasiphaë couldn't rest until she copulated with the animal and called upon the inventor Daedalus to help her execute her plan. He created a hollowed-out wooden cow, covered in real cowhide, leaving a hole in the back of it for . . . well, you know. Pasiphaë climbed into its empty centre and assumed the position.

The contraption was certainly lifelike enough for the white bull, who got to work doing what bulls do, and Pasiphaë's bovine-horniness was sated. From the bizarre union, she would birth a monster with the body of a human, and the head and tail of a bull, commonly known as the Minotaur.

Minos was deeply ashamed of his wife's actions (despite the curse being his fault) but decided that instead of having the bull-child murdered, he'd use it to his advantage. The royal family called on Daedalus once again, this time to erect a labyrinth in which the beast would be kept.

The Cretan royal fam had beef with the people of Athens after they'd killed their son, so to punish them, Minos ordered that seven sons and seven daughters of Athens would be sent to Crete every year, to be fed to the Minotaur. For an added bit of cruelty, the sacrifices would be dropped into the labyrinth that housed the beast to make a game of it. For Pasiphaë's part, she wasn't particularly maternal with any of her children, so it's unlikely she put up any real objections to the imprisonment of her son.

ASTYDAMEIA
(*ass-tee-dame-ee-a*)

When King Peleus accidentally killed his father-in-law during a hunt, he sought purification from Acastus, the ruler of Iolcus. Though purification was usually done in preparation for people approaching the gods or during funeral rites, it could also be done to expel blood-guilt as in Medea's story with Circe. Purification was a complex ritual usually involving a sacrifice, which the Ancient Greeks believed was sufficient to cleanse a person's soul. This meant that they could avoid a banishment or other punishments on the back of such crimes.

Acastus, happy to help out, invited Peleus into his palace, where he caught the lustful eye of Acastus' wife, Queen Astydameia. The queen was mad with desire for the hero, and it didn't take long for her to shoot her shot once her husband was out of the way. Peleus, though, was completely uninterested and rebuffed her advances. Furious, Astydameia penned a letter to Peleus' wife telling her that her husband had left her, and was to marry Sterope, Astydameia's daughter. After reading the letter, the woman was heartbroken and immediately hanged herself.

Still not satisfied with the damage, the queen went to her husband and falsely accused Peleus of attempting to rape her. Acastus believed his wife wholeheartedly, but worried about breaching the rules of *xenia*, which was a custom that forbade hosts from harming their guests for fear of facing the wrath of the Furies (vengeance goddesses that lived in the Underworld). To get around this, the king invited Peleus on a hunting trip, but abandoned him once they were in the depths of the woods, knowing he was likely to be picked up and killed by the vicious centaurs (mythical creatures with the upper body of a man, and the lower body of a horse, known for their lairy and violent tendencies) that resided in the area. Luckily for Peleus, Chiron, the one peaceful centaur, was on hand to help him, along with the messenger god Hermes. He returned to Iolcus unscathed, plundered the city in revenge, and tore Astydameia limb from limb.

ILIONE (*ill-ee-own*)

A few years prior to the kick-off of the Trojan War, King Priam and Queen Hecuba of Troy gifted their daughter Ilione to their neighbour and friend, King Polymestor of Thrace. Thrace was a staunch ally of Troy, so the marriage would be advantageous on both ends, further securing their bond to each other.

Ilione was the eldest of Priam and Hecuba's many children, and by the time war came, her parents had asked her to keep and protect her baby brother, Polydorus. This was a sort of insurance policy, as it meant if Troy did fall, there would be at least one surviving prince to rebuild their city. They had also given the royal couple a stack of gold to keep aside for the boy, to be used for a possible restoration. Ilione had by now borne Polymestor a son, who was around the same age as Polydorus. Although her arranged marriage was a sound political decision on the surface, Ilione knew from watching the power-dynamics of her own family to trust no one. With this in mind, she switched the children, raising her own son as though she were his sister, and presenting Polydorus as her own child. She even changed their names, thinking, should the worst happen and one of the babes meet a nasty end, the other would still be around to claim the Trojan throne and carry on her family's legacy. Polymestor was none the wiser that the son who had grown up in his own home literally had a different face all of a sudden.

Time passed, Troy fell, and Polymestor chose to kill his supposed brother-in-law so he could keep the gold for himself. Of course, he had actually killed his *own* son - the real Polydorus was currently travelling, and on his journey consulted an oracle for guidance. He was told that his city had fallen, his father killed, and his mother enslaved. Horrified that something terrible had happened in his absence, Polydorus returned immediately to the very much intact Thrace. Confused, he went to Ilione and relayed to her what the oracle had said.

Ilione, knowing it was time to come clean, told Polydorus who he really was, and advised him to take revenge on her husband. Very much on the same page, he slaughtered Polymestor. Later, unable to live with the grief of losing most of her family, Ilione killed herself.

RHEA (*ree-a*)

As the mother of the majority of the Olympians, Rhea was quite the force to be reckoned with. After she put a stop to her brother-husband, Cronus, swallowing their children, she became even more so.

While baby Zeus was busy growing up and preparing to take over as king of everything, Rhea had some time to spare. So she turned her attention to finding a new abode – she'd had her eye on the prime real estate that was Mount Olympus for a while, but it was currently inhabited by fellow godly couple, Ophion and Eurynome. No matter, Rhea thought, and pulled her husband along to the great big mountain in the sky to acquire it by force. Rhea was particularly skilled in the art of wrestling, and Eurynome was quickly floored by the Titaness, while Cronus KO'd Ophion without so much as breaking a sweat. The unlucky pair were thrown from Olympus into the sea, and Rhea started picking out paint samples.

That's not to say Rhea and Cronus' marriage was a happy one (as evidenced by the whole 'him eating her children' saga, and the eventual plan of hers to overthrow him), and as Zeus matured, Cronus continued to be a general scoundrel to all, especially his wife. When Rhea caught him in the act with his concubine Philyra, Cronus simply transformed himself into a horse and galloped away from the scene, neighing, 'it wasn't me!' Philyra would fall pregnant to the god, birthing the man/horse hybrid Chiron. Creeped out at the sight of this mutant child, she abandoned him. Afterwards, Philyra begged the higher gods to transform her into something else so that she didn't have to think about the unpleasant child she had given birth to. The gods granted her wish by making her into a linden tree.

Eventually, after the Olympians had beat Cronus and his cronies during the Titanomachy, Rhea would be able to start the next phase of her life. She raised the god Dionysus, gifting him a magical amethyst that allowed him to enjoy as much of his beloved wine as he wanted without feeling the effects of the alcohol (and, perhaps more helpfully, the *after*-effects). As Dionysus grew into a man, Rhea enjoyed partying it up with him and his followers, particularly delighting in the feverish dancing that they were known for.

IPHIMEDIA (*if-ee-meed-ee-ya*)

When a son of Poseidon, Aloeus, married the mortal Iphimedia, he wasn't expecting her to be quite so interested in his family tree. The truth was, Iphimedia had always had a bit of a *thing* for the sea king, and she would do anything to get closer to him, even if that meant marrying his son.

Every day, Iphimedia would walk up and down the beach, purring a prayer that Poseidon would hear what was truly in her heart and come to her. Poseidon, who usually needed no persuasion to bed anyone, really wasn't keen, and left his daughter-in-law to want.

Finally accepting that he wasn't coming, Iphimedia sat at the shore and poured ocean water into her lap. Perhaps the god now felt a bit sorry for her, or maybe he was just sick to the back teeth of hearing her incessant prayers, but he allowed the seawater to impregnate her with his twins, Otus and Ephialtes. It's unknown whether Aloeus knew of their true parentage (that would make him Otus and Ephialtes' brother), but they were referred to as the Alodae after him, which was a common custom in Ancient Greece for the collective children of a man. Otus and Ephialtes grew very rapidly due to their divine blood and had reached the height of thirty feet by the time they were nine years old.

To Aloeus, she had a beautiful daughter called Pancratis. When Pancratis was of age, mother and daughter travelled to partake in an orgy to celebrate Dionysus, which isn't weird at all. While they were there, Pancratis attracted the attentions of a group of pirates, who abducted both ladies and took them to Naxos. Here, they were given to the king of the island and his lieutenant as wives. Just as they were settling into their new lives, Iphimedia's twins arrived. In an epic rescue mission to retrieve their mother and half-sibling, they killed the captors and returned home as one big happy family.

PHAEDRA (*fee-dra*)

One of the daughters of Pasiphaë and Minos, Phaedra, became queen of Athens when she married the hero Theseus. To him, she had two sons, Acamas and Demophon. While the boys were still small, the family had a visit from Hippolytus, Theseus' grown-up son from another marriage.

Hippolytus was a devoted follower of the virgin goddess Artemis and had decided many years ago to take a vow of lifelong chastity in her honour. It was even said that the youth avoided images of sexual relations, finding the whole thing disgusting beyond measure.

Phaedra couldn't help but feel the pull of attraction to Hippolytus. This could have been down to a little intervention from Aphrodite, taking issue with Hippolytus for being so scornful of everything she stood for, but Phaedra had also become rather unenamoured with her aging husband as of late.

Phaedra went back and forth over what to do for a while. Her feelings for her stepson occupied her every waking thought, but she'd always been a good queen and wife, understanding her duties as a woman. Giving in to these feelings would risk everything – her throne, her family, and her status, and she was no stranger to the ramifications of taboo love – her mother was Pasiphaë, after all.

In the end, she decided that she couldn't fight the connection. Running down to the stables where Hippolytus spent most of his time, she threw herself at him. Between her desperate advances,

Phaedra made promises to the young man that nobody would find out – living under the same roof, they'd have many opportunities to enjoy each other undiscovered. Hippolytus pushed her away, and so Phaedra told him not to worry about the ramifications of their great love affair – the gods married their kin all the time, and she and Hippolytus weren't even blood relations! Again, though, Hippolytus told her to stop. Phaedra's hands still pawed at his youthful body – she asked him if his father hadn't already hurt both of them enough, by killing his mother and being generally cruel to Phaedra over the years. Hippolytus needn't feel any guilt for betraying this man. And besides, knowing how strong their connection was, she was sure that the goddess of love herself would support them.

What Phaedra hadn't considered was that her stepson would simply not be interested in her. Despite all of her reassurances, Hippolytus fiercely rejected her, making it clear he wouldn't be breaking his vow of chastity for anyone, least of all her. Phaedra was embarrassed and angry, but she was also scared – Theseus may have been a celebrated hero to all of Greece and beyond, but he could also be brutish and wicked when the mood took him. If Hippolytus were to tell her husband she'd tried it on with him, who knows what he'd do to her. In her dread, she decided to get in there first, going to Theseus and claiming that Hippolytus had tried to rape her.

Theseus, who had previously been granted three wishes by his father Poseidon, was raging. He rounded on Hippolytus, who vehemently denied the accusations, yelling that Phaedra wasn't even good-looking enough for him to feel inclined to break his vow of chastity (oof), and that he didn't care for the politics of being a king, so what reasoning could he have for doing this? Theseus wouldn't listen to what his son had to say, though – he wanted him dead for his disrespect, and decided to use one of his wishes to make it happen. He called out to Poseidon, and together, they came up with a plan.

Waiting until Hippolytus was out riding his chariot near the sea, Poseidon summoned a bull-like sea monster to rise up out of the ocean. The horses were frightened by the sight, veering off course and upending the chariot. Hippolytus was caught up in the reins and dragged to his death by the startled animals. Phaedra felt some guilt over the death of her stepson, but this was overshadowed by the sheer relief of knowing her husband wouldn't find out her terrible secret.

It wasn't over yet, though, as Artemis was angered by the loss of her loyal follower, especially considering the cause. She appeared to Theseus and revealed the true story, but before the king had the chance to harm his wife, Phaedra killed herself to avoid punishment.

Racked with guilt over his rash actions, Theseus would go all-out to give Hippolytus a proper burial and extravagant funeral rites. The same courtesy would not be extended to his late wife, who he left to rot where she hung.

CYDIPPE (*sid-ip*)

When Acontius, a boy from the island of Ceos, attended a festival in Delos to honour Artemis, he found himself enamoured by a woman he spotted in the temple.

Cydippe was a high-born Athenian beauty, and Acontius assumed (likely correctly) that he wouldn't have any chance if he were to simply offer himself to her, so he used a different tack. He took an apple and wrote on its flesh: *I swear by Artemis that I will marry Acontius*, which he then rolled over to her. It bumped against her foot and, without thinking, she picked it up and read the inscription aloud. As the words were said in front of Artemis' altar, both Acontius and the goddess took Cydippe's words as gospel, and she was tied in.

Cydippe, however, didn't feel such a way. When Acontius confidently introduced himself as her betrothed, Cydippe told him not to be so ridiculous – someone of her stature could never be wed to such a low-born dosser. Besides, she was already engaged to a much better social match. Secretly, Cydippe *did* feel a familiar pull of attraction to Acontius, but heaven forbid she acknowledge it. Instead, she returned home, resolving to never think of the strange man and his stupid apple ever again.

As her wedding day approached, Cydippe was overcome by a terrible fever that resulted in the nuptials being postponed. Unfortunately for the noble couple, each time the new wedding date came around, Cydippe would again have to take to her bed with another bout of illness. Finally, her father decided to consult the oracle of Delphi to find out the problem. What her father didn't know, though, was that Cydippe and Acontius had been in cahoots of sorts. Although adamant that she was marrying her betrothed, over time her feelings for the bold Acontius had grown, and they'd been passing each other love letters, with the help of her nurse. The oracle revealed that her illness was caused by offending Artemis as she'd gone back on her sacred vow. Her father felt he had no choice but to agree to the marriage between Cydippe and Acontius. This time, the wedding went ahead without a hitch. To give the couple their dues, Cydippe ended up very happy to be coupled with the cheeky chap, and they had a great marriage.

LEUCONE (*loo-cown-ee*)

When the young maiden Leucone fell in love with and married the beautiful hunter Cyanippus, she couldn't believe she'd bagged such a capable, handsome partner.

As the pair settled in to married life, though, Leucone found herself spending her days alone as Cyanippus hunted with his friends. When he would eventually return home, her husband would be so exhausted from a day of hunting that he'd fall straight into bed, sometimes not even speaking to her before he was snoring.

This truly wasn't what Leucone had signed up for – she wanted a partner, someone to love and love her in return. Was it so much to ask that the person you promise yourself to might want to have a conversation every now and again? She decided she had to see for herself what had such a pull on Cyanippus, so one morning when he left for the hunt, she sneaked out behind him.

Leucone stayed at a safe distance as she watched her husband thrive doing what he loved best, and she had to admit, he did make it look fun. At some point, Cyanippus and his party doubled back on themselves, so she had to hide in a bush. His hounds, who were rather savage, picked up her scent and began tracking her. She couldn't alert Cyanippus to her whereabouts – how would it look if she was caught snooping? So, instead, she closed her eyes and prayed to the gods that the dogs would lose interest and leave her alone.

It wasn't to be, though – the dogs sniffed right up to her bush and, seeing something living within, couldn't help themselves. They attacked, tearing Leucone to pieces. By the time Cyanippus caught up with them, she was already dead. He was heartbroken that he had caused his wife's frightful fate, and immediately began constructing a pyre so he could honour her with a fitting funeral. After he lit the fire and sent Leucone on her way, he led his dogs into the flames, then he followed them, and they all burned to death.

2

Femme Fatales

'Seductresses' who bring about
the downfall of the men
they encounter

HERO (*hee-ro*)

A virgin priestess of Aphrodite, Hero, first locked eyes with a boy called Leander when they both attended a festival for the goddess. Hero lived in a tower on Sestos, on the western shores of Hellespont, and Leander lived across the water from her, in Abydos. Young, handsome, and above all keen, Leander saw Hero and instantly fell for her.

While the story of these lovers is told as a romantic one for the most part, it's worth mentioning that Leander went to great lengths to convince Hero to give up her virginity. He told her that, as the goddess of love and sex, Aphrodite would expect someone worshipping her to succumb to their own carnal desires, and she would be disappointed in Hero for denying exactly what she stood for above all else – pleasure. Pressured to the extreme, Hero let him pop her cherry. As mad as the couple were for eachother, they knew their love (or likely, lust) must remain secret, or Hero's priesteshood would be called into question.

The pair had a long, hot summer together. Every night, Leander would swim across the waters to meet Hero, guided by a candle that she'd leave lit in the top window of her tower. The waters between them weren't exactly timid, but Leander was a strong swimmer and didn't face much hindrance as he passed. They'd make love through the night, and Leander would swim home afterwards. As winter approached, they decided it was best to pause their escapades and resume again in the spring, knowing that the choppy waters could be lethal. They were sad to be parted, but both stuck to this very sensible and justified agreement. That is, until Leander noticed Hero's light in the tower across the water one stormy night.

Instead of stopping to consider that his lover was simply using the light to see, he took it as his cue to immediately dive into the hazardous waters, and haul ass to see her. As he swam, the violent winds blew out Hero's light and he lost his way. It wasn't long before he was completely overwhelmed, and he drowned. Hero witnessed everything from her tower and, devastated, threw herself out of the window into the perilous waters below. Once the storm cleared, the pair washed up on the shore entwined in an embrace and were buried together in a lover's tomb.

ERIS (*eh-riss*)

When Eris, goddess of strife and discord, got word that every deity in existence was invited to the wedding of the year, she had a serious case of FOMO. It wasn't like she didn't know people (and her fellow gods and goddesses) didn't like her – everyone always avoided Eris if they could help it, the only exception being Ares, who couldn't resist a troublemaking gal. Still, though, even the god of DEATH was invited to the union of King Peleus and the goddess Thetis but she wasn't? She decided that she could stay at home stewing over it, or she could ignore the snub and attend anyway . . . Guess which she chose.

The gods showered the royal couple with wondrous gifts, and Eris had brought one of her own. Not only was it a present for the newlyweds, but a gift for the whole wedding party! From under her cloak, she produced a golden apple, inscribed *for the most beautiful*, and tossed it into the crowd.

Aphrodite, Athena, and Hera all bent down to retrieve the generous gift, and each were surprised to see the others making a claim for it. The three goddesses started scrambling for the apple, and things got a bit heated. Eventually, Zeus stepped in, but he was smart enough to not make the decision of who truly deserved the apiteth himself. Instead, he appointed a mortal to settle the dispute. The job fell to Paris, a Trojan prince. What happened next is known as the Judgement of Paris and would lead to dire consequences.

Paris looked at the three lovely ladies in turn, scratching his chin in concentration. The goddesses saw that he was torn, and quickly turned to bribery. Athena, goddess of war, offered him great wisdom and skill in combat, if he were to choose her. Queen Hera promised that she would make him king of all of Europe and Asia. Lastly, Aphrodite guaranteed him the most beautiful woman in all the world, should he name her the fairest. Perhaps thinking with a certain appendage rather than his brain, he took Aphrodite up on her offer and handed over the golden apple. The massive ramifications of this decision would come in time, but it's safe to say this little outburst put quite a downer on the wedding party. *My work here is done*, thought Eris.

HELEN (*hel-len*)

Helen may be best kown as the highly sought-after babe that started the Trojan War, but she began her turbulent life in Sparta.

Helen's mother, Leda, was married to the king, Tyndareus, when she attracted the attentions of Zeus. Throwing it back to his bird-ish 'wooing' of Hera, he transformed into a swan, then attacked and raped Leda. Try not to focus too much on the logistics of it all, but swan-Zeus managed to impregnate the queen. That night, she also slept with her husband and got pregnant to *him*. This wasn't any normal pregnancy (obviously) and Leda didn't give birth per se, but laid two eggs. From one hatched the boy Castor and the girl Clytemnestra, the children of Tyndareus. From the other, Pollux and Helen, the offspring of Zeus. Whether or not Tyndareus felt a particular way about his wife birthing eggs is unclear, but he brought all four children up as his own.

When Helen was still a child, she suffered her first abduction. Athenian friends Theseus and Pirithous decided that as sons of gods, they deserved divine spouses. Theseus chose Helen, who at the time was believed to be seven years old, while Pirithous chose Persephone, wife of Hades and queen of the Underworld. They say aim high, but that does seem a little *too* high.

You may be familiar with the heroic exploits of Theseus (if not, you will be soon) and you'd be forgiven for thinking this story comes from his younger, angsty years. But Theseus was a full-grown man,

45

which makes his choice of bride-to-be even weirder. This all went down *before* his marriage to Phaedra, FYI.

The duo easily secured Helen, and when it was time for Pirithous to fetch his wife-to-be, the pair set off for the Underworld. Theseus left Helen with his mother, Aethra, who was happy to watch over his new child-bride – a very early example of how mothers think their sons can do *no wrong*.

Down in the Underworld, Hades learned of their plan and almost wet himself laughing. He trapped the men with minimal effort and kept them as prisoners for their insolence. While they were otherwise indisposed, Helen's brothers invaded Athens and took their sister (who, since they were born at the same time as Helen, were also presumably still children, but sure), as well as her sort of mother-in-law, back to Sparta.

The rest of Helen's childhood passed with minimal trouble. However, as soon as she came of age, Tyndareus decided to marry her off properly. Helen had grown into what many reported to be the most beautiful woman in the world, and men from all over wanted her hand. Tyndareus was unable to choose a winner, but was also unwilling to turn anyone away for fear of causing a political shitstorm, and it wasn't long before the suitors started to get restless.

One of Helen's potential paramours was the wily Odysseus, who upon realising that he had no chance with Helen, turned his attentions to her cousin, Penelope. Odysseus told Tyndareus that he'd resolve his sticky situation, as long as he had his support in pursuing Penelope. The king readily consented.

Odysseus got all the men to agree not to kick up a fuss if they themselves were not chosen, and they swore a binding oath that if anyone were to jeopardise the marriage of Helen and the successful suitor, they would all come to the couple's aid. Everyone agreed, and the promise would become known as the Oath of Tyndareus.

With the oath in place, Tyndareus granted the honour of his daughter's hand to Menelaus. Menelaus' brother, King Agamemnon of Mycenae, was already married to Helen's sister Clytemnestra, so this was a politically strong pairing. After their marriage, Menelaus became king of Sparta, and Helen became queen. They ruled together for a few years, having a daughter who they named Hermione.

Meanwhile, on Mount Olympus, Zeus had decided that he'd had enough of these exasperating humans, especially the heroes. He determined that the most efficient way to start obliterating them would be with a legendary war. Plus, it would give him and his fellow deities some light entertainment.

It was during Helen and Menelaus' marriage that the Judgement of Paris would come to fruition, and it seemed obvious to the prince that the Spartan queen was the woman he'd been promised by Aphrodite, especially if the rumours were true about her great beauty. When King Priam sent Paris across the sea on peace talks, the prince decided to take a little detour to Sparta. When the king and queen warmly welcomed him, his expectations of Helen's beauty were blown out of the water. She was absolutely exquisite. As Paris made himself at home over the next few days, he found that he couldn't stay away from her, flirting and showing off with stories of his life back home. Helen was no stranger to the attentions of men, but there was something different about Paris. Try as she might to resist, she found herself hanging on to every word that passed his lips throughout the day, and fantasising about those same lips when they parted of an evening. Later, Menelaus announced that he had to leave Sparta to attend his father's funeral. He asked Helen to stay behind and keep their guest company. Without the threat of her husband finding them, Helen and Paris got to know each other more intimately. The pair made love and stayed up into the early hours sharing their secrets and dreams for the future. When Helen expressed that she'd be sad to see him go, Paris revealed he had no desire to leave without her. Helen knew it wasn't the proper thing to do, but she couldn't fight her heart, and they made arrangements to smuggle her out of Sparta and bring her to Troy.

When Menelaus returned, he immediately invoked the Oath of Tyndareus, and all his wife's previous hopefuls joined forces to get her back. And so began the Trojan War. It lasted a decade and included many legendary stories that make up a good chunk of Greek mythology.

Helen was certainly the face of the war, but realistically it was much deeper than a man getting his feelings hurt. Troy was a powerful, previously untouchable capital with some serious wealth, inspiring jealousy and greed among its rivals. It was convenient for the commanders of the Greeks that Helen and Paris had set the wheels in motion, especially as it gave the soldiers someone to direct their anger at.

Many years into the battle, Paris was mortally wounded and died. Helen would quickly be married to his brother, Deiphobus, a particularly cruel man who'd fancied himself a piece of her even before his brother's death. By this time, Helen was feeling dreadful. As handsome and exciting as Paris was when they met, it hadn't taken long for him to show his true colours, and they were that of a spoiled little prince. The sweet nothings he'd whispered to steal her heart and body quietened to nothing once she was his officially. She felt very much like a trophy rather than a beloved partner, and now he was dead, who knew what lay in store for her? At least with Menelaus she knew where she stood, and she would be home in Sparta, the kingdom of her own family. It's actually thought that Helen may have betrayed the Trojans around this time, perhaps even being the one to kill Deiphobus, or at least ratting out his whereabouts so that the Greeks could do it for her.

In the end, the Greek army pretended to surrender, clearing out their camp and leaving nothing behind but an apparent 'gift to the gods' for safe passage home. When the Trojans went to investigate, they found a massive wooden horse on wheels and decided to bring it into the city for their celebrations. What they didn't expect was that the horse would be hollow, and inside its belly, thirty of the best Greek soldiers sat patiently. Everyone in Troy partied heartily into the night, thrilled that they could finally put this terrible war behind them. Later, as the city slept, the Greeks sneaked out of the horse and opened the gates to let their comrades in. With the element of surprise on their side, Menelaus and the Greeks quickly won the war.

The Greek soldiers rallied for Helen's blood, and Menelaus ordered that it should be him to carry out her killing. He raised his sword but just as he was about to bring it down, Helen disrobed. One glimpse of her glorious naked body was enough for Menelaus to forgive her for everything, and she returned to Sparta on his arm. By most accounts the couple lived happily ever after, both apparently choosing to gloss over the minor bump in their marriage that was the Trojan War.

If you're looking for something a bit less anticlimactic, there are also accounts to say that Helen was:

- deified and spent eternity on Mount Olympus with the demi-god Achilles
- driven from Sparta and later betrayed by a girlfriend, subsequently killed by hanging
- sacrificed to the gods
- killed by Achilles' mother for her part in his death.

SELENE (*seh-leen-ee*)

Selene was the Titan goddess of the moon, and sister to both Eos (the dawn) and Helios (the sun). It was her job to drive the moon across the sky every night. As a lunar goddess, she was also associated with female menstruation, and was worshipped particularly on a full or new moon. The phases of the moon were very important to the Ancient Greeks, who relied on Selene's work so that they could plan their planting and harvesting. Lunar eclipses in particular struck fear into them, as they were thought to signify the gods' anger with mortals. They even had a story for why the moon was filled with craters. It's said that Selene was once attacked by the vicious monster Typhon, who scratched at her with his sharp claws. Selene was able to fight him off, but he marked the goddess forever, the craters being scars left over from their fight.

She had various consorts in her time, including her own brother Helios, and Zeus himself, but her most epic love story is that of her and a shepherd called Endymion. The pair were completely obsessed with each other. Selene would visit him regularly in a cave on Mount Latmos, where they'd make love through the night (after she'd done her duties, of course). But the threat of time panicked Selene greatly – she had seen how quickly the lives of these mortals came and went, and the thought of losing Endymion to old age or disease terrified her. Desperate for their love to last forever, Selene went to Zeus and asked him to grant her beau immortality, so that they would never be parted by death, and he would never lose his beauty to age. Zeus granted Selene her wish, but thought to put his own spin on it. Indeed, Endymion would remain youthful forever, but he'd do so only in an eternal sleep. It's also possible that Zeus misunderstood the lunar goddess' request accidentally on purpose, as it's thought Endymion might have had a bit of an eye for his own wife, Hera.

So, Endymion was put into a dreamless slumber from which he'd never age a day, and Selene took him back to the cave where they'd fallen in love and had their steamy liaisons. The ageless Selene would visit him every night and weep over the loss of their love.

POLYXENA (*pol-lick-sin-a*)

Polyxena was a Trojan princess during the war.

A prophecy had said that if Polyxena's brother Troilus lived to the age of twenty, Troy would not fall during the battle. The enemy got wind of this and, when the siblings were out collecting water from a local spring, sent Achilles himself to murder him. As the very best soldier of the Greeks, he completed his mission easily, but immediately fell for the sister of his victim. Polyxena was extremely beautiful and wise beyond her years, plus it's likely that Achilles was on the rebound after losing his best friend and lover, Patroclus, in the war efforts.

Despite the fact that he'd just killed her brother and probably doomed Troy to fall, Polyxena appeared to love Achilles right back. The pair spent many nights consorting, whispering stories and secrets to one another. In fact, Achilles told her his biggest secret: that when his mother dipped him into the river Styx to make him invincible, she'd left the place she held him vulnerable – his heel.

One afternoon, Polyxena left Achilles a message asking him to meet her at Apollo's temple. Likely expecting a few blissful hours of canoodling, he came eagerly. However, he was ambushed by her other brothers, Paris and Deiphobus, who shot him in the heel with a poison arrow. Of course, it's possible that Polyxena never loved Achilles at all, and was looking for a way to avenge her family and save her city.

When the Greeks emerged victorious, the ghost of Achilles appeared to the army, telling them that, to have sailable winds on their return home, he required the sacrifice of Polyxena.

Queen Hecuba, who had already lost so much in the name of this war, begged the victors not to make her go through the death of another child. Polyxena reasoned with her mother. She knew that, as a Trojan princess, she'd likely end up enslaved by the Greeks once the city fell (it was common practice to divvy up the surviving women of war as concubines and slaves. While a practical, if sexist, way to deal with the prisoners, it also added insult to injury to have noblewomen humiliated in such servitude). She declared she'd rather die as a sacrifice to allow others safe passage than to meet this fate. Polyxena stood at the foot of Achilles' grave, resolute, as her throat was slit.

Hecuba mourned once again, but was comforted by her daughter-in-law, Andromache. She told Hecuba that she'd witnessed Polyxena's sacrifice, and once the Greeks moved on, she'd been able to quickly perform funeral rites for the girl, ensuring her safe passage into the afterlife.

PANDORA (*pan-dor-a*)

At one point in time, the earth was populated only by men (according to Greek mythology), as women hadn't yet been created. Back then, Zeus was unhappy with mankind discovering fire, and wanted to punish them. He decided that he would create a new race to live alongside man – one that would torment and plague earth's OGs forevermore. That race was woman.

He ordered the forging god, Hephaestus, to mould a woman in the image of a goddess, using dirt and water. He explained his vision to his fellow deities and asked that they each bestow upon it a gift of their own.

Aphrodite gifted her grace, beauty, and longing. Athena clothed her in a shimmering silver gown and veil, giving her the skills of weaving and needlework. Hermes gave her a voice, as well as a deceitful mind. The Graces adorned her with jewellery, and the Horae a crown of garlands (more on these two to come). Finally, Hermes circled back around to name her Pandora, meaning 'all-gift'.

She was brought down to earth and presented to Epimetheus, who'd been pre-warned by his Titan brother, Prometheus, not to accept any gifts from the gods. One look at Pandora, though, and any logic disappeared. 'Yes please' and 'thank you' were all he could muster. Suffice to say, the other mortal men of earth were equally awestruck. As Epimetheus was to be the lucky groom, he insisted they be married as soon as possible (when there's only one woman in the whole world and she's *this* fierce, you've got to lock it down).

At the wedding party, Zeus pulled Pandora to one side and gifted her a beautifully decorated jar. The catch? She wasn't allowed to open it, though he wouldn't tell her why. Zeus slipped away, all mysterious and whatnot.

Of course, Pandora, who the gods themselves had designed to be curious, couldn't help having a peek – what harm could it do, after all?

She carefully prised open the lid and lifted it slightly. Quick as a flash, *things* started escaping, jumping into the air around her and seeping into the world. Pandora panicked, quickly jamming the lid down and twisting it tight, but it was too late – all the personifications of suffering and evil, formerly contained within the jar, were now free to ravage humanity. All descendants of Nyx (night) and Erebus (darkness), they were:

- **Limos** (starvation)
- **Neikea** (arguments and feuds)
- **Makhai** (war and combat)
- **Adroktasiai** (manslaughter)
- **Phonoi** (murder)
- **Dysnomia** (lawlessness)
- **Algos** (pain)
- **Pseudea** (lies)
- **Ponos** (hardship and toil)
- **Amphilogiai** (disputes)
- **Hysminai** (fights)

Only one thing was left inside: Elpis (hope).

Nowadays, the story of Pandora and her nosiness is used as an explanation of why evil exists in the world. It's all women's fault, naturally.

THE SIRENS (*sigh-rens*)

Daughters of the river god Achelous and Melpomene (a Muse, goddesses of the arts), the Sirens were huge birds with the heads of women that would lure sailors to their deaths with their sweet song.

The Sirens resided on their own island, Anthemoessa, which was surrounded by mountains and jagged rocks. The Sirens would use these to their advantage, causing the shipwrecks of their victims. As the sailors tried to swim to the safety of the island, the bird-women would attack, drowning them with their clawed feet.

At some point, the goddess Hera persuaded the Sirens to enter into a singing competition with the Muses (who were the Sirens' mothers and aunties). The Muses won, and plucked out their opponents' feathers in order to make themselves crowns, which they flaunted in their victory.

We only know of two instances where sailors were able to escape the feathery clutches of these temptresses. The first were the Argonauts – the Sirens sensed their approach so started belting out their tunes, and the men started to fall under their spell. Luckily for them, though, they had the musician Orpheus on board, who whipped out his lyre and played his own song for the crew. Distracted by this, they were able to safely navigate far away from Anthemoessa.

It was also a close call for Odysseus and his gang, though they sailed near the Sirens of their own accord. Odysseus had heard stories of the mystical creatures from the witch Circe and was desperate to hear the beguiling call for himself. He told his crew to fill their ears with beeswax to temporarily deafen themselves, and to bind him tightly to the ship's mast with ropes. When he heard the Sirens call, Odysseus thrashed and screamed to be released, but it all went unheard and, eventually, the sweet song faded into nothing.

After Odysseus escaped unscathed, the creatures jumped into the ocean, drowning themselves on the same shores as many men before them.

The story of the Sirens has since been used to (unfairly) suggest women possess temptations and dangers that they utilise to lead men astray.

EOS (*ee-oss*)

As Titan goddess of the dawn, it was Eos' job to rise each morning and open up the gates of heaven, so that her siblings could come and go with the sun and moon.

Eos and her kin were able to toy with the timings of the day and did so to suit them and their friends. During the Gigantomachy, when Gaia learned that her children were destined to die at the hands of the Olympians, she knew she had to do something to change their fate. Gaia began searching for a particular herb that would make them indestructible. Zeus, however, got wind of her plan, and asked Eos and her siblings to work their magic and delay the day. While the world was still dark, he harvested all of the herbs for his own army.

Eos married Astraeus, fittingly the god of dusk, and together they had numerous children, including the Anemoi (winds). We know she also had a steamy rendezvous with Ares, and was subsequently punished by Aphrodite with an insatiable lust for mortals. This would lead to many instances of her abducting young, handsome men and having her way with them (like Procris' husband, Cephalus). Eos was clueless about the curse, though, and thought she just had a type.

The most famous of Eos' abductions was Tithonus. A Trojan prince, Tithonus was the son of King Laomedon and a water nymph, Strymo. Eos was besotted with him, but by now had grown wise to the perils of loving a human, so she took some steps to protect her heart this time around. She went to Zeus and begged him to make Tithonus immortal. He agreed, but Eos missed his shifty smile as he bestowed the 'gift' upon her beau.

So, the prince was now immortal, and together they had two children, Memnon and Emathion. As time passed, though, Eos started to notice strange things about her lover. For an immortal, it was odd for him to be sprouting these grey hairs, or those crow's feet around his eyes . . . and what did he mean, 'his back was aching'?

It turns out that Eos wasn't specific enough when requesting his immortality. Zeus had indeed given Tithonus the gift of endless life, but he hadn't stopped the aging process. As the years passed, Eos stayed young and perfect, while Tithonus grew old and withered. As he couldn't die, he became completely helpless as he shrivelled up like a raisin. Eos looked after him tenderly, holding his sunken body in her arms and embracing him every night. Eventually, she couldn't bear it any more, and she went to Mount Olympus to ask Zeus for his help once again.

Zeus could not (or would not) undo what had been done, but could, apparently, do something else to help – he offered to turn Tithonus into a grasshopper. Eos, probably wondering where on earth that suggestion came from, quickly agreed, so that her love could be put out of his misery at last. It's said that this is why you can hear the call of the grasshopper accompanying the dawn.

Eos would face heartbreak once again, when their son, Memnon, was killed by Achilles during the Trojan War. When he died on the battlefield, Eos ordered Helios not to start his ascent into the skies to bring the day, and begged Nyx (goddess of the night) to stay in her place a little while longer, so she'd be able to remove her son's body under the cover of darkness. Zeus would make the hero immortal as he was so moved by Eos' grief – either that or he felt like he owed Eos one for screwing over Tithonus. After Memnon's passing, it's said that the dawn was always slightly less brilliant, and that the morning dew was her tears of grief.

CALYPSO (*cal-ip-so*)

A nymph that dwelled on the island of Ogygia, Calypso found a certain hero by the name of Odysseus washed up on her shores after the Trojan War, close to death after a run-in with Zeus. When he woke up in Calypso's embrace, he couldn't even find the energy to be thankful for his survival. His crewmates were long dead, and Odysseus longed for nothing more than his crown and slippers back home.

Calypso didn't particularly care about his wants, though. She liked the look of this lean, mean, hero-machine, so she used her mystical singing voice to keep him enchanted and trapped on her island. Odysseus might not have been able to leave of his own free will, but he was still very aware of what was happening, and while Calypso tried to convince him to stay with her sans enchantment, he made it very clear that he wasn't interested. Even her promise of immortality didn't waiver his resolve – he told her that he simply couldn't bear to be separated from his wife any longer, which would be nice if we weren't about to hear the story of his decade-long affair with Circe. Thanks to Calypso's magics, every night Odysseus' body would betray him and he'd be forced to sleep with the goddess.

After a full seven years of this captivity, right-hand goddess of Odysseus, Athena, decided to step in, and asked Zeus to command his release from Calypso's melodic clutches. He sent Hermes to give her the message, and Calypso was super vexed, giving a great speech about the gods and their double standards when it came to goddesses staking claims to mortal men, but having no such misgivings when they themselves wanted to make the females of the species their playthings. Honestly, she made a fair point.

Hypocritical or not, Zeus' word was law, and Odysseus was finally freed from Calypso's spell. She even begrudgingly gave him a few provisions and advised him on the best way to get home to his kingdom.

DEIANIRA (*dee-an-eye-ra*)

Deianira, a princess of Calydon, had been promised by her father to the river god Achelous. He was able to change his form at will, and while most people considered a pretty cool trick, it gave Deianira the ick, and she couldn't think of anything worse than being tied to this metamorphosising god for the rest of her life.

As she stewed over what to do one day, she bumped into the handsome Heracles. They were both smitten on sight, and she knew immediately that she'd much rather be with him than Achelous. However, Achelous wouldn't let her go without a fight.

Challenging Heracles to a wrestling competition for Deianira's hand, Achelous used the transforming powers at his disposal. When Achelous transformed into a bull, however, Heracles was simply stronger and shattered his horns. The fight was won. Heracles and Deianira were married, and as well as gaining a wife, Heracles had also inherited the kingdom of Calydon from her aging father, and its substantial army.

With a hefty legion of warriors behind him, Heracles decided to settle some old scores in Oechalia, where the king had previously promised him the hand of his daughter, Iole, but went back on it. He pillaged the city and murdered the king's sons. Iole, expecting to be next, scaled the cities walls and threw herself from the peak. Conveniently, the dress that she was wearing acted as a parachute, billowing out and allowing her to land safely on the ground below.

Heracles found her at the bottom and was delighted to be reunited with her. Iole, apparently unbothered by his murdering of her entire family, was also happy to see him. Heracles brought Iole back to his and Deianira's kingdom, where the pair began a steamy affair under the radar.

Deianira had long suspected Heracles wasn't the most faithful husband (and she was right – aside from Iole, he'd been spreading his seed around all of Greece for the duration of their marriage). It just so happened that she had a trick up her sleeve to turn her husband's attention back to her.

Back in their early days, Deianira had been given assistance from the centaur Nessus, when she needed ferrying across a river. After he'd helped her pass, though, he tried to rape her. Luckily, Heracles was nearby and planted an arrow, poisoned by the blood of the Lernaean Hydra, into the villain. As he lay dying, Nessus whispered to the princess that she should take some of his blood and, should she ever worry her husband was straying, mix it with olive oil to create a love potion that would reinforce his devotion to her. Deianira gathered some of his blood as he died, tucking it away for safekeeping.

Deianira was worried by the prospect that Herc may leave her to marry the concubine, especially because if Iole were to bear him any children, they'd have just as much of a claim to her father's throne as her own offspring.

When Heracles was off doing his hero-ly duties (with Iole along for the ride), he wrote home to his wife, asking her to send him his favourite ceremonial robe for a sacrifice. Deianira seized her opportunity, mixing the potion as instructed, then steeping the robe in the solution. Next, she packed it up and sent it with strict instructions that nobody else wear it, and that it must be kept in the dark until Heracles was ready to put it on.

As she waited for her husband to return and declare his reignited passion to her, she started to wonder. Maybe the centaur who tried to assault her didn't have her best interests at heart?

It was too late to go back now, though – the robe had arrived, and as soon as it made contact with Herc's skin, the poison within the blood spread through his body, and he killed himself to escape the searing pain.

Deianira's name literally translates to 'killer of husbands', so maybe somebody should have seen that one coming.

As he lay dying, Heracles called for his eldest son with Deianira, Hyllus, and stated that his final wish was for him to marry Iole. Hyllus agreed, and the couple would go on to have three daughters and a son. As for Deianira, it wasn't long before the widow's grief and guilt got the better of her, and she committed suicide.

GALATEA THE
NEREID (*ga-la-tay-a*)

The Nereids were the fifty sea-dwelling daughters of Nereus and the nymph Doris. Each personifications of the beauties of the ocean, they were all lovely, with coral crowns and flowing white dresses. Residing in Poseidon's palace, when they weren't accompanying the god on his daily dalliances, they could be found assisting sailors, keenly giving tips on direction for survival, and maybe offering up a bit of *somethin' somethin'* to get them through those lonely, choppy nights at sea. Thought to be the loveliest of all of the Nereids was Galatea, who caught the eye (singular) of the Cyclops Polyphemus. Unfortunately for him, Galatea was madly in love with a handsome, mortal shepherd named Acis, from Sicily. He was also the son of the god Pan (god of the wild) and a wood nymph, so he really would have been dishy.

Galatea was well aware that the Cyclops desired her, but she was utterly disgusted by both the sight of him and the way he lived, deeming him a barbarian. Though it's true the Cyclopes were an uncivilised lot, Polyphemus found that the Nereid brought out a soft side to him. To please her, he'd trim his unruly hair and beard in an attempt to look a bit more presentable, and made up many songs about her beauty. In one of his ballads, he confidently belted out a verse on how much he hated the arrogant young Acis, and how he'd like nothing more than to dismember him and scatter his limbs across the mountains. Catchy. Polyphemus scorned the worship of any other gods, declaring that the only heavenly light he needed in his life was Galatea.

Unbothered by these declarations, Galatea and Acis' love affair continued. Once, as the pair lay post-coitus, Polyphemus came upon them and let out a jealous roar. Acis, terrified by the sound and sight, leapt up from the sand and fled, calling to Galatea to help. Using his raw strength, Polyphemus ripped a boulder straight from the rocks of Mount Etna and hurled it at his love rival. Acis tried to move out of the way, but wasn't quite fast enough, and he was completely crushed. As he died, Galatea, in her mourning, transformed his flowing blood into a river with his name, and Acis became the immortal god of the stream. For the most part, Acis the god looked very much like Acis the man, except he was larger, and his skin had a bit of a blue tinge. Deified, Acis and Galatea could now live a very long and happy life together. Polyphemus truly screwed himself over.

CORONIS (*coh-roh-niss*)

The Thessalian princess Coronis was a lover of Apollo who found herself pregnant to the god. Apollo was always coming and going on godly business, so he appointed a white crow to watch over his baby mama while he was gone, like a secret, feathery nanny-cam.

When she was nearing the end of her pregnancy, Coronis felt an undeniable attraction to a mortal called Ischys (maybe blame it on the hormones?) As a granddaughter of one of the Muses, it's likely that Coronis was extremely beautiful, and she had no trouble seducing Ischys. Her father tried desperately to persuade her to leave the man alone, knowing the damage that the wrath of a powerful god like Apollo could bring down on her and their family, but Coronis was having none of it – she knew what she wanted, and she was going to get it, wrath be damned.

Coronis and Ischys enjoyed a hot night together, and the crow immediately went a-squawking to Apollo. He was heartbroken over the betrayal, frying the bird's wings black as punishment for not stopping the union – it's said this is why crows are black to this day. Apollo is thought to have been one of the horniest gods, even outdoing Zeus with the notches on his divine bedpost, but the ashamed crow probably thought it wise to keep this point to itself. When Apollo tearfully relayed the news of his lover's infidelity to his sister, Artemis, she fizzed with rage on his behalf. Who was this mortal woman to treat her baby brother like this? Coronis was going down, pregnant or not.

By the time Artemis appeared before her, Coronis was just about ready to pop, but knew it was pointless to fight her fate. She faced the goddess head-on as Artemis shot her in the heart, then went on to kill her entire family.

When Apollo found out what his sister had done, he rushed to Coronis' side, but it was too late – she was already dead. He could still feel their child moving within her, though, so decided that if he couldn't save the mother, he could at least save the babe. He cut open her belly and pulled out their son, performing the first ever caesarean section, and named the baby boy Asclepius. Apollo put Coronis in the sky as the constellation Corvus, which means 'crow'.

CRESSIDA (*cress-i-da*)

Although she was the daughter of a Greek seer, Cressida resided in Troy. She and the Trojan prince Troilus had been together since childhood and had declared their love everlasting. To throw it back, her father, Calchas, told of the prophecy from Polyxena's story that said if Troilus lived to twenty years old, his city would never fall. During the war, Calchas decided that he simply must have his daughter back, and suggested to the leaders of the Greek army that they do a hostage swap – they currently had possession of Antenor, one of Priam's right-hand men, who would certainly hold a lot of sway. Both parties agreed, and the changeover was arranged. Troilus, though admittedly saddened to see his lover leave, didn't fight particularly hard to keep her. Cressida, now little more than an object to both armies, was handed over to the soldier Diomedes, who delivered Antenor to the Trojans.

As the hero and Cressida walked the path back to the Greek camp, they couldn't help notice that there was an undeniable spark between them. By the time she was reunited with her father, Cressida was quite smitten with Diomedes and likely wouldn't have been able to pick Troilus out of a line-up.

In the evenings, after the army returned from the battlefield, Diomedes would find himself shunning the company of his comrades to sit and flirt with Cressida. During one of these sessions, Troilus finally grew a pair and decided to go and rescue Cressida from the enemy. He managed to sneak into the Greek camp without much trouble, but when he found his fiancée, quite unshackled and free, whispering sweet nothings into this much older, more powerful man's ear, he moodily slipped off back to the palace. Not long after, he was ambushed and killed by Achilles.

Diomedes survived the decade-long war of Troy, but it's not known whether the relationship between him and Cressida blossomed, and whether or not she accompanied him home as his concubine.

Cressida's story has been used to perpetuate a sexist trope (as with the Sirens) claiming that females can be extremely fickle and their inconsistencies persist to cause poor men so many problems.

ANOTHER GALATEA

When the Cypriot Propoetus refused to worship Aphrodite, the love goddess, she punished him by turning his daughters into the world's very first prostitutes.

The Propoetides, as they were collectively called, became so immune to shame that the blood in their cheeks hardened and they could no longer blush. Eventually, they became so unfeeling that they turned to stone.

In the same town, we have perhaps the earliest known account of incel-dom. A sculptor by the name of Pygmalion had witnessed the Propoetides carrying out their business, and was so appalled that he decided to swear off women forever, choosing instead to dedicate his life to his art. He proclaimed that woman had, in his own words, 'immeasurable faults that came naturally to them', and he for one wanted nothing to do with them. A devastating loss for the women of the ancient world.

However, it's unclear just how much Pygmalion *could* hate women, when all of his art seemed to centre around them. He worked so hard on one of his sculptures depicting the female form that by the time he was finished he thought it to be so perfect that he fell in love with it.

Pygmalion loved his statue so much that he began, in the privacy of his own home, to treat her as if she were his living wife. He'd dress her in beautiful clothes and jewellery, talk to her about his day, and bring her presents from his travels that he thought a woman may enjoy, like pretty shells, feathers, and flowers. Whenever he had to leave her, he'd plant a passionate kiss on her cold, unyielding lips and promise to return soon.

When the time came for Aphrodite's annual festival, Pygmalion brought the goddess offerings but was too embarrassed to speak his true desires out loud. Instead, he prayed, intensely but silently, that the goddess would consider sending him a woman as beautiful, perfect, and modest as his marble mama. When he returned home, he greeted the statue with a peck.

Was it just his imagination, or did the marble seem warmer to the touch? He kissed her again, and swore that he smelled the sweet skin of a woman. He watched in amazement as the statue's features softened and filled with life. Before him was a living, breathing girl. He named her Galatea, and they were quickly married. Aphrodite herself blessed the union, and the couple never forgot to honour her. Despite her simple, stone beginnings, Galatea was able to bear Pygmalion a daughter, who they named Paphos.

They lived happily ever after, with Galatea never displaying the inconsiderable faults of her gender *according to Pygmalion*.

OENONE (*ee-no-nee*)

When people hear of Paris, the Trojan prince, the first woman that comes to mind tends to be the beautiful Helen and their love story that launched the war. However, the Spartan princess wasn't the first lady he had pledged his heart to.

When the pregnant Queen Hecuba dreamed that she gave birth to a lit torch entwined with snakes, they took it to mean that the baby growing within her would bring on the fall of their great city. To avoid this, she and the king rejected little Paris, ordering that he be left on a mountain to die of exposure. Luckily for the tot, he was rescued and raised by a shepherd well into his late teens. During his modest beginnings, he would meet and fall in love with one of the nymphs of Mount Ida, by the name of Oenone. The lowly shepherd's boy couldn't believe his luck at landing such a beauty, believing her to be the most gorgeous creature in existence. *For now.*

Oenone and Paris had a son, who they named Corythus. The trio lived a simple but comfortable life, with Paris going out to work with his adoptive father, and Oenone raising their child at home. That is, until Paris was herding his sheep one day and was approached by a group of men from Troy. They'd come to Mount Ida to take his best bull to use as a prize in their kingdom's upcoming funeral games. It was, in fact, Paris' own funeral games, which the Trojans had held annually since he'd 'died in childbirth', as was the official line. Paris was sore to lose such a fine bull but knew there wasn't anything he could do about it. He thought he'd try his luck by entering the games himself, and hopefully win his cattle back fair and square.

Paris was strong from his life of manual labour, and did spectacularly in the competition, besting two of the royal sons, including Deiphobus. Embarrassed by being beaten by this nobody, Deiphobus rounded on him with his sword. Paris fled the scene, holing up in a temple of Apollo for protection. At the same time, Princess Cassandra the seer was also pottering about the temple, and thanks to her gift, she recognised her long-lost baby brother straight away. She couldn't help but embrace him and tell him all about his true roots.

It wasn't long before Paris got better acquainted with the wider family, who seemed to have forgotten all about the terrifying prophecy that his being alive would fulfil. The new-found prince returned to Mount Ida, where he told Oenone what he'd learned. They packed up their limited possessions and prepared to move to Troy on the royal family's request.

Sometime between the discovery and the big move, Paris was called upon to settle the dispute of which of the three gorgeous goddesses was the fairest. We know that Paris chose Aphrodite and therefore accepted her bribery of 'the most beautiful woman in the world', despite Oenone waiting for him at home. He didn't think twice about revealing Aphrodite's promise to a rather surprised Oenone – not only was her husband uprooting their happy life in favour of a family who had abandoned him, he was also going to travel to another foreign city to collect a concubine to come and live with them!

Irrespective of her outrage, Oenone couldn't imagine her life without him, so she agreed to move to Troy. Paris did manage to officially marry Oenone before he set off for Sparta, which perhaps counts for something. Possibly. Probably not. Oenone waited impatiently for his return, and when she finally clapped eyes on her new love rival, she knew it was pointless to fight for her marriage. Seeing the way that Paris flaunted the lovely Helen, and the way that the people of Troy reacted in the face of her beauty, Oenone had to accept that it was curtains for her. She moved back to her home on Mount Ida, with Corythus in tow.

Being separated from her husband, Oenone's sadness quickly festered into anger. What stung Oenone the most, though, was how she – a goddess – had never questioned whether the lowly shepherd was good enough for her, but now that Paris had a bit of stature, she was no longer valued high enough for him alone. She may have loved him deeply, but she hated him, too.

When Corythus came of age, Oenone couldn't stop him from following his father to Troy. When he arrived, he went straight to the palace in search of Paris, but happened upon his stepmother first. He started to explain who he was and how he wanted to help, clutching at Helen's hands in his desperation to get his words out. As he did, Paris entered the room and saw this handsome youth seemingly groping at his wife and stabbed him. Helen, by this point completely unenamoured by her second husband, calmly told him what he'd done. Once again, his rash actions had disastrous consequences.

When Paris was mortally wounded, he struggled to Mount Ida to beg his old flame to use her powers to heal him. Oenone, not believing the gall of him, told Paris to get his precious Helen to cure him. Paris would die on his way back down the mountain, and Oenone would quickly grow to regret her rash response. In despair, she threw herself onto his funeral pyre as the flames burned his body, joining him in death. The pair would be buried next to one another, with their headstones facing opposite ways.

SALMACIS (*sal-mack-iss*)

The Naiad (water nymph) Salmacis could have gone down the same path as most of her sisters by becoming a follower of Artemis, but instead she chose a life of vanity and idleness. Her friends tried to pique her interest by introducing her to various hobbies like dancing, singing, and making flower crowns, but she had no desire to indulge in anything past languidly wallowing in a stream and brushing her long, exquisite hair.

One day, though, her attentions were roused when a handsome youth happened upon her waters. He was the son of Aphrodite and Hermes, who they'd named Hermaphroditus (a super subtle blending of their names) and had been raised by other Naiads on Mount Ida. At fifteen years old, he was on his first adventure away from his nurses. On seeing him, Salmacis suddenly forgot all about her self-involvedness, and knew beyond a shadow of a doubt that she would dedicate her life to loving him.

She popped her head out of her pool and shouted over to the youth that he surely must be a god, seeing as he was so beautiful. The young Hermaphroditus went a deep shade of red and scowled as he tried to walk on by, but the nymph floated alongside him, demanding that he kiss her and take her to bed this instant. Still embarrassed, he snapped at her to leave him alone and that he wasn't interested.

The stunned Salmacis was distraught at the rejection, but felt certain that she could change his mind if only he would give her a chance. She crouched in wait behind a bush and, when he walked past, jumped out and latched on to him.

Hermaphroditus struggled fiercely to escape her grip, but Salmacis' burning passion had made her surprisingly strong. She peppered his face with kisses while he tried desperately to untangle himself from her. Not able to understand why he wasn't returning her enthusiasm, she cried out for help from the gods, asking to make it so that they would be together forever. The gods obliged immediately, and the nymph and the boy were fused together, leaving one body with both reproductive organs.

Now forever unable to escape his overzealous mate, Hermaphroditus cursed the waters that surrounded them so that anyone who bathed within them would meet the same fate as he had. It's said that any man who took a dip in the pool of Salmacis would become more soft-hearted and feminine.

PEITHO (*peeth-oh*)

The goddess of persuasion and seduction, Peitho was, perhaps unsurprisingly, a close companion of Aphrodite. They were so close, even, that Peitho was thought to have nursed the Olympian's children, the Erotes, while she was out doing her godly business. Though Peitho's personification is mainly linked to love and sex, she also had influence over other matters that needed a bit of persuasion, like politics.

She was considered the opposite of the goddess Bia, personification of force, and preferred to concentrate mainly on matters of love, friendship, and sex. One of her most notable displays of persuasion was when she successfully convinced the hero Cadmus, who was supposed to be looking for his sister, Europa, to take a bit of a detour in order for him to meet his future bride, Harmonia.

As well as being the strings behind their union, Peitho was also on hand on the actual wedding day, attending to the bride-to-be. This is a role she took on in many noteworthy nuptials that we'll soon come to hear about, including that of Dionysus and Ariadne, and Thetis and Peleus. She was actually one of the five deities that newlywed couples would pray to for prosperity, and the only minor goddess amongst them.

Peitho was often depicted in art, especially pieces concerning the abduction of Helen by Paris, implying that the Trojan prince may have needed her to coerce Helen into fleeing with him.

A particular group of mortals that were linked to the goddess were sex workers, who were referred to as 'servants of Peitho', as they practiced their own powers of persuasion when it came to their employment.

3

Good (ish) Gals

So pure of heart, they just can't help but attract trouble

PYTHIA (*pith-ee-a*)

In an ancient world dominated by men, it was a woman that they all went to for advice.

Prophesied to become one of the greatest cities in history, Delphi was considered the centre of the world. It was originally guarded by a huge python, sent by Gaia for protection. When the snake died at the hands of Apollo, its body fell into a giant crevice. As it rotted, from the crack leaked an intoxicating gas (dubbed 'Gaia's breath'), and anyone who inhaled it was overcome by 'visions of the future'.

But they couldn't have just anyone sniffing up the goods, so the people of Delphi decreed that this job must be given to one person at a time, specifically a woman. She would be known as 'Pythia', the go-between for humans and the divine gaseous source.

There were certain prerequisites for the job: she must be over fifty, lest she attract the sexual attentions of men who couldn't be expected to control themselves; if the chosen woman was married and/or a mother, she had to shed her former identity completely to serve; finally, she'd have to undergo a period of purification before assuming the role, during which time she'd fast, bathe in a sacred spring, and drink holy water.

Now ready, she would be positioned near the fragrant fissure, and be available for questioning on the seventh day of the nine warmest months of the year. The vapours would overcome her, and she would become the Oracle of Delphi.

As word spread, people would travel from all over to speak with Pythia. As she was only available for a limited amount of time, priests would have to thin the crowd. First, they'd interrogate potential questioners as to whether their query was good enough to receive the oracle's attention.

Next, they'd be required to donate money, which would be spent on the erection and improvements of a temple, and the city in general. This palm-greasing helped Delphi in becoming a great city, so in that way it fulfilled its own prophecy.

The final requirement before gaining access to the (wo)man behind the curtain was to make an animal sacrifice. If the spilled innards were deemed favourable by the priest, you'd be allowed to see the oracle. If not, you'd be sent home on the spot (no refunds, sorry).

The prophecies themselves could be vague or worded in a way that could be interpreted as correct no matter what the outcome. People often left with more questions than they arrived with, but of course you didn't dare query the reliability of the oracle, as that would essentially be akin to doubting the gods themselves.

DRYOPE (*dry-oh-pee*)

A princess of Oeta, Dryope was the daughter of King Dryops, who clearly liked the sound of his own name.

Once, when she was tending to her father's sheep in the mountains of the kingdom, she caught the interest of a group of tree-dwelling nymphs, called Hamadryads. These Hamadryads recognised Dryope's kind and gentle spirit and took a real liking to her. They revealed themselves and taught her the songs and dances of their people, which Dryope delighted in. From then on, the princess would visit as often as her royal schedule allowed. In truth, she wasn't really cut out for the unavoidably political life of a royal, and frolicking in a field would win over fancy banquets and peace talks any day.

One day, as they all played together, a huge tortoise wandered over, seeming to take a particular interest in the mortal. It was certainly a strange sight, but Dryope and her friends were thrilled with their new pet, stroking its hard shell and looping flower garlands around its long, wrinkled neck. Dryope brought the tortoise to her lap for a snuggle, when all of a sudden it transformed into a snake. The Hamadryads fled in terror, leaving the princess alone. The tortoise was actually Apollo, and when Dryope tried to run with her friends, the Apollo-snake coiled himself around her, holding her tightly, before assaulting her. Dryope was impregnated with a son.

Although devastated by the attack, Dryope gave birth to and raised the boy, who she called Amphissus. Now a mother, Dryope tried to put her days with the nymphs behind her, even getting married and making sure that her son knew of his divine parentage. When Amphissus grew up, he built a temple and dedicated it to his father, and Dryope became a priestess of it.

Years passed, and eventually the Hamadryads would come down from the mountains to visit Dryope. She held no anger towards the nymphs for abandoning her that day and was pleased to see them. Promising to make her a nymph like them, they asked her to join them in the mountains and she positively jumped at the chance. Dryope was promptly whisked away, and in her place the Hamadryads left a fully grown poplar tree. Two women were watching the strange exchange and tried to relay the story to the people of Oeta, but as they started talking about the apparent abduction, they were transformed into a pair of fir trees. Everyone decided it was best that the disappearance of Dryope remained a mystery after that, lest they start feeling a bit tree-ish.

THE HORAE (*haw-ree*)

The Horae, or 'Hours', existed twice in Greek mythology.

The first set of Horae were the personifications of the believed three seasons at the time. There was Thallo (the bringer of blossoms), Auxo (the increaser of plants), and Carpo (the bringer of food). Essentially, they represented the budding of crops, their ripening, and the eventual harvest. They were particularly worshipped by farmers, who relied on the changing of the seasons for a fruitful income and referred to the passing of the seasons as the 'dance of the Horae'. The personification of winter wasn't represented in the Horae, as the season didn't exist before Persephone shacked up with Hades and brought out Demeter's frosty side (more on that later). Back then, it wasn't particularly important to follow time in terms of which point of the year or even hour of day it was, but it was vital to know when the weather would change.

These Horae also guarded the entrance to Mount Olympus. First to welcome the Olympians when they returned from their travels, they hid the entrance from view of other gods with clouds whenever they got close. It was also their job to rally the stars and constellations across the sky. It's thought that these sisters, along with the Graces (their sibling goddesses that embodied charm, beauty, nature, and creativity), assisted Aphrodite when she emerged on the coast of Cythera. They dressed her in fabrics dyed with flowers of spring, the same garments that they wore themselves. Adorning her in all manner of gold and jewels, they then led her to Olympus to introduce her to her new friends (or frenemies, at least).

The second lot of Horae were daughters of Zeus and the Titaness Themis, and they represented law and order. First was Dike, who was the personification of justice in mortals. Then there was Eunomia (order and good law), and Eirene (peace and wealth). Eirene in particular had quite the following, especially in Athens, where they had a cult specifically for the path of peace.

Although relatively minor goddesses and not super involved in any of the myths, both sets of the Horae were highly respected. They both had influence over order and balance, whether it was the passing of time or the moral structures followed by society to maintain civility, which is about as important as it gets.

CASSANDRA (*cass-an-dra*)

When Apollo tried to win the affections of one of his fiery-haired priestesses, he presented her with the gift of prophecy. Cassandra, though flattered to receive the attentions of the god she revered higher than any other, politely declined his advances. Apollo wouldn't accept a simple 'no thanks', though, especially since he'd given her such a wondrous gift, so as punishment, he cursed her. While he wasn't able to revoke his gift of sight, he instead made it that no matter how accurate, nobody would ever believe her prophecies.

As the daughter of King Priam and Queen Hecuba of Troy, Cassandra was also the sister of Paris, and she vividly predicted the bloodshed that her brother's little dalliance would cause. She warned her family that if Paris went to Sparta, he would bring on the fall of their great city. Of course, they didn't listen, and off he went, returning with his missus, Helen. As the rest of the city rejoiced in the arrival of their new princess, Cassandra attacked Helen on sight, knowing the pain and suffering her presence would inevitably cause. Still, though, nobody wanted to heed her warnings, rolling their eyes at *classic crazy Cassie.*

Just as Cassandra predicted, retribution came to the city in what would be remembered as the most epic war of history so far. In the final days of the fight, she cautioned the people of Troy that the city would burn due to a clever wooden contraption in the shape of a horse. Who cared? Nobody. Too busy celebrating their apparent win, citizens jeered and booed at her trying to kill their buzz. Even when she attempted to uncover the Greeks by taking an axe to the horse, the Trojans pulled her away, calling her hysterical. As we know, the opposition descended from said contraption and attacked in the night, obliterating most of the remaining Trojans.

During the final battle, Cassandra hid in a temple of Athena, clinging to a statue of the goddess for protection. Ajax the Lesser (not to be confused with Ajax the Great – must have been pretty disappointing receiving *that* nickname) took no notice of the divine security this should have provided, dragging her away and viciously raping her.

Cassandra stumbled out of Athena's temple and straight into Agamemnon, commander of the Greeks. Unfortunately for the princess, her troubles were far from over . . .

PYRRHA (*pirra*)

When Zeus decided that it was time to end the bronze age of man, he did so with a great flood. Pyrrha's husband Deucalion was the son of the Titan god Prometheus, so was *in the know* as it were, and his father advised him to build an ark for himself and Pyrrha.

What do you mean, this story sounds familiar?

So, build he did. Together, Pyrrha and Deucalion boarded and were protected by the ravaging waters that wiped the surface of the world.

Once the waters calmed, the pair moored the ark on the banks of Mount Parnassus, the only spot high enough to remain untouched by the flood. Zeus would have usually been royally pissed that Prometheus had gone behind his back, but Pyrrha and Deucalion were god-fearing people that lived a life without sin, so he let it slide. As the couple climbed to higher ground, Zeus cleared the storm clouds and considered his next steps. Calling for the sea god Triton to blow his magic conch, the waters receded, uncovering the severely bogged world once again.

Pyrrha and Deucalion looked at one another and wept. This new, soggy existence was sure to be lonely, and though they were grateful to the gods for their survival, they weren't sure they wanted to live out the rest of their days with nobody to talk to except each other. Spotting a cave in the face of the mountain, they sought shelter and prayed to the gods for advice. It was the goddess of prophecy, Themis, who would hear their call. She told them that it was their task to repopulate the earth. As they weren't quite up to the job of doing it the old-fashioned way, Themis instructed them to throw the bones of their mothers over their shoulders, as that should have the desired results. Pyrrha in particular was appalled, not wanting to dig up and disrespect her mother in such a way, regardless of the importance of the task. Deucalion gently suggested that Themis might be speaking figuratively. He took 'mother' to mean Gaia, the mother of 'the world' and 'bones' to be the rocks of the earth. So, Pyrrha and Deucalion walked the land and tossed as instructed.

Where Deucalion's rocks landed, men appeared. Where Pyrrha's landed, women were created. These newbies would become a respectful, hardworking race that Zeus was happy with, for the time being at least. With the earth repopulated and drying out, Gaia worked on reproducing other natural forms of life, like vegetation and flowing waters.

IPHIGENIA (*if-uh-jen-eye-ya*)

When Iphigenia's father, King Agamemnon of Mycenae, was sailing with his army to invade Troy, he accidentally killed one of Artemis' sacred deer en route. As punishment, she stopped all winds, preventing the ships from sailing further than the port town of Aulis. Agamemnon consulted his seer, Calchas, for advice, and was told that the only way to appease the goddess was the human sacrifice of his daughter. He refused initially, but peer pressure from his crew (and fantasies of glory, likely) soon changed his mind. He sent word home to his wife, Clytemnestra, to bring the girl to Aulis, under the guise that he'd arranged for her to marry the hero Achilles.

On arrival, Iphigenia set about getting ready for the would-be wedding (probably getting an ancient mani-pedi or something) while her mother sought out her son-in-law-to-be. She found Achilles and began chewing his ear off about the upcoming nuptials. 'Should I have the chicken or the fish? I wonder who will catch the bouquet. Isn't it weird how my husband's suddenly so concerned with marrying off his daughter when he's meant to be going to war?', etc. – typical wedding chat. Achilles, having no idea what she was talking about, told Clytemnestra that she wasn't here to witness a wedding, but a sacrifice. Annoyed that his name had been unfairly used in such a lie, Achilles agreed to help save Iphigenia. They rushed to tell her, with Clytemnestra expecting to swiftly head home and avoid any sacrificing, but the two were surprised to find that the young princess accepted her fate calmly.

She reasoned that, as a mere mortal, she had no right to go against the will of the gods, and if sacrificing herself would serve the needs of Greece, then she would do so willingly. Achilles was astounded at the bravery and selflessness of Iphigenia, offering to fight for her honour, and *actually* marry her if she wanted to change her mind, but she was resolute. She told her mother not to cry for her, or to be angry at Agamemnon (who had always revered Iphigenia as his favourite child). Despite loud and passionate protests from Clytemnestra, Iphigenia walked up to the altar that she thought would make her a wife, ready to die.

NYX (*nicks*)

Nyx was the primordial deity of the night, one of the earliest 'things' to ever exist. As the world grew, she married her brother, Erebus (the personification of darkness), and they had lots of calamitous children, including Hypnos (god of sleep), Nemesis (divine retribution), and Thanatos (death). She resided in the depths of the Underworld, in Tartarus, with her family. With her huge black wings, flowing inky robes, and crown of misty darkness, Nyx was the one to bring the veil of night down onto earth to signify the end of every day. As the goddess of night, she was rather widely feared, but realistically didn't express any particular evil in comparison to other gods and goddesses. However, due to the nature of her powers and the mystery that surrounded her, people tended to think of her as a malevolent being (or maybe they were just scared of the dark).

In fact, even Zeus feared Nyx, who was significantly older than him. Zeus even suspected that Nyx might be more powerful, too. This was exemplified when Hera called upon Nyx's son Hypnos to make her husband fall asleep, so that she could torment Heracles without his continuous interruptions. When Zeus found out what Hypnos had done, he took off after him, wielding a thunderbolt and hell-bent on making him pay for his insolence by throwing him into the sea. Hypnos dived straight down into Tartarus and took refuge under his mother's skirt. When Zeus realised where he'd fled to, he didn't dare invoke Nyx's wrath, so had no choice but to let it go.

Hypnos learned his lesson, though, and was quick to tell Hera where to go next time she asked him for a favour.

Nyx's palace in Tartarus was wrapped in dark clouds, giving it a real gloomy vibe, and she lived there with her daughter Hemera (the day), though they were never thought to be home at the same time, with one going out to do their business just as the other returned. Nyx was often depicted in art alongside Helios, Selene, and Eos, other deities responsible for moving the day along. She was also tasked with keeping up a constant dark veil above the sky that stopped the shining blue light of Mount Olympus poking through. Busy lady.

FLORA (*flor-a*)

The nymph Chloris fell in love with Zephyrus, the god of the west wind. By becoming his wife, she was elevated to minor-goddess status, and with that came new responsibilities. Chloris was now responsible for making flowers bloom on earth each spring, and would be renamed Flora. She dressed in glorious white robes embroidered with the flowers that she looked after.

When it wasn't her time to shine, Chloris lived in the Elysian Fields of the Underworld, where only the crème de la crème of humanity were permitted to spend eternal life. It's thought that these fields were a sea of flowers, with every species imaginable at full bloom all the time. She was somewhat of a groundskeeper there, and she took great pride in keeping the sacred place at its peak of beauty with magic and tenderness.

Her life as a goddess was generally quite an idyllic one, but even she would experience loss. Once, when Flora was going about her duties on earth, she stumbled upon the body of an unknown nymph. The sight upset the goddess greatly, and she mourned for her fallen sister. To honour the nymph, she transformed her into a new flower, but that wasn't quite enough. Flora cried out to Aphrodite for assistance and, hearing her plight, the Olympian donated radiant beauty for the flower. That was better, Flora thought, but there was still room for improvement. Next, she called for Dionysus, who dropped some of his sweet nectar onto the bud, creating an intoxicating fragrance.

Then, Flora asked if the Graces could possibly gift her new creation something of their own, and they obliged, bestowing allure and brilliance. Almost there, Flora lastly asked her husband for his own gift. Zephyrus, who would do anything for his wife, blew apart the clouds so that the flower could be touched by the light from Helios' sunny chariot, making it bloom spectacularly. The new flower flourished and revealed stunning deep red petals that gave off the most scrumptious scent she'd ever sniffed. It was simply perfect, and she named it 'rose', understanding it would come to be known as the queen of all flowers. Using her own powers now, Flora multiplied the rose and spread it across the globe, so that everyone could enjoy it.

Flora is thought to be the deity behind the metamorphosis of some of the most popular Greek myths, responsible for helping to transform the likes of Adonis into his flowery form after his untimely death.

HESTIA (*hes-tee-ya*)

Olympian goddess of the hearth and home, Hestia was a pure and peaceful deity who was not there for her sibling's incessant drama. She was the first-born child of Cronus and Rhea, but when her father was forced to regurgitate his children, she was last out, so some consider her to be the youngest.

Hestia is usually depicted as a modest woman of middle age, wearing a veil and holding flowers. She's not hugely involved with much of the mythology as she was commonly at home, tasked with keeping the fire in the hearth of Olympus burning strong, using the fats of the sacrifices that were always pouring in from earth. Although she may not have had many temples dedicated to her, it could be considered that every dwelling with a hearth was technically devoted to her.

Greatly worshipped and respected by mortals, they called on her divine protection for their own homes. At banquets, Hestia was honoured with wine and prayers both first and last, as well as given first pick of any sacrifice made within the home. As it goes, she was particularly fond of pigs.

It was considered an insult to Hestia if a hearth's fire were to peter out due to inattention, and relighting it would involve rituals and purifications to appease the goddess. As the typical homemakers, it was usually down to the eldest woman of the household to pay proper respects to Hestia and tend to the flames.

Hestia had no interest in coupling up, but was still pursued by her fellow Olympians, Poseidon and Apollo. Both wanted to make her their wife, but she was having none of it. Instead, Hestia went to Zeus and pledged to live her entire existence as a virgin. Even Aphrodite, who we know didn't take too kindly to anyone saying no to her, had no influence over her decision. Aphrodite's son Priapus (of the lolling tongue and bulging erection) would try to take her anyway. As she slept peacefully one day, Priapus sneaked up on her, but a nearby donkey suddenly let out a bray and the goddess woke up. Alerted to this terrible disrespect, the other gods banned Priapus from all their gatherings, and he was exiled to the woods.

Eventually, growing tired of everyone else's theatrics, Hestia graciously stepped down from her duties, handing her Olympian status over to the newer, keener god, Dionysus. Even after this, Hestia always had a place to call home on Mount Olympus, and she'd continue to keep its fire strong. A true unproblematic queen.

CALLISTO (*ca-liss-toe*)

As a hunting companion and close friend of Artemis, Callisto had taken a vow to remain a virgin her whole life.

Although Zeus greatly respected his daughter's own vow of chastity, the same could not be said for the rest of the women of the world, including Callisto. He appeared to the girl in the form of Artemis, who Callisto loved so much that she couldn't help but respond tenderly when the 'goddess' put the moves on her. Callisto didn't have any experience with sex, but something about the mechanics of this run-in felt a bit off even to her, especially since she ended up pregnant. Realising that she'd obviously been tricked, not only was Callisto devastated, but she was also terrified of her friend finding out and condemning her. She tried her very best to hide the pregnancy from Artemis, and it worked for a little while, but eventually she came upon Callisto when she was bathing in a spring and saw her swelling belly.

Artemis was enraged that such a close friend and apparently devout virgin could do something so blasphemous. Callisto was swiftly kicked out of their hunting party and shunned by her favourite goddess. As the heavily pregnant Callisto moped about her fate, Hera descended on her. She pulled the girl's ponytail, called her a whore, and transformed her into a bear. Bear-Callisto gave birth to her son, Arcas, who remained human. Later, a gaggle of shepherds came across mother and son and feared greatly for the boy's safety. In order to protect him from the vicious beast, they took the baby away with them. Years later, the group returned with a hunter amongst them – the hunter was in fact Arcas, now all grown up. Callisto couldn't help but try to get a closer look at her son, but to Arcas she just looked like a wild animal on its way to batter him. With shooting skills that would have rivalled his own mother's, he killed the she-bear, having no idea of their connection, receiving congratulations from the shepherds.

Zeus, who had watched all of this drama unfold (but didn't bother to step in), put mother and son in the stars as Ursa Major and Minor, also known as 'big bear' and 'little bear'.

TETHYS (*teh-this*)

As one of the Titans, Tethys didn't exactly have an idyllic childhood. Along with her siblings, she was hidden away inside of Gaia by her father, for fear of overthrowing him.

Beautiful and wise, she was the personification of fresh water, and when she married Oceanus, her brother and god of the ocean, the pair didn't let their poor upbringing affect their own parenting. Together, they were very nurturing and kind parents, which was no easy feat considering they had over six thousand children, all of whom ruled over their own rivers, lakes, streams, or rain clouds.

Their best-known offspring were the Oceanids (sea goddesses) and Potamoi (gods of rivers and streams). Tethys also looked after the world's sea creatures, with the couple overseeing the comings and goings of the underwater metropolises.

The eldest of Gaia's children, Oceanus, had no interest in conflict. When his siblings started planning to topple Uranus, he would have no part in it, though it's assumed he was also tired of his cruel father's ways. Despite not joining in on the action, Oceanus was still awarded a nice slice of the pie, as it were, as his brother Cronus put him in charge of all the water on earth (he'd have to hand this over to Poseidon after the Titanomachy).

Tethys and Oceanus spent a few more years popping out water babies, but they were starting to get a bit worried. Even for Titans, their family tree was looking substantially overgrown. Meanwhile, complaints were being made about Cronus' reign, too, and out broke the next war. Again, the aqueous couple didn't partake. They would be called upon, however, once Zeus started retrieving his siblings from his father's stomach. After their release, their sister Rhea asked them to watch over and raise Hera while the rest of the plan was carried out. Tethys in particular bonded greatly with the queen-to-be of the heavens, and this relationship endured as Hera grew into a woman. When Zeus' lover (see: *victim)* Callisto was put into the sky as a constellation, Tethys demanded that her stars should never sit below the horizon (and thus touch the ocean), out of respect for Hera as Zeus' long-suffering wife.

After the war was won, Tethys and Oceanus retained their respected status. They also decided that, despite their enjoyment of each other, it was time to split – the continuous floods they were instigating with their overflow of offspring was causing too many problems. They divorced amicably, and it's not known if Tethys ever moved on with any other men, godly or not.

ECHO (*eck-oh*)

One thing we can be sure about the mountain nymph Echo is that she was a horrendous chatterbox. Her incessant mouth got her into trouble when she kept Hera talking for so long that she couldn't spy on Zeus with his flavour of the month. Enraged that she missed out on catching him (for the thousandth time), she cursed Echo by taking away her ability to speak. Now Echo could only repeat the last few words that were spoken in front of her by others.

Echo was mooching through a forest on earth one day when she came across the most handsome man she'd ever seen. The man was Narcissus, who admittedly was rather magnificent, and had been separated from his hunting party. The enchanted Echo hid behind a tree and watched him, desperate to be able to introduce herself.

Narcissus heard a rustle and called out, 'Who's there?'

Echo, well, echoed, *'Who's there'*.

He said, 'Come here'.

She repeated, *'Come here!'*

He announced: 'We must come together'.

'We must come together!' she agreed, springing out from her hiding place and pouncing on the beautiful stranger.

Echo tried desperately to express herself without words, but the youth was uncaring of her feelings, and was rather harsh in his rejection of her. Echo fled in shame. Heartbroken, but having possibly made the worst first impression in ancient history, she resigned herself to watching from afar as she pined desperately.

It just so happened that the goddess of divine retribution, Nemesis, had been watching this whole exchange. She was an especially remorseless deity, who took a special interest in matters of the heart.

Nemesis deemed Narcissus' nasty rejection of Echo worthy of her wrath, so she cursed the hunter to fall in love with his own reflection in a nearby spring. Narcissus' heart swelled at the sight of himself. He decided that nothing else could possibly measure up to this feeling, and he never moved again, eventually transforming into a flower (with a little help from Flora).

Just as Narcissus couldn't pull away from his reflection, Echo couldn't leave the real thing, either. She watched on as the love of her life became consumed with himself, and she eventually withered away.

It's said that you can still hear the doomed Echo's voice to this day, repeating your own words when you call out in empty spaces (*spaces . . . spaces . . .*)

EUROPA (*you-roh-pa*)

When Europa, a beautiful Phoenician princess from Tyre, was playing with her friends on a beach, she caught the attention of the one and only Zeus. As with anything (or anyone) Zeus wanted, he would get it. He transformed himself into a white bull and moseyed on over to where she was picking flowers, acting like a simple friendly bovine, curious of the humans. Europa was transfixed by the bull and began stroking its soft white hair, noting that its breath had the intoxicating smell of saffron. Even as her friends moved on, Europa couldn't pull herself away, making a flower crown for the animal and looping it lovingly around its horns. Eventually, she climbed on the back of the bull-Zeus, wanting to take a ride. Maiden secured, Zeus ran full pelt into the sea and started swimming. He swam all the way to the island of Crete and, once Europa had dismounted, turned back into his human(ish) form.

Meanwhile, in Tyre, Europa's family were completely frantic over her disappearance. Her parents commanded that her four brothers scour the earth for her and to not even think about returning home without her in tow. Ever.

They each set off on their own quests, but while they got themselves into various situations along the way, they never did retrieve their only sister.

Back in Crete, Zeus was completely enamoured with the young princess, and Europa in turn was apparently agreeable with both her abduction and relocation. He showered her with his godly affection and extravagant gifts, including a necklace forged by Hephaestus himself, the magical dog Laelaps (the same from Procris' story – Europa had it first), and the javelin that never misses (ditto). To protect his new beau, Zeus had the bronzed giant, Talos (from Medea's story), circle the island shores three times a day looking for any potential dangers. From their union came three sons, including Minos, who would grow up to marry Pasiphaë and rule over Crete.

Once Europa and Zeus had their fill of each other, she went on to marry the king of the island, Asterion, who adopted the three boys and raised them as his own. As well as being the first ever queen of Crete, Europa's string of descendants would scatter and become key influencers in many important Greek myths, earning her the title of 'godmother of Europe'.

HARMONIA (*har-moh-nee-ya*)

Goddess of harmony and concord, Harmonia was born from the union of Aphrodite and Ares (love and war). She would eventually go on to marry Cadmus, founder of Thebes, but he had some trials and tribulations to get through first (starting with attempting to find his sister, Europa).

As we know, he was unsuccessful, probably because he abandoned his search to establish the city of Thebes. In his defence, he was told to do this by Pythia herself, and who was he to deny her? Later, he found himself in Samothrace, dining with the stepmother of Harmonia. Cadmus and his host got on fantastically, and when Hermes appeared to the woman and told her to offer him the hand of Harmonia without a dowry, she did so. When she told Harmonia the news, the young woman refused to go along with it – Cadmus might boast of royal blood, but he looked positively poor, and she was the daughter of two very important gods!

Aphrodite decided to step in, knowing this would be a great match for her daughter. She took the mortal form of a local girl and gave Harmonia a long speech about Cadmus' beauty (both outside and in), and encouraged her to look at the stranger in a different light. Taking after her mother in the looks department, Harmonia was lovely, and Cadmus needed no such pep talk to accept from his side.

Their wedding was a huge celebration, and all the gods attended alongside mortals, showering the couple with beautiful gifts.

Aphrodite loaned Harmonia her magical girdle (there's various arguments for what this piece might be – for the sake of this story, imagine it as a knock-out sexy lingerie set). It was a huge success, too, as they went on to have five children.

Another gift came from the forging god, Hephaestus – an intricate necklace, its chain linked together by golden snakes, with their jaws clamped around an eagle. Garish as that may sound, the bride loved it and fastened it on immediately. Heph told her that the piece would keep any woman wearing it eternally young and beautiful, and thus, the necklace became much coveted amongst the women of the house of Thebes and beyond.

What nobody stopped to think about, though, was that Hephaestus may have had a hidden agenda. Let's not forget that Harmonia's mother, Aphrodite, was actually Hephaestus' *wife*, and her father, Ares, had humiliated him countless times by bedding his spouse so unashamedly. Indeed, Hephaestus had in fact cursed the necklace so that it would bring terrible luck to whoever owned it.

And so the newlyweds, though happy in their relationship, faced challenge after challenge, including the city of Thebes' civil unrest and their families' tendency to land themselves in sticky situations. The necklace would be passed down through the generations, scorching a path of bad luck throughout the Theban family tree. We'll get to know some of these stories soon, including the fate of the couple's daughters Autonoë, Agave and Semele, as well as Jocasta and her unfortunate lineage.

Eventually, Cadmus and Harmonia bowed out of the picture. They'd always fancied seeing more of Greece, so decided to spend their twilight years travelling. They did so quite humbly – usually royals would stay at other palaces as they toured, enjoying lavish banquets in their honour and rubbing shoulders with similar hoit and toit, but they were happy to go without. That said, they did bring with them a small staff, so they weren't exactly slumming it. Akin to choosing the Hilton over the Savoy, but it was hardly a Holiday Inn.

Wherever they went, though, they made sure to pack their favourite trinket, the necklace forged by the gods. Because of this, luck never seemed to be on their side no matter what they did. The pair would eventually take their retirement in Illyria, but it wasn't long before Cadmus angered Ares (this time the result of an offhand remark that the god of war took the wrong way), who transformed him into a snake. Harmonia said, 'if you're a snake, I'm a snake' and with the help of Athena, joined him in serpentine form.

They slithered off into the sunset, finally free of the curse that had plagued their wedded life, and when their time was up, Zeus allowed the couple to transform back into their human forms. They died peacefully, together, and in the afterlife, they were permitted into the Elysian Fields.

After ruining some more lives, the cursed necklace would be placed in a temple in Delphi that was dedicated to Athena, where it couldn't cause any more trouble.

MELISSA (*mel-liss-a*)

The wedding of Zeus and Hera was set to be the grandest party to have ever been. Hera was feeling pretty pleased with herself – Zeus was finally going to take the vows and pledge fidelity to her, and surely even *he* wouldn't dare to go against them!

In the run-up, Zeus announced that there would be a competition. Gods, goddesses, nymphs and the like were invited to bring a dish of their own making. The bride and groom would taste everything, and whoever they jointly decided was the winner would get one wish granted from Zeus himself. The whole of Olympus and beyond really rose to the challenge and got to work creating what they thought to be the perfect dish for their king and queen.

The big day came, and an extra-long table groaned with the weight of hundreds of dishes. The gods and goddesses scouted out the foodstuffs with interest, marvelling amongst themselves at the impressive culinary delights on offer, hoping Zeus and Hera might allow them to enjoy any leftovers when they were finished.

Just before the tasting was due to start, the strangest little nymph approached the table. She was called Melissa, and she was positively tiny. Her whole body was covered in black fuzz, with a yellow stripe along her middle. She rose up to the table on translucent wings so small they shouldn't have reasonably been able to carry her, making a bizarre buzzing noise as they did just that. Next to plates of shining gold and bowls studded with rubies and amethyst, Melissa plonked down a small, white container, about the size of your average watch-face, filled with a dollop of gold liquid. The other deities averted their eyes in embarrassment for the poor thing.

Zeus and Hera got to tasting, starting at the other end of the table, mmm-ing away as they crunched, licked, slurped and swallowed their way through so many delicious dishes. Melissa's was the final offering of the day, and the couple shot each other doubtful glances as they each dipped their pinkies into the golden goop. As they tasted it, their eyes widened in disbelief. This was absolutely the most delicious thing either of them had ever tasted. Without the need to even discuss it, Zeus declared this dish the winner of the competition, and urged the deity responsible to step forward.

Melissa shyly buzzed to the front of the room as the audience gave a stunned round of applause. Zeus decreed that this delicacy would be the food of the gods, and he dubbed it 'ambrosia'. He then turned to Melissa and asked what her wish would be. Melissa started to tell of what she so desired – making her honey was exceptionally difficult, made more so by her small frame, as well as the constant threat of other creatures trying to hurt her and steal her produce. It had taken weeks for her to make just this tiny amount. What Melissa wanted, she explained, was a weapon – something that would allow her to protect herself against predators, so that she wouldn't have to worry about meeting a sticky end as she went about her business.

The mood in the hall suddenly became thunderous (literally, as Zeus was fuming). How dare this nymph ask for something so violent on this joyful day. He'd show her. He couldn't kill her, of course – she was the only one who knew how to make ambrosia, and he couldn't live without it now that he'd experienced its delights. In fact, he was keen for it to be mass-produced as quickly as possible.

Zeus conjured up a colony of nymphs just like Melissa and told her that she'd be their queen. Melissa thanked the god and tried to buzz off, but he grabbed her by her wing and pulled her back.

'I think you're forgetting your weapon, little nymph,' he sneered. Suddenly, Melissa felt the worst pain she'd ever experienced in her life. As she writhed on the floor, screaming in agony, she was able to register that her new colony were doing the same. There was a horrible stabbing pain coming from her backside, and she was appalled when she looked behind her to see a huge, barbed stinger poking out. With the pain still present but less urgent now, Melissa stood up, whimpering.

Zeus told her to enjoy her longed-for weapon, which she was free to use to ward off any attacks from enemies. If she did, though, the stinger would stay within the body of the receiver, pulling her insides out with it.

ERIGONE & MAERA
(*eh-rig-oh-nee* & *mee-ra*)

When Athenian man Icarius showed kindness and respect to the god Dionysus, he was taught the art of winemaking as a reward. So was his generous nature, Icarius wanted to share the joy, and did so with a group of local shepherds. Together they drank heartily and enjoyed the sweet treat. However, as the shepherds were gripped by the unfamiliar side-effects of intoxication, they began to feel unbalanced and unruly. To them, the only reasonable explanation was that Icarius must have poisoned them. In their panic and anger, the shepherds stoned him to death and buried his body under a tree.

That night, Icarius' daughter Erigone had begun to worry when her father didn't return home at his usual time. She set off to look for him, bringing along with her their faithful dog, Maera. After searching for a while, Maera caught the scent of her master and led Erigone to the tree, where she began to dig until the body was uncovered. Distraught, Erigone climbed the tree and hanged herself over her father's body. Maera, unwilling to be without both beloved members of her family, leaped off a cliff to join them in death.

When Dionysus got wind of the tragic loss of such a noble man and his household, he was furious. As was often the case with these vengeful gods and their unfair punishments, though, it wasn't the vicious men who would directly feel the vino god's smite. He cursed all the unmarried women of Athens with a psychosis that made them all want to end their own lives in the same way that Erigone had, and the population of the city quickly started dwindling. No matter how hard the Athenians prayed, the madness wouldn't relent. Eventually, one of them thought to pay a visit to an oracle, who instructed them to give Icarius and Erigone (and hopefully Maera) respectable burial rites. After this, the women woke up from their mania, and the city would later start a festival in the departed families honour (or perhaps just to keep Dio on-side).

Satisfied that everyone had sufficiently suffered, Dionysus put the trio into the skies: Erigone was transformed into the constellation Virgo; Icarius would become Boötes; and Maera, the star Procyon.

BAUCIS (*baw-sis*)

An elderly couple of Tyana, Baucis and her husband, Philemon, didn't have much in the way of money or possessions. What they had in spades, though, was kindness and compassion.

When Zeus and Hermes disguised themselves as peasants to test the people of Tyana, they went door to door asking for some hospitality and a bed for the night. At each place, they were turned away, often cruelly, by the townspeople.

Lastly, they arrived at the modest cottage of Baucis and Philemon. The couple had little to give but gave what they did have willingly. The mysterious guests were served food and wine, all the time chatting amicably with the poor but friendly couple. At some point, Baucis came to realise that although she'd refilled all four of their goblets plenty of times, the pitcher of wine remained full. Discreetly, she pointed this out to her husband, and they came to the shocking realisation that they were playing host to a couple of gods.

Baucis was suddenly extremely embarrassed of their inferior home and felt foolish for serving such significant guests such paltry rations. Philemon rushed into the garden and began chasing after a goose thinking Baucis could make a meal more befitting for their guests with it. The goose hid behind Zeus, who laughed cheerfully. He told the couple not to worry, but that he and Hermes must leave now, and instructed them to follow. As they walked, the pair were ordered not to look back until they reached the top of the mountains surrounding the city.

Baucis and Philemon obliged, and when they were finally able to take a peek, they realised the entire city had been wiped out by a flood. The only tangible thing remaining was their once modest cottage, which had been transformed into a stunning temple. The townsfolk had been punished for their disregard of xenia, and the kind couple had been the only ones spared.

As Baucis and Philemon gazed upon what was left of their home, they dared to ask the gods for two things. First, that they may be guardians of the temple. This wish was granted. Secondly, that when it was time for one of them to die, the other may go as well. When they did pass, the two were transformed – one into an oak tree and the other a linden, the two intertwining with each other in the boggy remains of Tyana.

AMARYLLIS (*a-ma-rill-iss*)

When the young woman Amaryllis fell for the local shepherd
Alteo, she would soon learn that he had a very specific key to his
heart.

Alteo was strong and extremely handsome, with an all-encompassing
obsession with botany. When he wasn't tending to his herd, Alteo
loved nothing more than to look upon beautiful flowers and learn
everything he could about them, and there wasn't a single woman in
town (or, he suspected, the world) who could thrill him more than
his hobby. And so, he announced that he would never take a lover
or wife, unless a potential paramour could bring him a flower that
he'd never seen before.

Amaryllis was desperate for him to return her love, but she knew
nothing of flowers, never mind how she'd go about finding one that
others before her had not. Instead, she decided her best bet was to
consult the gods for help, so she went to see the oracle of Delphi.

For once, the oracle gave her a straightforward albeit nasty solution
to her problem – to win Alteo's love, she must make a blood sacrifice
for him. Despite the fierceness of her passion Amaryllis could not
bring herself to harm someone or something to win Alteo's heart, so
she went about this sacrifice another way. Amaryllis made the journey
to Alteo's cottage every night, puncturing her own heart continuously
with a golden arrow. Her blood trickled down her body and into the
earth below as she did so.

It seemed that her heartache, both figuratively and literally, would never end, but Amaryllis was prepared to continue with the routine every day for the rest of her life if it meant she had a shot with the beautiful shepherd. Then, on the thirtieth night, a crimson flower bloomed from the pool of blood at her feet. Ignoring the pain, Amaryllis bent down, gently plucked the new flower from the ground, and ran to present it to Alteo. The young man was overjoyed with the beautiful gift, and equally smitten by the woman who'd made it a reality. With his floral condition fulfilled, Alteo and Amaryllis were married, and he named the crimson flower after his new wife.

DORIS (*do-riss*)

Sea deities in general were known for being rather cold and, honestly, a little bit mean to humans. It wasn't their fault, really – living in the ocean meant that they didn't spend much time with us, and they didn't understand the ways in which we lived, laughed, and loved.

One Oceanid who wasn't like her sisters though, was the lovely Doris. Mother of the Nereids, she was married to Nereus (also called the Old Man of the Sea). They were somewhat of a power couple, mostly concerning themselves with making their waters (and thus, the world) a better place.

From fellow divinities to creatures, it was Doris' responsibility to make sure everyone in the ocean had sufficient housing and food – not an easy feat at all, considering how often one sea critter is the main food source for another. She doesn't have much in the way of mythological stories, but she's worth a mention, since without her we wouldn't have the many tales of her offspring, more of which we'll meet soon.

AEGINA (*ah-gee-nah*)

When Aegina, daughter of the river god Asopus, was abducted by Zeus, he carried her to an island far away. Asopus witnessed the abduction from afar, devastated that his daughter had had her virtue stolen, but despite his watery roots, he wasn't able to swim fast enough to catch them. He missed Aegina terribly and wanted her back with him. So, he travelled all over, looking for breadcrumbs that might lead him to her whereabouts. Eventually, he wound up in the kingdom of Sisyphus in Corinth. Sisyphus told Asopus that he did indeed know where his daughter was, but it was going to cost him (Sisyphus was a bit of a scallywag like that). Asopus didn't care for riches and gave the greedy king everything he had in exchange for whatever information he could get. Sisyphus showed the god the location of the island where Zeus had sequestered his daughter,. The island now bore the name Aegina, after her. Asopus set off in a very rapid breaststroke, but Zeus saw him coming and sent a flurry of thunderbolts to the waters around him as he swam – not to kill him, but to push him back and away from his latest conquest. Try as he might, Asopus just wasn't strong enough to fight the currents, and had to admit defeat. He returned home to his river, never to see Aegina again.

Aegina went on to give Zeus a son, Aeacus, who would grow up to be the king of the island. He'd also father the hero Peleus making Aegina the great-grandmother of Achilles.

Hera would eventually find out about the affair, but her detection skills must have been having an off few years, as it wasn't until Aeacus was well into manhood and Aegina was dead that she made the discovery. Unconcerned by the years that had passed, Hera sent to Aegina a devastating plague that killed everyone except the king. As he sat under the shade of a tree feeling sorry for himself, Aeacus prayed to his father, Zeus, that he might transform the army of ants currently skittering about the trunk into people, so that he could repopulate his island. Zeus granted his wish, and the Myrmidon tribe was created, the men of which would fight alongside the Greeks in the war against Troy, led by Achilles.

PENIA (*pen-ee-ya*)

Penia was the goddess of poverty, so any offering she received was likely to have been of the humble variety. She was the sister of Ptocheia (beggary) and Amechania (helplessness), and all three were primordial deities.

She married Porus, the god of plenty (they do say opposites attract), who was the son of the Titaness Metis. The couple apparently met at one of Aphrodite's birthday parties, and as would be expected from this goddess, love was in the air. Porus was decidedly sloshed on nectar from the open bar, and Penia used this as an opportunity to seduce him. Considering she'd only attended the party to beg for scraps, it was definitely a night to remember. Penia and Porus are sometimes considered the parents of Eros who, as the god of love, was a direct combination of the two – always in need (Penia) and existing in abundance (Porus). Generally, though, he's thought to have been born from Aphrodite and Ares.

People who weren't in the grips of hardship wanted nothing to do with this particular goddess lest they attract her attention, and Penia was well aware that she was given a wide berth. It didn't really bother her, as she was more than comfortable with her place in the world, believing that she was a vital player in all of mankind.

Once, she got to reasoning with two men who were debating the consequences of allowing everyone in the world to have great wealth. Penia argued that if everyone had enough riches, no care or consideration would go into the making of a product, as it didn't matter if anything was *good*, because nobody would need the reputation that comes with providing an excellent service. In this respect, her job was just as important as any of the other deities when it came to keeping the world balanced.

ANDROMACHE
(*an-drom-a-kee*)

Andromache and Hector, the Trojan prince, were very much in love. Although he had a reputation for being rather cold to everyone else, Hector was thought to have showered his bride in luxurious gifts and romantic words in private.

Though Andromache was believed to have been a perfect example of wifely obedience, she was also on hand – especially as the Trojan War approached – to give her husband advice and guidance on battle strategies. Despite her willingness to help where she could, she was terrified of losing her darling husband, and continuously begged him to take more of a back seat in the fighting. Hector wouldn't hear of it, though, always wanting to be on the front line of every battle.

When Hector was killed by Achilles, Andromache, like most of the surviving Trojan women, was captured as a slave. The hailed hero Odysseus then took Andromache and Hector's only child, baby Astyanax, and hurled him from the walls of Troy, to ensure there would be no surviving heir to the kingdom. Andromache was inconsolable, and the women of the city bargained with the Greeks to allow them to bury their littlest prince. They laid him on his father's shield, tucked in with some salvaged ornaments from the capital.

The man to claim Andromache was Neoptolemus, the son of her husband's murderer, who had actually chosen her based on her stellar reputation. As a devout Trojan woman and a doting mother and wife, it's unlikely that Andromache took her capture lying down, especially as she expressed her hatred in the past of women who 'cast off old love for new', perhaps a dig at a certain sister-in-law of hers who she believed was at fault for all of this. However, she would have at least two children to her captor, who much preferred her to his actual wife, Hermione.

AMPHITRITE
(*am-fi-try-tee*)

The eldest of her fifty sisters, the Nereid Amphitrite was a true romantic at heart, often fantasising about falling in love and living happily ever after.

God of the sea Poseidon loved to watch the flowing dancing of the Nereids and one day decided that he simply must have the beautiful Amphitrite as his wife. When he came forward to claim his bride, though, Amphitrite quickly swam away. She swam so quickly and so jaggedly that Poseidon could not find her, no matter how hard he looked. He scoured under every barnacle and inside every cove, but the lovely lady was nowhere to be found. Needing to return to his sea business, he recruited a band of aquatic creatures to take up the search for him. One of his dolphins eventually found Amphitrite, who was catching her breath on the shore.

Amphitrite was sat weeping, and when the animal popped up from the sea and revealed himself, she cried to him about her worries. She told him she didn't *want* to marry the sea king, as she'd always dreamed of marrying for love. The dolphin listened to her woes and talked to her at length about her situation. It told her that, in fact, Poseidon loved her very much, and enticed her with visions of how her life could be, should she accept his proposal. As steadfast in her resolve as she was, Amphitrite wasn't immune to the rush of desire when she thought of the wealth and comforts that would be afforded to her as Poseidon's queen.

Once convinced that she really could have both love and marriage with the god, she returned to the sea to accept the proposal. Poseidon was overjoyed at having secured such a beauty, and he threw a lavish underwater celebration for their nuptials. In gratitude to the dolphin for his help, Poseidon put him in the skies as the constellation Delphinus.

As queen of the sea, Amphitrite lived a relatively quiet life, and though we know Poseidon had many other conquests, it seems that they remained married throughout. She's often depicted sporting crab-claw horns, either sitting on her underwater throne with her husband, or riding with him in their massive seahorse-drawn carriage as he goes about his duties. To him, the Nereid birthed many sea creatures and monsters, as well as a son, Triton, who was a merman.

4

Mad Mothers

*They won't stop on their path
to vengeance, leaving behind
a trail of traumatised offspring
in their wake*

CIRCE (*sir-see*)

Powerful and enchanting, Circe was a witch whose speciality was the transfiguration of others, whether they liked it or not. Using herbs and incantations, she was able to harness the power of nature, and animals were obedient to her will. The sister of Pasiphaë, she was known as the mistress of magic, thought to have been the most powerful witch of natural alchemy. She's said to have had beautiful red hair that resembled fire, and flashing, golden eyes that she inherited from her father, Helios.

In her earlier days, Circe was famed for her jealous streak. She fell hard for the sea god Glaucus, but sadly for Circe, he was completely blinded by his infatuation for the nymph Scylla. He even had the nerve to ask her for help to win her love-rival's heart, who was uninterested in him. Circe agreed to 'help' and, honestly, if Glaucus believed that then he's just as much to blame for what transpired as she is. Circe journeyed to Scylla's favourite bathing spot, dumped some of her magic herbs into the water and muttered a sneaky incantation. When Scylla next took a dip, she transformed into a hideous sea monster with a heart full of rage and six horrifying heads. Eternally cursed, Scylla would reside on the rocks opposite Charybdis, another sea monster, and feast on passing sailors.

Later, Circe became enamored with the mortal King Picus – this was destined for doom, too, as he was already married to a woman called Canens, whom he loved dearly. Enraged that she was being rejected again, Circe transformed Picus into a woodpecker. Canens, heartbroken over the loss of her husband, killed herself.

Circe resided on the secluded island of Aeaea, with only her wild animal companions (some of whom used to be men) for company. She lived in an immense stone palace in the middle of the island, surrounded by woods rich in the herbs she needed to create her magics.

Circe is perhaps best known for her tryst with the hero Odysseus. While travelling home from the Trojan War, his crew ended up mooring on Aeaea's shores. While planning their next move, they found themselves drawn to the centre of the island by the sound of Circe's beautiful singing. Odysseus, sensing that something shady was afoot, decided to stay back with the ship. As they proceeded towards Circe's palace, the crew were surprised to find a menagerie of wild animals – lions, wolves, and bears, sprawled around the place like tame, loyal pets. As they approached the entrance, the red-haired witch appeared to welcome them in, offering up a delicious feast and a night of warm hospitality. Weary from their travels, the men jumped at the chance of some R & R. What they didn't know was that the sorceress had laced the food and wine with her magical herbs. With their bellies full, the men looked to satisfy themselves in other ways, turning their attentions to their gracious host. This prospect was short-lived, though. As Circe drew her wand and gave a practised flick of her wrist, the men were transformed into pigs. Still with their human minds, the swine-soldiers were shepherded to her sty on the isle, squealing and crying all the way.

Only one of Odysseus' men remained un-pigged, as he'd decided to hang back and observe from outside, and he ran back to tell his captain what had happened. As the hero power-walked to the palace to save his squad, Picus the woodpecker sprung up and tried desperately to warn him against the dangers of the witch. Odysseus told him to buzz off, sure that he could handle it. As the palace came into view,

Odysseus was met by Hermes, who'd been sent by Athena. She knew what had befallen the crew and wanted to help. Hermes gave Odysseus a moly plant, which was unpickable by humans, but made those in possession of it immune from dark magics. Hermes warned the hero that Circe was wily, and that he wouldn't be safe in her presence unless she swore on the gods not to hurt him.

At the palace, Odysseus was welcomed in, and Circe was looking forward to having another little piggy to add to her collection. Just as Hermes had promised, though, the magic-laced wine and meats that Circe offered him had no effect, and when she pulled out her wand, he drew his own weapon – a sword. Foiled, Circe made a vow not to harm her guest. Actually, she was kind of turned on by his bravery. Odysseus managed to convince her to undo the transformation of his crew. After this, they promptly tumbled into bed together.

Odysseus and his men stayed with Circe for a year, though we must wonder how his comrades felt, being around the witch who had so readily given them tails and snouts. Hopefully it gave them pause next time they fancied taking something that wasn't theirs.

Eventually, Odysseus admitted he was eager to return home to Ithaca, not only to his people but to his wife, and the son who'd not long been born before the war began. Circe helped him prepare for his journey, before he and the crew left her to her own company once again.

At the time of his departure, Circe was pregnant with Odysseus' child. She gave birth to a boy, Telegonous. Telegonous was born curious, often asking about his parentage. As he matured, Circe eventually told him the story of his father. Desperate to meet him, he decided to travel to Ithaca. Knowing of the dangers he was likely to face, Circe visited the immortal stingray, Trygon, whose poisoned tail was lethal to any human, and would cause any god that touched it eternal agony. Trygon told her that in order to obtain his tail as a weapon for her son, she'd first have to touch it herself. Willing to do anything to protect Telegonous, she reached out her hand. Trygon quickly pulled his tail away, telling her that her willingness was good enough for him. Hephaestus crafted the stinger into a spear for the youth.

When Telegonous landed on Ithaca, his significantly aged and now rather paranoid father mistook him for an enemy and tried to kill him. During the struggle, Odysseus was brushed by the poison spear and died.

Telegonous brought his father's body back to Aeaea, along with Odysseus' widow, Penelope, and her son, Telemachus. As awkward as this might sound, the foursome got on spectacularly – after a modest cremation of the man who connected them, Circe made the other three immortal, like her. She would go on to marry Telemachus, and Penelope would wed Telegonous. Double dates were sure to be a scream.

Circe was seen as a figure of fear and desire, and one of the first examples of a predatory female. It's rich that she's usually the one painted as the monster, when the men that she cast against are the ones who rocked up to *her* private island and decided to bother her, but that's the patriarchy.

THETIS (*thee-tis*)

The leader of the Nereids, Thetis was able to change her form at will;
and could prophesise. A foretelling played a big part in her own life,
too. It was said that when Thetis gave birth, the child would grow
up to be more powerful than their father. Originally, both Zeus and
Poseidon were interested in pursuing her, but they quickly changed
their minds when they found out about this little catch.

And so, to protect the gods and their fragile egos, Thetis was
married off to a mere mortal (albeit a king) by the name of Peleus (the
same one from Astydameia and Aegina's stories). In a bizarre act of
courtship, Zeus told Peleus that in order to secure his bride, he must
surprise her on the beach as she relaxed, and embrace her tightly, not
letting go no matter what. Peleus did what he was told, and while
Thetis screamed and thrashed about, she changed into multiple forms,
including a serpent, a flame, and a lioness. Despite her godly strength
and slippery transformations, Peleus locked on tight, and the goddess
was unable to buck him off. Eventually, she tired herself out and was,
apparently, ready to wed. This was Peleus' second wedding, but it
was to be a grand affair, with all the gods on the guestlist (except for
Eris, goddess of strife and discord, because . . . well, her penchant
for strife and discord).

Thetis and Peleus would go on to have seven children, six of whom
would not make it past childhood. The one who did, though, was
a little-known demi-god named Achilles. Wanting to give her son the

best chance possible, Thetis took him to the river Styx, flipped him upside down, and dunked him like a biscuit into its magical waters. By the powers of the river, Achilles was invigorated and made almost invincible, except for the heel that his mother had held him by. Peleus was appalled that his wife had done such a thing without consulting him and tried to have it out with her, but the goddess was turned off completely by her husband's lack of faith and left him, returning to her home in the sea.

When Thetis heard the prophecy that Achilles was destined to die in the Trojan War, she took further measures to protect him. Taking him to Scyros, she told Achilles he was to live as though he were female and play lady-in-waiting to the king's seven daughters. Under the name of Pyrrha, off he went to the king's court, and Thetis thought he was finally safe. Generally, Achilles never did anything unless it involved having a bit of fun for himself, so it wasn't long before he'd struck up a flirtationship with one of the daughters, Deidamia, who he'd revealed his secret identity to. Deidamia would end up pregnant by the demi-god with a son, who they named Neoptolemus (the future captor of Andromache).

Just when Thetis was starting to relax, Odysseus got wind that Achilles was hiding from the coming conflict. As young as he was, the demi-god was already rumoured to be an impressive fighter, and the fact he was almost completely invincible would be a massive plus for the army. And so, the hero travelled to Scyros and convinced Achilles to join their ranks, allowing a brief hiatus for him to marry Deidamia.

Meanwhile, Thetis had been squirrelling away favours from various powerful gods: When Hephaestus was temporarily evicted from Mount Olympus by Hera (for generally being what she deemed 'unsightly'), Thetis and her Oceanid friend Eurynome looked after him; and when the Olympians were planning an uprising against

Zeus, Thetis tipped off the Hecatoncheires to watch over him. Later, when god of wine, Dionysus, was sneaking around, avoiding Zeus' wrath for one misdemeanour or another, Thetis housed him in her underwater haven, eventually encouraging him to return to life on land. As the Trojan War broke out, Thetis used the favours she garnered from these gods to try to bargain for her son's safety. This included calling up Hephaestus and having him make Achilles an entirely new set of armour when his was taken in battle.

When the inevitable happened and her son died, he was buried at sea as a nod to his roots. Thetis and her companions rose up out of the water to join the mortals in their grief over the fallen hero, singing so mournfully that there wasn't a dry eye in the house (or, rather, camp).

CLYTEMNESTRA
(*clie-tem-nes-tra*)

Back in her youth as a Spartan princess, Clytemnestra was no stranger to power-politics, and the complications of being part of a royal family. She would have been a great match for Agamemnon, the soon-to-be king of Mycenae, as they both had similar elite heritage. Though perhaps not head over heels in love, the royal couple rubbed along together for many years, having several children and ruling Mycenae reasonably smoothly.

The queen knew that her husband had a hunger for power, and in the past she had taken solace in this, expecting it would serve her well by protecting her family and ensuring the comfortable life she had become accustomed to. However, when Agamemnon used their eldest daughter in a human sacrifice to give his army favourable winds to Troy, it was never going to be something the couple could recover from.

As soon as their daughter Iphigenia had been sacrificed, the previously absent winds began to blow, and Clytemnestra's husband conveniently had to leave. So off Agamemnon went to save his sister-in-law from the Trojans, thinking his wife would appreciate the time to cool off before he returned home. Oh, how wrong he would be.

During the wait for his return, a lot went down in Mycenae. Agamemnon's cousin, Aegisthus, travelled to the kingdom seeking revenge for the throne being stolen from his house many years ago. He and Clytemnestra bonded over what a scoundrel Agamemnon was, and it wasn't long before their joint passion for revenge graduated into passion for each other. Together, they came up with a plan to end him.

Post war, Agamemnon arrived home to Mycenae with his slave, the Trojan princess and seer Cassandra in tow. A ballsy move from Agamemnon, considering the last time he'd seen his wife, he'd been wiping their daughter's blood from his hands, and here he was bringing a sex slave into their home. Ten years had passed, but Clytemnestra's rage hadn't cooled a single degree. Naturally, Cassandra knew what awaited and warned Agamemnon not to return, but as usual it fell on deaf ears. Arriving at the palace, he told Cassandra to wait for him to collect her and shouted out a reminder to his people that the war was caused by an unruly woman. Clytemnestra was apparently thrilled at her husband's return, telling him that she'd prepared a relaxing bath and that he should go and take a load off. Agamemnon was pleased with his reception; clearly his wife had understood that their sacrifice was for the greater good. Presumably forgetting about Cass, he stripped off and jumped into the tub. As he bathed his aching limbs, Clytemnestra sneaked up behind and threw a net over him. Unable to free himself, he was powerless to avoid the axe that his wife plunged into him, over and over again.

Once Agamemnon was good and dead, Cassandra calmly walked into the palace and accepted her own fate. With everyone she'd ever loved now gone, she was ready to join her family in death. After a violent passing at the hands of the queen, the princess descended to the Elysian Fields, where the worthiest souls were granted eternal rest.

Clytemnestra and Aegisthus ruled over Mycenae for a further seven years. That is, until a certain son came to seek revenge . . .

JOCASTA (*jo-cass-ta*)

Queen Jocasta and her husband, Laius of Thebes, were struggling to conceive an heir to their throne. As tended to be the case, when Laius visited an oracle to find out why, he got more than simple advice. She informed him that should Jocasta ever bear him an heir, the child would go on to kill its father and marry its mother.

Horrified at the prospect, Laius swore to never have sex with his wife again. The pair lived quite a content, abstinent life for a while. A familiar tale, however, would come to pass – after a few too many goblets of wine, the couple threw caution to the wind and got down and dirty. Jocasta fell pregnant, and what do you know, it was a bouncing, father-murdering, mother-marrying baby boy! The king handed him to one of his shepherds, instructing him to take the babe to Mount Cithaeron and leave him there to die of exposure. Not super keen on being responsible for the death of a newborn baby, the shepherd instead passed him to a friend who worked for the king of Corinth. The baby was brought to the king and queen who, since they had no children of their own, decided to adopt him.

Oedipus was raised to believe that King Polybus and Queen Merope were his true parents, but as he grew, so did whispers amongst their people to suggest that may not be true. Eventually, sick of speculation, Oedipus consulted an oracle to find out for himself. The oracle, as per usual, didn't give him the straight answer he was looking for, and instead repeated what she had told Laius years ago:

that Oedipus was destined to kill his father and marry his mother. Although he didn't *want* to do either of those awful things, he knew prophecies had a way of coming true no matter how hard you tried to avoid them, so he vowed to get as far away from his parents as possible, just in case. During his travels, he had a confrontation with another man on the road over who had right of way. Things got heated, and Oedipus killed the stranger. It seems road rage was a thing even in ancient times. Of course, this stranger was his biological father, Laius. *Prophecy, one – Laius, nil.*

Eventually, Oedipus arrived in Thebes. The town was guarded by the Sphinx – a mystical creature with the body of a lion, wings of an eagle, tail of a serpent, and face and breasts of a beautiful woman. The only way to defeat the beast was to solve its riddle. Many had tried, but failed (and subsequently were eaten by her). Oedipus fancied his chances, though. He squared up to the Sphinx, who licked her lips at the prospect of another delicious man-meal.

To him, she asked, 'What goes on four feet in the morning, two feet at noon, and three feet in the evening?'

Oedipus answered, 'A man – as a baby in the morning of his life, he crawls on four feet. As an adult in the noon, as he walks on two. Then, when he is old and in the evening of his life, he walks with a cane.'

Distressed at being bested, the Sphinx threw herself off a cliff and into the sea.

Overjoyed to be rid of the terrorising creature, the people of Thebes crowned Oedipus their new king. Luckily for him, someone happened to have killed their previous ruler a little while ago, so there was a vacancy. Surprisingly, Oedipus hadn't quite made this connection. Along with the crown, he also inherited their widow queen, Jocasta. Oedipus was thrilled with his new life – he had a palace, adoring people, and a super-hot-cougar wife who bore him four children.

Things seemed to be going swimmingly, until a horrific outbreak of disease struck the city. No matter what they did, Thebes couldn't heal, so once again, the royal family sought the oracle's advice.

She was all, 'Well yeah, I told you what would happen, but you didn't listen – and now the gods are punishing you for killing your father and bedding your mother, sicko'. The pieces finally slotted together in the couple's minds, and they were appalled. Jocasta immediately hung herself, and Oedipus gouged out his own eyes, using the pins from her dress. Blind but still disgusted, Oedipus exiled himself from Thebes.

Jocasta's brother, Creon, would temporarily take the throne. This . . . would not work out, but we'll get to that.

LAMIA (*lay-mee-ya*)

Lamia was once a beautiful queen who ruled over Libya. A familiar story by now, she would attract the ever-wandering eyes of Zeus. Naturally, this resulted in her facing Hera's wrath, in what may be her most brutal punishment ever.

Hera killed Lamia's children (or hid them away, but realistically, it's Hera – she killed them). She then cursed Lamia so that whenever she gave birth, she'd be inflicted with madness that would have her kill the newborn. This was to be the case for any child of hers, whether it was with Zeus or not. To add salt to the wound, Hera also took away the queen's ability to sleep, meaning she'd have no respite from grieving her lost children.

Lamia, completely mad with grief and sleep deprivation, began stealing other women's babies from their cots and eating them. The wickedness of her actions were so severe that she became physically disfigured, eventually turning into a hideous monster. There're minimal records of her appearance, aside from being described as generally terrible and possibly serpentine, which likely added to the mystery and terror surrounding her tale.

Eventually, Zeus took pity on his ex-lover, deciding to give her the gift of prophecy and, perhaps more helpfully, the ability to remove her eyes. In the safety of the cave she now called home, Lamia was able to pluck out her peepers through the day, popping them in a jar, and giving herself and the mothers of Libya some much-needed rest.

The legend of Lamia would become somewhat of a bogeyman, used to coax children into behaving. Her story evolved again over time, becoming in part a warning tale for young, lustful men. Likely shapeshifting either back into her original, beautiful form or generally disguising herself, Lamia is said to have seduced young men and, when she'd had her sexual fill, feasted on their flesh.

HELLE & INO (*hell-ee* & *eye-no*)

Remember way back when Zeus crafted a Hera-lookalike out of the clouds to humiliate King Ixion? Well, that woman came to life (obviously) and was named Nephele. She wed King Athamas of Boeotia, and they had a handful of children, including the twins Helle and Phrixus. They later seperated, and Athamas would take a second wife, Ino, who immediately took a disliking to the children. Ino was the daughter of Cadmus and Harmonia, so you can imagine how this might end.

Ino plotted a way to get rid of them without getting her hands dirty. Secretly scorching the newly sown seeds in the area, she caused farmers to panic that famine had come to Boeotia. The farmers sent a few men to consult a nearby oracle, and Ino intercepted their journey and bribed them to say that the oracle had advised a sacrifice, and that the gods would only accept Phrixus.

When they were told of the 'prophecy', the farmers rounded on the young prince, hell-bent on presenting him as an offering to fix their issue. Luckily, Phrixus' cloud-mother was watching, and sent a flying golden ram to rescue him and his sister from harm. The pair grabbed on tight as the animal took to the skies, flying them to safety. As they soared, Helle looked down to the waters below, spooking herself so much that she let go and fell into the sea. Instead of letting her die, though, Poseidon transformed her into a sea goddess, and they had a couple of kids together. The stretch of water that she fell into was renamed Hellespont after her (where Hero and Leander would meet their doom much later).

Phrixus managed to hold on and was flown to the safety of Colchis. Once there, King Aeëtes welcomed him with open arms, giving him his own daughter, Chalciope. In gratitude, Phrixus sacrificed the golden ram to his sister's new lover, and gifted its fleece to Aeëtes, who would guard it until Jason and his Argonauts came a-knocking. *Thanks for saving us, magical ram, but you're just lunch, now.*

Back in Boeotia, Ino took it as a win – the annoying step-kids were out of her hair. She was just kicking it back, being queen and popping out heirs, when she heard news of her sister Semele's demise (coming up). Ino took it upon herself to help raise Semele's child, Dionysus. As he was the son of Zeus, this was bound to bring on Hera's wrath, and so it did when she struck Athamas and Ino with a blood-lusting madness. Athamas hunted one of their sons down like an animal, while Ino boiled another alive. Then, she jumped into the sea, clutching his dead body.

With the damage done, the madness was lifted. Athamas possibly mourned for a day or two, but a man without a wife wouldn't be proper, so it didn't take him long to remarry – this time he took a Thessalian princess, Themisto. Unfortunately for her, the ink on the marriage certificate wasn't even dry before Athamas learned that his late wife wasn't actually that late – she had survived the jump and was alive and well. Athamas, still in love with Ino, disguised her as a servant of the palace to keep her close.

Ino, however, wasn't the only one who could harbour massive amounts of undeserved anger towards her stepchildren – Themisto despised the children that remained of Athamas' second marriage. When she got wind that her new husband's eye may be wandering to a certain servant, she roped in said servant to help her with her devious plan. *Two birds, one stone* as they say, if the birds were a group of helpless children, and the stone was cold, hard murder.

She ordered the disguised Ino to dress her own children in black, and Themisto's children in white, then organised the killing of the first lot. Ino, of course wise to the plan, switched the children's clothing, resulting in the wrong set of tots' deaths. Themisto, overcome with grief, killed herself.

In another version of the story, Ino still jumps from the cliff clutching her son, but as she hits the sea, Aphrodite pities her and asks that Poseidon turn her into a sea goddess. Ino would become Leucothea, meaning 'white goddess'. She'd spend her days swimming languidly and occasionally helping out a distressed sailor who'd floated himself into a pickle. One of these lost seafarers was the hero Odysseus, who Leucothea buoyed to safety after his raft was destroyed in one of his exploits.

Leucothea was also given the gift of prophecy during her transformation, and she would go on to have her own sanctuary, where humans could visit to get help interpreting their dreams, which was her speciality.

PELOPIA (*pell-oh-pee-ya*)

Brothers Thyestes and Atreus both thought it their destiny to take the Mycenaean throne. The pair spent years trying to outdo each other in a game of who can be the nastiest, and eventually Thyestes would consult the oracle of Delphi for a way to avenge his brother's wrongdoings once and for all. He was advised to father a child by his own daughter, Pelopia, as the offspring would go on to be the undoing of Atreus. When Pelopia was washing her clothes in a river, her father donned a mask to hide his identity and attacked her. During the struggle, Thyestes dropped his sword, and Pelopia kept it as a grim reminder of her assailant.

Pelopia couldn't bear the thought of raising a child to the masked aggressor, so she abandoned the baby in the woods. A nanny-goat would find it, giving her own milk to ensure its survival. It was later found by a shepherd, who presented it to Atreus. Atreus, who by this point was sitting comfortably on the Mycenaean throne, decided to raise the abandoned child as his own, naming him Aegisthus.

Pelopia was living in Sicyon at this point and would meet her uncle as he passed through in search of her father. As the two didn't recognise each other, Atreus mistook her for a princess of the city. He thought she was very beautiful, so asked the king, Thesproutus, for her hand. Thesproutus knew Pelopia's identity but agreed, knowing it was wrong but wanting to protect the young girl, lest she meet a stickier end altogether.

With uncle and niece now in Mycenae and living as husband and wife, Pelopia became the adoptive stepmother (but actually *birth* mother) of Aegisthus. Eventually, Atreus struck gold when his brother was finally captured and in his clutches. He'd told his son stories of their rivalry over the years and, by this point, Aegisthus hated Thyestes just as much as his adoptive father. When asked if he would be the one to kill their nemesis, Aegisthus was only too willing.

Entering Thyestes' cell, Aegisthus raised his sword (a handsome thing, gifted to him by Pelopia) over his head. Thyestes called out for him to wait – he'd seen that sword before, owned it even. He asked the prince how it had come to be in his possession, and when he was told it was a gift from his stepmother, the prisoner insisted that he bring her down there.

The complicated web of lies unravelled behind Pelopia's eyes, as she realised not only who had raped her, but who her adopted son really was. She grabbed the sword right out of Aegisthus' hand and threw herself onto it.

With his true parentage revealed, Aegisthus killed Atreus, returned the kingdom to his birth father and ruled alongside him. Later, Agamemnon would rock up and forcibly eject the pair from Mycenae, and we know Aegisthus would take it back, bed his wife and help to kill him. Complicated family dynamics, for sure.

CASSIOPEIA & ANDROMEDA
(*cass-ee-oh-pee-ya* & *an-drom-eh-da*)

Queen of Aetheiopia, Cassiopeia was very beautiful, but also vain and obnoxious. When she boasted that she and her daughter, Andromeda, were more beautiful than the Nereids, she brought the wrath of Poseidon down on her kingdom.

As punishment for this act of hubris, the sea god flooded the coast of Aetheiopia and sent a monster by the name of Cetus to ravage the land and make flesh-kebabs out of the city folk. The queen and her husband, Cepheus, consulted an oracle for a way to make things right, who told them that to appease the gods, they must sacrifice their daughter to the beast.

Andromeda, unsurprisingly, was not thrilled with this turn of events, and fought like mad the whole way. Regardless of her efforts, her parents managed to strip her and chain her to a rock. They retreated back to the palace, crossing their fingers that Cetus would find their offering in time for him to spare the remaining Aetheiopians. The princess was still vocalising her unhappiness when the hero Perseus was passing by and heard her cries. He perched on a rock near to where she was bound and the pair spent some time flirting and shooting the breeze, despite the fact that Cetus was well on his way. Andromeda asked the budding hero if he fancied saving her at all, and Perseus confirmed that yes, that sounded fine. Andromeda was thrilled at the prospect of being able to continue living, telling him that she'd be happy if he'd have her as a servant, slave, or wife. Perseus quickly went to the palace and asked if he could possibly have the hand of the daughter that they'd chained up and left as monster-chow, in return for removing the threat of the scaly beast terrorising their city.

King Cepheus readily agreed, although Andromeda was already engaged to be married to his own brother and her uncle, Phineus. The royal couple added an extra sweetener, too, by offering the kingdom as Andromeda's dowry. Perseus charged towards Cetus, using his sword to lop the monsters head off (Perseus had somewhat of a fixation with beheading, FYI). Job done, he was granted Andromeda as his prize. The king and queen rejoiced and proceeded to throw the couple a huge royal wedding, which apparently wasn't awkward at all after the whole 'shackling the bride to a rock and leaving her to die' thing. What *was* awkward, though, was Andromeda's ex-fiancé-come-uncle getting a bit too overzealous with the free table wine and picking a fight with the groom in an 'it should have been me!' moment. Cepheus pointed out that Phineus was nowhere to be seen when it came to saving his daughter (rich, coming from him), but Perseus was more than happy to settle this in the way he was fast becoming accustomed to – with violence.

Phineus' men attacked the groom and his companions, but Perseus had a trick up his sleeve – he'd recently slain Medusa (a Gorgon whose gaze would turn anyone that met it to stone) and had kept the head to use as a weapon. He whipped out his weapon, turning the clamouring crew to statues. Phineus begged for his life, clamping his hands over his face to avoid the stony gaze of the severed head, but Perseus wasn't in a forgiving mood. He seized him by the hair and forced open his eyes, leading to Phineus also being Gorgoned in a rather pitiful cringing position. With that nasty business out of the way, the celebrations resumed. After the wedding, Phineus' statue would be stationed inside the palace for everyone to enjoy.

Andromeda would accompany her husband back home then on to Argos where he took the throne and she became queen. This didn't last long, as Perseus killed his grandfather (by accident, this time), and they needed to move along to the neighbouring Tiryns.

Andromeda and Perseus had a happy life together, raising seven sons and two daughters, and Perseus continued to rack up more heroic-type dealings. Andromeda was particularly fascinated with Medusa and longed to be able to see her head without losing her life. Perseus, wanting to please his wife, came up with the idea that he could hold it over the water of a calm pool and Andromeda could look at the reflection safely.

When they died, Athena turned the couple into constellations of their own names, and they were put in the skies beside Andromeda's parents. King Cepheus' constellation was pretty normal, but Cassiopeia's was in the shape of a torture chair. That's what you get when you insult the gods.

ALTHEA (*al-thee-ya*)

Althea was the wife of Oeneus, King of Calydon, but was known to dabble in a bit of extramarital activities with certain gods.

Although she had seven children to the king, it's thought that Oeneus gave her the green light for at least one of her affairs, with the god Dionysus, who made it clear he'd like to bed the queen.

Oeneus, either not wanting to bring the wrath of such a powerful god down upon his house, or just being a chill guy, excused himself to let the pair . . . get to know each other better. Dionysus was so pleased with the hospitality that he gave the couple the gift of the vine, decreeing that the fruit it produced would be called *oinos* after his host. Althea had her own little keepsake of his visit, currently growing in her womb.

With Dionysus she had a daughter, Deianira, who would grow up to be the third wife and eventual killer of Heracles. She had two sons to other gods – one with Poseidon, by the name of Ancaeus, and her most well-known offspring, Meleager, with Ares.

When Meleager was born, the Fates appeared in Althea's bedchamber and delivered a prophecy: the child could grow up noble and brave, but would only live as long as it took a certain log, currently on their hearth, to burn to ashes. On hearing this, Althea jumped up and quickly extinguished the fire. She hid and preserved the log, essentially making her son both invulnerable and immortal.

Meleager grew into a fine young man, but would come to make an epic slip-up by missing out Artemis during a sacrifice. The scorned goddess sent a massive wild hog to ravish the city, known as the Calydonian Boar – it completely devastated their land and killed many citizens. Meleager requested external help to clean up his mess, and thus, a party of hunters came together.

The boar was eventually defeated, but when Althea's brothers took issue with who Meleager awarded its hide to, he killed them. When Althea found out, she was so angry that she retrieved the log that preserved his life and burnt it. Meleager immediately dropped down dead, and Althea was gripped so hard by regret that she ended her own life in sorrow.

By now, Artemis was feeling pretty satisfied with her vengeance, but as a last eff-you, she turned Althea's mourning daughters into birds.

HECUBA (*heck-you-bah*)

A princess of Phrygia and half Naiad, Hecuba was given in marriage to King Priam of Troy. This was to be Priam's second marriage (he was first wed to Arisbe, a seer who bore him a son who could also, er, *see*), but Hecuba would go down in history as his 'chief' wife.

Together they had many children, some of whom were the best-known amongst the Ancient Greeks, like Hector, Cassandra, and Paris. After her birthing premonition, we know that Paris would go away, then come back, then abduct a beautiful Spartan queen by the name of Helen.

After that, it wasn't long before Menelaus and co were beating on the city's gates, promising war. Despite the overwhelming feeling of foreboding, the king and queen refused to return Helen – while she made their son very happy, Troy was a powerful city and it would look weak for them to bow to another. Most of her sons were of age to fight at this point, and as the Greeks made their way to the shores of Troy, Hecuba and Priam stashed their baby Polydorus with his big sister Ilione in Thrace. As war ravaged her city and her children were killed one after another, Hecuba at least felt safe in the knowledge that one of her children would be out of harm's way.

Hecuba, though protective of all her children, particularly favoured her son Hector. When the hero Achilles demanded that Hector fight him one-on-one for murdering his lover, Patroclus, Hecuba pleaded with him to refuse. Hector would not be persuaded, and Achilles emerged victorious. To exacerbate the family's grief, he tied Hector's corpse to the back of his chariot and dragged him around the Greek camp for nine days.

After the Trojan War ended in victory for the opposition, the now elderly Queen Hecuba would be taken as a slave for no other than the hero Odysseus. As her once great city burned, she tried to encourage the other surviving Trojan women to join her in jumping into the flames, but the Greek soldiers held her back, telling her that she was Odysseus' property now, and that meant they had to keep her safe for him. As she and the last of her people were dragged to the ships, Hecuba kissed the ground of her fallen city.

Along with the crew, Hecuba and Odysseus sailed back through Thrace, where they stopped to rest. Hecuba, after so much heartbreak over the loss of her children so far, sneaked away to the palace to finally lay eyes on the one son she hadn't lost.

Of course, King Polymestor had already killed the child (or so he thought – remember Ilione's crafty kiddie-swap? The real Polydorus was swanning around on his travels and would later return to kill Polymestor). Hecuba was wild with grief and rage – she dived on Polymestor, clawing and scratching at his face and gouging his eyes out with her bare hands.

Hecuba wasn't willing to take her new fate as Odysseus' slave lying down. On their return journey to Ithaca, the fallen queen swore and snarled at the hero so much that the gods transformed her into a dog, which allowed her to escape his clutches.

POLYPHONTE
(*pol-ee-fon-tee*)

Young Polyphonte, a granddaughter of Ares, was a beautiful girl who desired nothing but a simple life. Certainly not in her plans was a man or the amorous acts that came along with keeping one. She left her home for the mountains with big plans of becoming a companion of the goddess Artemis.

However, when Aphrodite got wind of the girl shunning what she considered her 'responsibilities' as a woman (or maybe just looking for an excuse to punish any descendant of Ares that didn't come from her), she was furious. She inflicted Polyphonte with a voracious lust for one of the bears that she'd met on her travels. Polyphonte couldn't help herself, nor could she feel any shame for the sexual acts she partook in with the wild beast. When Artemis witnessed this for herself, she was disgusted. Using her own powers, she turned the bear against Polyphonte, which chased her from the mountain that she'd begun to think of as her home.

Disgraced and back in her hometown, Polyphonte discovered that she was pregnant to the bear. She went on to give birth to the twins Agrius and Oreius, who were completely savage. As they matured, the two discovered that they particularly enjoyed the taste of human flesh and became cannibals. The twins grew so tall that they were able to literally pluck humans from the ground and chomp them down in one.

Zeus absolutely despised these freaks of nature, so recruited the god Hermes to put a stop to them. Not fussy on how they met their end, he told Hermes to use his imagination. Planning to sever their hands and feet, Hermes was interrupted by the twins' great-grandfather. Ares stepped in and asked his fellow god to show mercy (a bit rich considering Ares' affinity for violence himself). The messenger god agreed and instead transformed the pair into birds, along with their mother.

Hermes' choice of birds may have been a little passive aggressive: Oreius was turned into an eagle-owl, thought to be an ill omen, and Agrius a vulture – a widely hated bird in general. Polyphonte was turned into a strix and would never eat or drink again, instead spending her time hanging from a tree, announcing the arrival of wars or other similarly horrible comings.

ADRASTEIA, IDA &
AMALTHEA
(*ad-ras-tee-ya, eye-da*
& *am-al-thee-ya*)

Adrasteia and Ida were mountain nymphs, known collectively as the Oreads. Oreads were generally associated with Artemis, since she loved hunting in the mountains so much, but before she was born, it was the Titaness Rhea that held them in regard. Rhea tasked Adrasteia and Ida with raising the newborn Zeus while the stage was being set for him to overthrow his father.

The goddesses stayed with little Zeus in a cave on Mount Dikte, where they nursed him on milk from the she-goat Amalthea. Adrasteia made him a toy sphere out of golden hoops linked together, the likes that even the forging god Hephaestus couldn't replicate, to keep him occupied. When thrown in the air, it would leave a trail of glorious fire in its wake, which delighted the future king of the skies. When other gods passed by, the sisters would protect him by performing a dance involving the loud clashing of shields. This would mask the baby's cries and gurgles to ensure that he wasn't uncovered.

Once, when Zeus and the nanny-goat were playing, the infant reached up and accidentally snapped one of her horns clean off her head. Even as a toddler, Zeus was coming into his own powers, and as he clutched the horn in his chubby little hand, Amalthea's and the nymphs' eyes widened in wonder as they saw the horn fill with food. Thinking it a nifty trick but not much more, the ladies and Zeus shared the nourishing goodies from the horn that night. The next morning, however, they were astounded to see the horn full to the brim once again. No matter how heartily they ate, the horn would never run empty, and it would come to be known as 'the horn of plenty', or 'cornucopia'.

When Amalthea died, Zeus was devastated, and decided to honour her by skinning her and incorporating her hide into his own shield. *Thanks?*

ENDEÏS (*en-dice*)

When Aeacus (the son of Aegina) met and married Endeïs, she bore him not one, but two great heroes. We already know of Peleus, but she also had Telamon, who'd grow up to be a close friend of Heracles. The royal family was set to become quite the dynasty, if it wasn't for Aeacus and his fondness for nymphs.

Psamathe, a Nereid, was a helpless victim of Aeacus' desires, which resulted in his third son, Phocus. In fact, she was so unwilling that she tried to transform herself into a seal to escape, but Aeacus overpowered her in the end. He brought Phocus back to Aegina to live with him, but Endeïs hated the boy immediately. To make matters worse, it was clear that Aeacus preferred his youngest son, and Endeïs just knew that he'd end up giving him the throne over her two precious boys, despite them being before him in line.

Endeïs made sure to whisper poisonous thoughts into her children's ears about their younger half-brother, and by the time they were adolescents, they hated him just as much as she did. Time was getting on, and as the king and Phocus grew older, Endeïs' sons risked losing their birthright, so they made a plan. Peleus and Telamon persuaded Phocus to enter a discus-throwing competition, telling him that if he won, it would be a great honour for the kingdom, and their father would be hugely impressed. Phocus, who looked up to his brothers, was keen to do anything they suggested, but knew he wasn't very good at the discus. 'No matter,' said Telamon, 'we'll teach you.'

The trio practised throwing and catching for a while, so it could reasonably appear a complete accident when Phocus was hit fatally in the back of the head with a discus.

Phocus' body was soon discovered, and the king exiled his sons from Aegina. It's not known what happened to Endeïs, but we can't imagine it was good.

Psamathe would have her revenge, too. Once Peleus was ruling his own kingdom, she sent a pack of murderous wolves to eat his livestock and his subjects. Peleus, who had grown up into a good king, had the humility to pray to the goddess for forgiveness. She was loath to listen, but his wife, Thetis, who was much more powerful than her sister Psamathe, made her transform the pack to stone.

TYRO (*tie-roh*)

A Thessalian princess, Tyro was in love with the river god Enipeus. Unfortunately for her, the feeling wasn't mutual.

One water god *was* keen, though, and that was Poseidon. He knew that Tyro had a thing for Enipeus, so disguised himself as the god. Tyro would end up pregnant from this sly union.

She gave birth to twins and left them in the wilderness to die, but unbeknownst to her, a herdsman rescued and raised them. She carried on with life as best she could, working on her marriage with her husband (who also happened to be her uncle), and tried to put the brief affair behind her.

Once her sons had grown, they figured out their parentage, and journeyed to the palace to be reunited with their mother. Tyro told them all about her life, including how her father's second wife, the wicked Sidero, had made each day a living hell. The boys vowed to avenge their mother.

Sidero, now getting on a bit, realised she was no match for two young men so she started running. Flinging herself at a temple of Hera, she claimed sanctuary. This didn't deter the twins, though, who had no problem killing her in the sacred place. Of course, this invited the wrath of the queen goddess, but what else is new?

Tyro's husband, now wise to her affair, left her, and she lived peacefully for a little while, until her other uncle, Sisyphus, came sniffing around. Sisyphus and Tyro's father, Salmoneus, absolutely hated each other. Not the kind of hate that you often find with siblings, filled with petty squabbles, but unadulterated 'if you pegged it, I would throw a huge celebratory party' kind of hate. Sisyphus was desperate for his brother to die (preferably horribly), but didn't fancy the consequences of killing a family member. Instead, he went to an oracle who told him that if he were to father a son to his niece, that boy would grow up to kill Salmoneus. Sisyphus truly understood the assignment and seduced Tyro. He had *two* sons to her, just to make extra sure one of them would go the distance. What he wasn't expecting was Tyro to overhear him bragging about his master plan. Tyro killed both of her children to Sisyphus by drowning them, leaving their bodies on a nearby riverbank for her uncle to discover. By the time he found them, she was well on her way back to her father's palace.

CREUSA (*cree-you-sa*)

Creusa, an Athenian princess, married Xuthus, a Phthian prince.

Long before their marriage, Creusa had once been raped in a cave by the god Apollo. She would end up pregnant from the attack, but she knew her father would go ballistic if he found out she was no longer a virgin. Apollo helped Creusa keep her pregnancy a secret with his magic, and made it so her labour was painless. After she gave birth in the place that she conceived, Creusa left the baby in a basket and fled. Apollo called on Hermes to bring his son to his own temple, and the half-brother obliged. The boy would be brought up there by a priestess of Apollo, who named him Ion. Quickly regretting the abandonment, Creusa returned to the cave but her son was gone. She assumed a wild animal must have come along and eaten him, so tried to put the whole sorry situation out of her mind and get on with her life.

After she married Xuthus, the pair struggled to conceive. By now, Creusa was nearing the end of her childbearing years and getting quite desperate, so the couple travelled to Delphi to consult with Pythia. The prophecy said that whoever Xuthus should encounter on leaving the temple would be his son. As he exited, he bumped straight into the young priest Ion, who he excitedly told he was adopting. Ion, knowing fine well not to go against the word of the oracle, said, 'sure, Pops'.

Xuthus rushed to tell Creusa the good news – they had a son! Creusa was decidedly less enthusiastic, though, assuming this meant

Xuthus had cheated on her (if you conveniently skip over the fact that the boy was clearly too old to have been conceived during their marriage).

The woman concluded that she would poison the vile lovechild of her husband and some rando. As she handed a tainted goblet over to Ion, however, a bird swooped in and drank some of the wine. It immediately dropped down dead, so Ion was now wise to her plan. He knocked over the drink and began chasing Creusa with a view to kill her, but she ran straight to the temple of Apollo and took shelter there. A priestess who knew of the prophecy gently explained to the pair that Ion was actually Creusa's real son, who she conceived with Apollo. As proof, she presented the babe's basket that Creusa had stashed him in. She went on to clarify that Apollo sent the false prophecy to Xuthus because he wanted him to be a proper father to Ion. Both mother and son were thrilled to be reunited, forgetting all about that silly attempted murder business. On the advice of the god, they agreed to never tell Xuthus the complicated truth.

TIMANDRA & BULIS
(*ti-man-dra* & *bew-lis*)

When Timandra got herself a toyboy by the name of Aegypius, her son was decidedly grossed out. Neophron couldn't bear to think of his ageing mother getting her rocks off with someone his own age, so he decided it was his duty to put a stop to it.

To put his plan in motion, Neophron went to Aegypius' own mother, Bulis, and seduced her. Once he'd convinced Bulis they had something special going on, he invited her to his home for some canoodling. He made sure to choose a time when Aegypius was due to visit his mother.

Aegypius arrived at his lover's house and let himself in as always, assuming that the darkened room he was faced with was something new Timandra was wanting to try out. *Suits him*, he thought. When he heard the front door open, Aegypius stripped off and silently began caressing 'Timandra', putting his finger over her lips so they could enjoy each other in silence.

After their lovemaking, they fell asleep wrapped in each other's arms. As the sun streamed through the next morning, Bulis was the first to wake, and as you can imagine got quite the surprise. Although she wanted to scream and/or projectile vomit, she tried desperately to think logically. What she should do, she thought, was blind her son and kill herself, so he'd never have to know the horrific act they'd committed. Just as she bent over to do it, though, Aegypius woke up and realised what had happened. Now, they both began shrieking in shame. Disgusted by what they had done, Aegypius shouted up to the gods to make him and his mother disappear forever. Sort of answering his prayer, Zeus turned all four of this love-square into birds. Not quite the outcome Neophron had hoped for . . .

5

Twisted Sisters

They're banding together to do harm with, or against, their own siblings

IPHINOE, LYSIPPE & IPHIANASSA
(*if-eye-no-ee, lie-sip-ee & if-ee-an-assa*)

When Queen Stheneboea falsely accused the hero Bellerophon of raping her, he chucked her on his flying horse, soared high up into the sky and hurled her to the ground below.

After this literal fall from grace, Stheneboea left behind three daughters: Iphinoe, Lysippe and Iphianassa. They were known collectively as the Proitides, after their father Proteus. When the sisters disrespected a statue of the Olympian queen, Hera, they were struck with a madness particularly unique to the deity cursing them. Stripping off their clothes, they revealed skin that had turned a deathly shade of white, and were covered in pussing wounds. As the curse took hold, the Proitides forgot they were princesses of Argos and started to believe wholeheartedly that they were cows (an animal sacred to Hera). The three sisters abandoned the kingdom in search of some cud to chew, leaving their father wondering what on earth his life had come to.

Since the madness didn't seem to be shifting, Proetus put a call out for assistance. The only person to answer was the seer Melampus, who was pretty sure he could cure the ladies of their strange psychosis. He had one condition though – in exchange for returning Proetus' beloved daughters to their senses, he wanted a third of the kingdom of Argos. Proetus refused to entertain the suggestion and sent the seer on his way. As time went on, though, the sisters' madness gave no sign of relenting, and they'd also started to sexually assault shepherds they encountered in the wilderness. What's more, other women in Argos began showing signs of following suit – perhaps letting out a faint *moo* and such.

The king called Melampus back, ready to agree to his demands in exchange for the cure. Now, though, it was going to be more costly. The seer wanted *half* of the kingdom, because he'd decided that he'd quite like to split the spoils with his brother, Bias, and half of a third just wasn't big enough in his eyes. Kicking himself for not accepting the offer the first time around, Proetus made the deal.

So, off Melampus went. It wasn't long before he found the ladies frolicking in Arcadia, and he began to round them up like the cattle they thought they were. He managed to get Lysippe and Iphianassa into a cave, but Iphinoe died in the pursuit.

Once safely inside, Melampus began cleansing the two remaining women with special herbs, giving them sacred baths, and doing something mysterious with a pig, apparently. The women were cured, and the seer brought them back to Argos where he claimed his prize. As an extra bonus, he and Bias married the sisters, and they all ruled together as one family.

CANACE (*ca-na-see*)

Canace, daughter of the wind god Aeolus, was no stranger to scandal. As a young woman, she'd been pursued by the sea god Poseidon, who had taken on the form of a wild bull to seduce her.

As she matured, Canace and her brother Macareus, grew . . . close. *Much* closer than is at all appropriate for siblings. This would eventually result in her falling pregnant. Initially, Canace tried to keep her condition a secret, attempting to end the pregnancy, but it was all to no avail as her belly continued to swell. Canace accepted her fate, and instead leaned on her brother to make an honest woman out of her in marriage. He agreed, but she wasn't ever able to pin him to a date.

Nine long months passed, and Canace had somehow managed to keep the pregnancy under wraps, most importantly from her father. As was fitting for his particular genre of godliness, Aeolus' temperament was dark and stormy, and Canace dreaded to think of the fury that would fall upon her if he discovered her terrible secret. As labour loomed, Canace decided that if her brother wasn't going to marry her any time soon, she didn't want to raise his child. When she gave birth, her nurse agreed to help take care of it, in the grimmest sense of the phrase. Swaddling the child tightly, she stashed it in a basket underneath a bunch of fruits and carried it out of the home in an attempt to pass it off as an offering to the gods. She very nearly got away with it, but as she passed her master, the baby mewed. Aeolus immediately knew what had transpired and roared confirmation to the entire kingdom. Unbothered by the shame of the union, only by what came of it, he seized the child out of the nurse's basket and threw it to the dogs for their dinner.

Unwilling to hear his daughter out, Aeolus sent a servant to Canace with a sword and the command that she use it to end her life. Heartbroken at her father's rage, the loss of her baby and the absence of a future with her brother, she obliged. Her only request was that her brother gather the remains of the child and bury it with her.

ELECTRA (*el-eck-tra*)

Seven years after the murder of Agamemnon, Clytemnestra's daughter, Electra, returned home and was devastated to find her beloved father long dead. It's uncertain why the sacrifice of her little sister, Iphigenia, was inconsequential to her, but she was absolutely distraught over Agamemnon's demise. However, Electra was smart, and had experienced enough familial politics to know that she had to use her head.

She knew, for example, that her brother Orestes would now be seen as a significant threat to the returning king of Mycenae, Aegisthus, so she shipped him off somewhere safe. It wasn't long before Clytemnestra got sick of hearing her daughter's constant carping over her father's murder, and she was swiftly married off to a poor local farmer. The farmer treated Electra well and respected her desire to not consummate their marriage, even if it did hurt his feelings a bit, but it was still a steep decline in quality of life for a former princess all the same.

When Orestes reached the age of twenty, he and his friend (and possible lover) Pylades returned to his hometown. Realising the risk, he arrived in disguise, presenting himself as a messenger and delivering the news that Orestes, true heir to the throne of Mycenae, was dead.

When Electra heard this, she felt completely defeated. She went to the tomb of her father to pray for guidance, and found a stranger there. Unable to contain himself, Orestes revealed his identity, showing Electra the ring he'd inherited from Agamemnon as proof. After much jumping up and down and squealing in delight, the siblings began plotting the demise of their mother and stepfather. Orestes, now re-disguised, delivered an urn to the palace (supposedly containing his own ashes). As his mother reached for the urn, Orestes revealed his true identity, drawing his sword and towering over her. Clytemnestra begged for her life, asking if Orestes had any respect or love for the woman who raised him. She exclaimed that she found it pretty rich that her remaining children had forgotten that their father had killed their beloved older sister, calling them hypocrites. Electra, ever the daddy's girl, argued Iphigenia's murder was justified, where Agamemnon's was a crime of passion, so that Clytemnestra could go on living immorally with Aegisthus. In order to shut her up for good, Electra held their mother still as Orestes forced a sword down her neck.

Soon, Aegisthus arrived home, to be confronted with the dead body of his lover, and his stepchildren covered in blood. He put up more of a fight than Clytemnestra, but was still no match for the young, lithe prince. With vengeance well and truly served, a madness descended upon Orestes, brought on by the wrath of the Furies.

In his mission to repent for the brutal slaying of his mother, Orestes would find himself in Tauris. After being captured by the locals, he and Pylades were taken to the temple of Artemis to be sacrificed. When the priestess in charge casually dropped into pre-sacrificial conversation that she was a former princess of Mycenae, Orestes couldn't believe his ears. Turns out Artemis had secretly swapped the princess Iphigenia out for a deer at the very last second during her sacrifice, sequestering her to Tauris and making her a priestess of her cult. Brother and sister were overjoyed to be reunited, and they fled Tauris.

As for Electra, she seemed to get off scot-free for the matricide – she would go on to marry Pylades and live happily ever after.

THE FURIES (*fyoo-rees*)

Also known as the 'Erinyes', the Furies were a group of vengeance goddesses, born from the blood of Uranus' castrated genitals as it hit the earth.

The Furies were driven by their need to punish mortals who went against the natural order, and they were particularly upset by those who killed their family members. There were three of them: Alecto (the personification of endless anger), Megaera (jealous rage), and Tisiphone (vengeful destruction). They presented as old women with the heads of dogs, their eyes shot with blood, and massive wings similar to those of a bat. The trio lived in Erebus (husband of Nyx, both a thing and a place), which was essentially perpetual darkness, but spent most of their time roaming the earth, disciplining wrongdoers by driving them to madness. It was thought that mortals dare not even say their names directly. Instead, they were referred to as the 'Gracious Ones'.

When they caught up with Orestes after Clytemnestra's murder, Athena organised for him to face a tribunal for his sins. Apollo acted as Orestes' defence, with the Furies being his accusers. Athena recruited ten of the most honourable men of Athens to serve as the jury, and the rest of the Athenian people gathered to watch the trial.

The court case started off competently enough, but soon disrupted into a heated debate on vengeance and the importance of showing respect to ancient goddesses like the Furies. The sisters argued that Clytemnestra's life was just as worthy as Agamemnon's, and that the boy's mother was exacting vengeance in their name. Apollo, on the other hand, argued that Agamemnon's life was obviously worth more, as he was a man. Athena agreed with this, musing how a woman may be able to bring new life into the world, but it was truly the man who provided the 'spark of light'. In the end, the jury was split, and Athena had to cast the final vote. She acquitted the mortal. Furious, the Furies began threatening to torment the people of Athens and poison their crops as revenge.

Athena, sympathetic to their frustrations, reasoned with them, offering them a new position as protectors of justice within the city of Athens. In this role, they would still be highly respected and receive great honours, but people wouldn't be quite so terrified of them. The Olympian could see that they were starting to sway, but weren't fully convinced, so she added a pinch of blackmail to secure the deal – helpfully reminding them that she held the key to the vault that kept Zeus' spare thunderbolts, the one thing in the universe that could put a stop to olden divinities like them. Unable to argue with that, they accepted her proposal.

ANTIGONE & ISMENE
(*an-tig-oh-nee* & *is-meen-ee*)

Concentrate now, because this family tree is particularly messy – Antigone and Ismene are the daughters of Jocasta and Oedipus, but since Jocasta was actually Oedipus' mother, the girls are also the grandchildren of their mother, and their father is also their brother. Got it?

Antigone and Ismene's brothers, Polynices and Eteocles, would inherit the throne of Thebes from their dad/bro after he exiled himself in the fallout of his prophecy being fulfilled. Actually, on his way out, the now blind king bestowed the throne to Jocasta's brother, Creon, who swore to look after the children in his absence. Oedipus specifically told him to look out for his daughters, who he loved dearly. Creon reigned for a while, and when the brothers came of age they agreed to reign jointly, with each one ruling for a year at a time. The first year fell to Eteocles, so Polynices had a year travelling, where he met and married Argeia, a princess of Argos.

Back in Thebes, the power had gone to Eteocles' head, so when Polynices returned to the city with his new wife, he was turned away. Furious, Polynices gathered a gang of great fighters who'd go on to be known as the Seven Against Thebes and, with the help of his new father-in-law, waged an attack on the city.

The battle between the brothers was fierce but ultimately pointless, as both would-be rulers died in the efforts. Their uncle Creon was quick to resume his position on the throne, now without the threat of any youngsters with a real claim. Creon decreed that while Eteocles would receive a hero's burial, the people of Thebes were not to hold a funeral for Polynices and weren't even allowed to mourn him, lest they be stoned to death. Instead, his corpse was left to rot where it fell on the battleground.

Antigone didn't accept this – despite their issues, she loved both of her brothers, and couldn't grieve one without the other. She urged Ismene to join her in giving Polynices the funeral he deserved, but Ismene was too scared to go against their uncle-king and urged Antigone to be discreet. However, Antigone wanted the city, and the king, to know that she believed both of her brothers had died nobly. She made no secret of her mourning or the funeral she held for Polynices.

When brought before Creon's court, Antigone faced him confidently. She told her uncle that she knew of the law forbidding her actions but defied it purposely. She also claimed that the people of Thebes agreed with her acts, but they were all too scared of Creon to speak up.

Antigone was sentenced to incarceration in an underground tomb. Ismene, unable to cope with the idea of losing another family member, tried to fake-confess to being in on the whole thing and demanded that she be punished, too. Antigone urged her to shut up, making her promise to live on, for all of their sakes. Antigone was sealed in her tomb behind a huge boulder, shouting her head off about how she was going out in glory and that her once great city was now ruled by a coward.

Soon after, Creon realised he was perhaps being a tad dramatic and sought to free his niece. When he unsealed the tomb, however, Antigone had already hanged herself. Creon's son, Haemon, was madly in love with Antigone, and on finding out the news of her death immediately fell on his sword. What's more, Creon's wife, Queen Eurydice, was so overcome with grief from the death of her son that she took a blade to her own heart. Basically, Creon killed his entire household by complete overreaction.

Years later, Ismene had started a bit of a romance with a man by the name of Theoclymenus. At the same time, Thebes was being attacked yet again by the descendants of the original army from Argos that assisted Polynices. Ismene and her beau had met outside of the city walls for some lovemaking, when Athena guided one of the warriors, Tydeus, to their location. He attacked the pair, and while Theoclymenus managed to leg it, stark naked, Ismene was captured. She begged Tydeus to show her mercy, but it fell on deaf ears as the ruthless warrior slaughtered her.

MNEMOSYNE & THE MUSES
(*nee-mos-en-ee* & *the myoo-ses*)

After his success in the Titanomachy, Zeus wanted to mark the occasion with a particular form of celebration. As it's Zeus, it'll come as no surprise what that meant . . . He had a nine-night fling with the Titan goddess of memory, Mnemosyne.

For each night of passion, Mnemosyne would birth a Muse – total babes who were responsible for inspiring arts in mortals and gods alike. They were:

- **Calliope** (poetry)
- **Clio** (history)
- **Erato** (love and erotic poetry)
- **Euterpe** (music)
- **Melpomene** (tragedy)
- **Polyhymnia** (hymns)
- **Terpsichore** (dance – always depicted sitting, ironically)
- **Thalia** (comedy)
- **Urania** (astronomy and astrology)

Apollo, as a god of the arts, liked to have these lovely ladies near, so although they resided at Mount Helicon, they spent the majority of their time on Olympus, where they'd entertain their divine buddies. For mortals, the Muses were on hand to help them forget the pain that was general life, allowing them to get lost in their various creative persuasions. It's said that any human the Muses favoured would be able to settle conflict with their words only, and that others would look to them and their skills as if they were gods themselves. The sisters were predictably revered especially by those interested in the arts, and poets would often call on the Muses for inspiration as they started writing.

Also known as the 'holy nine', they had a good handful of children between them, including the Sirens and the renowned music-man Orpheus.

When a king by the name of Pierus had nine daughters, he named them all after the lovely Muses. As such, the sisters grew up thinking they were equal to their namesakes. They believed this so staunchly that they dared to enter a singing contest alongside the holy nine. The Muses absolutely thrashed them, transforming the sisters into magpies for being so big-headed.

Their ruthlessness was sighted again when Thamyris, a musician from Thrace, bet the Muses that he could outshine their melodic talents. If successful, he said that he should be allowed to sleep with each of the sisters. The goddesses took immense pleasure in blinding the man for his rudeness.

Back in the early days of the universe, Mnemosyne had got a bit of a reputation as an airhead. As the personification of memory, she had little about her in the beginning (hardly her fault, since there was nothing for her to remember). It's only as time went on and memories became a 'thing' that the Titaness developed more knowledge. Eventually, as her personification grew, she was considered one of the wisest in all of creation.

THE GRACES (*gray-ses*)

The Graces were gorgeous goddesses that embodied charm, beauty, nature, and creativity.

Though opinions varied on their number depending where you were in Ancient Greece, it was generally thought that there were three of them:

- **Aglaea** (shining)
- **Euphrosyne** (joy)
- **Thalia** (bloom)

They were also referred to as the 'Charities', as they represented the act of charity itself; giving gifts and showing generosity. The Graces were daughters of Zeus and the Oceanid Eurynome (not the Titaness that got her house stolen and booty kicked by Rhea, but the one that helped Thetis look after Hephaestus). They were companions of Hera, who acted as their nurse (which doesn't sound like her really, considering their ancestry) and often attended to Aphrodite, like when she was getting ready to seduce Anchises.

They were mostly depicted either naked, or draped in splendidly flowing sheer garments.

They lived on Mount Olympus, where their role was to arrange parties for the Olympians. During the events, they looked after the gods, sometimes even entertaining their fellow deities with their glorious singing, dancing, and their general charm. They also performed at the wedding of Thetis and Peleus.

Aglaea would go on to marry Hephaestus, after he eventually separated from Aphrodite, and they shared a home on Olympus.

PHILOMELA & PROCNE
(*fil-oh-mee-la* & *prock-nee*)

Athenian princess sisters Philomela and Procne were very close throughout their childhood. Athens had been at war with Thrace for some time, so the king, Pandion, offered Procne's hand in marriage to Thrace's leader, King Tereus. Tereus accepted, and the cities were finally at peace. The sisters were sad to be separated, but this was a rational match and would keep the family's royal house strong.

For the most part, Procne and her husband got along quite nicely, and together they had a child, Itys. It's worth mentioning that the conception of Itys was attended by the Furies, and he was born under a dark omen, but the couple decided to ignore that. In their fifth year of marriage, Procne begged her husband to sail back to her hometown and bring her beloved sister over for a visit.

Tereus told Procne it would be his pleasure. Pandion was happy his daughters would be reunited but saddened to be separated from Philomela, who had remained unmarried and at home. He reluctantly agreed, but asked Tereus to promise to look after her, as if he were her own father. Tereus swore that he would.

Tereus, unfortunately, was a liar. He'd never met the princess on his first visit to the palace, and found that he desired Philomela very much. On arrival to Thrace, he dragged his sister-in-law from the boat and into the woods where he raped her. He swore Philomela to secrecy, but she was defiant, insisting that she would tell her sister and the world what a monster he was. Tereus wasn't counting on his victim being so headstrong, and he was suddenly worried about repercussions. To stop her telling, he cut out her tongue and abandoned her in the woods. He expected that she'd get lost and perish, likely by loss of blood. When he got back to his palace, he told Procne that her sister didn't survive the journey. She was devastated, ordering a tomb to be built in her honour and mourning greatly.

Back in the woods, Philomela may not have been able to tell her story, but what the king didn't know was that she was quite the weaver. She patched up her wound as best she could, then wove an intricate tapestry that told the whole sorry tale. She bundled the artwork in a cloth and recruited an old maid of Procne's to deliver it to the queen. When Procne looked at the tapestry and realised what had happened, she was enraged and deeply saddened for her sister. She asked the old woman to take her to Philomela immediately, and the siblings were finally reunited. Though happy to see her, Philomela couldn't look at her sister because she was so ashamed of what Tereus had done. Procne promised she would destroy her husband as vengeance for her. She spitballed some ideas on how to do it, including chopping off his penis, but in the end settled on a particularly nasty plan.

The two dressed Philomela as a male servant and went to the palace, where the queen dismissed the other staff for the night. When Tereus returned after a long day of king-ing, Procne told her dear husband that she wanted to cook him something special. She served up a meaty feast, and he gorged until he was full to the brim. Procne told him that she hoped he'd left room for dessert and stole off to the kitchen to collect the *pièce de résistance*. She emerged with her sister in tow, the pair of them working together to carry a covered silver platter to the table. Tereus was stunned, completely speechless as the pair placed the dish down. With a flourish, Philomela unveiled the final culinary delight – the head of Tereus' and Procne's son, Itys. With disgust, he realised he'd eaten his own child.

Tereus flew into a rage, grabbing a nearby axe and chasing the women out of the castle. As they ran, the ladies prayed to the gods to save them. Seeing their plight, Apollo transformed all three of them into birds. Tereus was turned into a hawk, while Philomela and Procne were turned into a nightingale and swallow respectively. Fittingly, although the nightingale is renowned for its singing, the females of the species are actually mute.

Poor Pandion would eventually find out the fate of his daughters and grandson. The pain of it all was so much that he died of a broken heart.

AGLAURUS, HERSE & PANDROSUS
(ag-lor-us, her-ss & pan-dro-sus)

The three princesses of Athens – Aglaurus, Herse, and Pandrosus – were spotted by Hermes whilst attending the temple of Athena.

Hermes was blown away by the beauty of Herse, so later decided to pay the girls a visit at home. Aglaurus would be the one to answer the door to the god, who confidently told her that he was there to put a baby in her sister. 'Fine,' said Aglaurus, 'but it's going to cost you'. Presumably she didn't know his true identity, or maybe she was just that bold. Hermes must have been without his godly purse that day, so left.

Athena had been watching the exchange, though, and was annoyed by Aglaurus' greed. She went to the goddess of envy and asked her to punish the princess by afflicting her with her vice. Envy crept into the girl's bedroom, stroked Aglaurus' breast and infected her with vivid green jealousy. As she slept, Aglaurus dreamed of the cold caller and her sister getting it on, then when she awoke found that she was absolutely seething with envy.

When Hermes returned, Aglaurus wildly threw herself in front of Herse's door, trying to block entry. Of course, Hermes simply walked through the girl and entered the bedroom. As Aglaurus screamed about the injustice of it all, the poison within her spread throughout her body and she turned to stone.

This trio of princesses had another myth linked to them, though they relate to one another in no way. We'll get to the why and how, but Athena had recently adopted a baby named Erichthonious when she was called away on patronly business in Athens. Needing a babysitter, she entrusted the child to the daughters of the king. She shut little Erichthonious into a chest and handed him over to the sisters, warning them not to open it under any circumstances.

Pandrosus was a well-behaved girl (evidenced already by her staying well away from the boy drama between her sisters) so steered clear, but Aglaurus and Herse just couldn't help themselves. They opened the chest to see the baby sleeping soundly, along with a terrifying snake (a sacred symbol of his adopted mother-goddess) wrapped around him. The sight drove the princesses into a frenzy, and they jumped from the Acropolis to their deaths.

After her disastrous foray into being a working mother, Athena stashed Erichthonious under Athens and protected him herself until he was grown.

THE HESPERIDES
(*hes-per-eh-deez*)

Nymphs of the evening sun and the personification of the golden light of a sunset, the Hesperides were daughters of the Titan Atlas. They were a trio of exceptionally lovely and charming women, who were tasked with tending to a gorgeous garden located in the far west of the world, which featured an orchard of golden apples. They were sometimes referred to as the 'Sunset Goddesses' or 'Daughters of Evening', though people can't seem to agree on what their individual names might have been.

The orchard that they oversaw belonged to Hera, who received one of the branches as a wedding present from Gaia when she married Zeus. She was so mesmerised by the golden fruit, which could restore youth, that she begged the mother goddess to plant them in her sacred gardens. Although entrusted to tend to the trees, the Hesperides had a case of sticky fingers, and were known to steal a golden apple from time to time. The apples must have tasted delicious, because the women were gods and therefore immortal, so had no reason to covet the anti-ageing effects of the fruit. As an extra layer of protection, and to stop the goddesses from getting greedy, Hera also stationed Ladon, the hundred-eyed snake-like dragon, in the grove, who wrapped himself around the trees and kept an eye on the comings and goings.

These apples appear several times in Greek mythology, like at the wedding of Thetis and Peleus, when Eris used one of them to wreak havoc among the Olympian ladies. When Heracles was in the midst of his twelve labours, he was instructed to steal some of the golden apples from the garden. There are two accounts of how the hero went about this mission. The first involved tricking the Hesperides' father, who was currently holding up the world as punishment for a past transgression, to get the apples for him. Heracles told Atlas that he'd take the weight of the world so he could have a break, maybe visit his lovely daughters, *maybe* pick an apple or two while he was there. Atlas jumped at the chance.

The other version of the story tells us that Heracles obtained the golden apples himself as the Hesperides were only too willing to gift them, and he stayed a while to let the goddesses fuss over him.

ARIADNE (*a-ree-ad-nee*)

Ariadne was the daughter of King Minos and Queen Pasiphaë, making her the sister of the ferocious Minotaur. She had quite the divine family tree, with her grandfathers (Zeus and Helios) being two of the most important gods, and the women being some of the greatest witches in Greek myth. As she was granted responsibility (by her father) for the labyrinth beneath the castle that housed her brother, Ariadne likely knew the maze better than anyone. Despite her royal standing, though, Ariadne was deeply unhappy. Between her father's power-mad reign, her bickering parents, and the pressures of being a princess, the gentle Ariadne wanted nothing more than to break free and start again somewhere far away.

Despite his bloodthirst, Ariadne loved her half-brother, but the annual sacrifices were unbearable for her. The royal family and the citizens of Crete were expected to witness and revel in the youths entering the labyrinth to their death, and Ariadne certainly hadn't inherited her father's cruel streak.

One year, a prince of Athens showed up as a tribute. Theseus had offered himself in the hopes of slaying the Minotaur and ending this barbaric practice once and for all. Luckily for him, as soon as the Cretan princess saw him, she fell head over heels. Ariadne desperately wanted Theseus to survive, so she made sure he learned the twists and turns of the labyrinth, and equipped him with both a sword and a ball of string. Ariadne advised him to tie the end of the string to the door and unfurl it behind him, so that he could use it to find his way out again. By doing this she was betraying not only her family, but her own kingdom. To Ariadne, though, Theseus' love and the promise of escape was worth it.

So, into the maze Theseus went, and thanks to Ariadne's assistance, he was able to slay the beast, rescue the sacrifices, and lead them out of the labyrinth to safety. With his prized weapon gone for good, Minos had no choice but to let the Athenians go, and his daughter stole away with them.

The new couple set sail for home and excitedly began planning their life together as the future king and queen of Athens. Dionysus, however, was on hand to throw a spanner in the works of their happy ending. He'd been keeping an eye on proceedings and thought the princess would make an ideal wife. The wine god appeared to Theseus on his ship and announced that in fact *he* had chosen Ariadne as his own bride, so tough luck. The hero wasn't about to come out of one life-threatening battle just to irk a powerful god, so he agreed.

Theseus moored their ship on the island of Naxos under the pretence of getting some rest on solid ground. As Ariadne slept, her lover abandoned her, being led back to his ship by Athena herself, who we know was always keen to assist a hero on his way. It's possible that Athena would have been pleased to see Theseus get rid of his bride-to-be – as an outsider, she likely wouldn't have been an ideal match for the soon-to-be king of her favourite city. When the princess woke, Theseus was nowhere to be seen. She called his name and ran around the island hysterically, eventually surmising that her lover had ditched her. Ariadne was heartbroken – not only had she been abandoned, but she was sure to die on this barren island. As she resigned herself to her fate, though, Dionysus appeared, and told her his plans for them. Although she didn't have much of a say in it, Ariadne accepted his proposal, and the god hosted a lavish wedding to celebrate their union. She would be a faithful wife to Dionysus, bearing him numerous children. The constellation Corona Borealis is said to be a crown of stars, gifted to Ariadne by her husband on their wedding day.

As we know, Theseus would end up married to Ariadne's own sister, Phaedra. There's an argument as to whether Theseus abducted Phaedra (classic Theseus, tbh) or if it was an arranged marriage to repair relations between their respective kingdoms.

Ariadne later accompanied Dionysus to Tiryns, where he was looking to spread his cult. When he arrived, King Perseus (his half-brother by Zeus, slayer of Medusa, saviour of Andromeda, etc., etc.) refused to allow him access to the kingdom, and a fight broke out. Dionysus' followers were overpowered, and Perseus killed Ariadne in the struggle, turning her to stone with the head of Medusa.

Ariadne was now bound for the Underworld, where she met her mother-in-law, Semele, whose untimely end we'll get to later. Dionysus travelled to the Underworld and was allowed to take the pair to Mount Olympus, where they were both granted goddess status and immortality.

IRIS & ARKE
(eye-riss & ark-ee)

The twin daughters of an Oceanid, Iris and Arke were divine messenger goddesses. They travelled via a rainbow (which linked heaven and earth), and each possessed a glorious set of wings – Iris' were a shimmering gold, whereas Arke's were pale and iridescent.

When the Titanomachy broke out, Iris stayed loyal to her Olympian family, but Arke betrayed them, going to work for the Titans. She assisted the enemy in secret for a while, but was eventually found out. The sisters, who before the conflict were extremely close, were now bitter enemies. When the Olympians eventually won the war, Zeus seized the rival goddess and violently ripped the wings from her back, banishing her to Tartarus, along with the Titans that she had favoured. He would (much later) gift her magnificent wings to Thetis and Peleus on their wedding day, and Thetis would later give them to their son, Achilles. It's thought that, from then on, Arke was represented by the less vibrant, secondary rainbow we sometimes see alongside a first.

After this nasty business, Iris was given various other jobs on top of her messengering. One of these tasks, requested by Zeus, was to carry back and forth a jug containing the water of the river Styx, which she used to put mortals who had committed perjury to sleep. Iris was also assigned the job of filling the clouds with water from the sea, allowing the rain to fall. As times changed and earth was eventually occupied by humans, Iris' job as the messenger expanded, and she carried communications from the gods to their favourite mortal playthings. Iris was the one to break the news of Helen's flit from Sparta to Menelaus, and on the order of Hera, had Lyssa (goddess of frenzy) inflict Heracles with his madness. She assisted by passing her reports and communications during the Trojan War, as well as in Heracles' various labours.

Iris was a loyal assistant of Hera, often depicted by her side, and prioritising her memos over any other for delivery. Although the queen of the skies and her godly buddies kept her busy, Iris still found time for romance, often consorting with the wind god, Zephyrus, and giving him a son, Pothos.

Although Hermes is more widely known as the messenger of the heavens in Greek mythology, it's believed that Iris was the OG, once side by side with her twin sister.

THE FATES (*fay-ts*)

The Fates, also known as the 'Moirai', were the three goddesses responsible for dictating the destinies of mortals.

Mainly depicted as three women weaving over one spindle, they were thought to be extremely powerful, and even beyond the influence of the likes of Zeus. The three sisters were:

- **Clotho** (the spinner of the thread of life)
- **Lachesis** (measurer of the thread and decider of the length of it)
- **Atropos** (snipper, decider of how one would die)

Seven days after a new life came into the world, the Fates would appear at the home's hearth to do their spinning. They were almost always silent while working; one of the only times they spoke was when they told Althea about the burning log that would determine her son's life. Interestingly, their appearance on the seventh day would often coincide with when the baby would receive their chosen name from their parents, a tradition that is still sometimes held to this day in Greece.

There's only one occasion when a destiny assigned by the Fates was changed, and that was in the case of King Admetus of Pherae. Admetus was renowned for being an all-round nice guy and excellent host, so when the god Apollo was sentenced to one year of servitude under a mortal, he chose the king as his captor. It's thought that the pair graduated from master and servant to friends then lovers over the course of his stay, so when Apollo got wind that the thread of Admetus' life was coming up short, he decided to step in.

Apollo went to the Fates and plied them with wine until they were blind drunk. Then, he laid on the charm and managed to convince them to agree that, should the god provide a suitable replacement to die for him, Admetus would be allowed to go on living. When he returned to the kingdom to tell his companion the good news, though, he didn't get a chance to scout out a viable substitute. When Admetus' wife, Alcestis, overheard the condition, she selflessly offered herself up. The Fates, hungover but unable to go back on their word, had to accept Alcestis, and she was led to the Underworld in his place. This isn't as sad an ending as it may seem, though. Years later, after the king hosted the hero Heracles, his guest was so grateful for the exceptional treatment he received that he ventured into the Underworld and retrieved Alcestis, bringing her back to her husband and kingdom.

The Fates were highly respected and immensely powerful, not to mention an essential part of life. They were thought to be very serious and stern, not to be messed with by either gods or mortals. Unless you're Apollo, apparently.

THE HARPIES (*har-pees*)

With the bodies of massive, fearsome birds and the faces of twisted, angry women, the Harpies enjoyed nothing more than bringing pain and suffering to mortals. They were hugely feared throughout Ancient Greece, and it was their job to abduct and carry people to the Furies, so they could exact their vengeance against whatever wrongdoing the victim had committed.

They were nicknamed 'the Hounds of Zeus', but were more than happy to take assignment from any god, really, as long as they got to inflict some torment. They'd be blamed for anything that went wrong in a person's life, especially for things going missing, and it's believed the touch of their talons would immediately spoil food, giving it a grotesque stench.

One of the Harpies, Podarge, mated with Zephyrus (the west wind) and birthed two immortal horses, Xanthus and Balius. The stallions would be given to Thetis and Peleus at their wedding, and would later be controlled by Achilles, who used them to pull his chariot in the Trojan War.

The best-known story involving the Harpies is that of King Phineus of Thrace (he's a different Phineus to the uncle-statue of Andromeda). After being given the gift of prophecy by Zeus, Phineus used it to uncover the plans of the gods, and reveal them to mankind. As punishment, Zeus blinded the king and banished him to a hidden island, filling it with delicious and fragrant foods.

Then, Zeus employed the Harpies to plague the disgraced king. The creatures snatched every morsel away from him whenever he got close, or made it smell so foul that he could no longer stomach it.

Phineus lived in this waking hell for some time, gradually getting weaker from lack of food and constantly dodging the Harpies. That was until the Argonauts found themselves lost on the island. The desperate Phineus promised that he could help them find safe passage home, if only they would save him from these horrendous, winged creatures. The Argonauts agreed, and two of the crew, the Boreads (sons of Boreas, god of the north wind and his wife Orithyia) used their gusty powers to throw the Harpies across the island. When they realised they'd been bested, they flew home to their cave in Crete to await their next torturous mission.

Nowadays, 'harpy' is more likely to be used to refer to a woman in a derogatory way, with connotations of being heartless, annoying and cruel.

THE PLEIADES (*ply-ad-eez*)

The Pleiades were the seven lovely daughters of the Oceanid Pleione. All staunch worshippers of Artemis, they would have planned for a life of purity, but it didn't work out that way.

They were:

- **Maia**, eldest of the Pleiades, who had Hermes to Zeus. The baby grew so rapidly that by the time he was a day old, he looked closer in age to her than a newborn. She was also given the baby Arcas, son of Callisto, to raise after he was taken from his mama-bear.
- **Electra**, who had Iasion (lover of the Olympian Demeter) and Dardanus by Zeus. When Zeus took her by force, she clung to Athena's statue for sanctuary. Zeus simply laughed at her and threw it down from heaven. It landed near Troy, where its founder built a temple in Athena's honour.
- **Taygete**. As Zeus was chasing her, she called out to Artemis for help. The goddess listened and transformed her into a beautiful doe with golden horns. Unfortunately, this metamorphosis didn't even slow Zeus down, and she bore him Lacedaemon, a founder of Sparta.
- **Alcyone and Celaeno**, who both bore various children to Poseidon.

- **Sterope**, who had Oenomaus by Ares (we'll meet his scheming daughter soon).
- **Merope**, who was the youngest of the sisters, and would marry Sisyphus, the founder of Corinth.

Although the rest of the Pleiades had relations and children with mortal men over time, it was only Merope who bore no divine children.

One day, when the Pleiades and Pleione were out frolicking, the hunter Orion discovered them. He was immediately obsessed with the girls and their mother, who politely rejected his advances. That wasn't acceptable to Orion, though, who began to chase them. The girls ran for seven years, not knowing any peace as they ducked, dived and hid from this pest of a man. Eventually, Zeus took pity on them (ironic, given his reputation for pursuing women who didn't want him, including almost half of these sisters) and turned them into stars, the faintest of which would be Merope, who is said to be shying away from her shame at never birthing a child with double-divine parentage. Merope's star is sometimes called 'the lost Pleiade' by astronomers.

Artemis was furious at losing such devoted ladies, sending a giant scorpion down to earth to kill Orion. After his death, he was put into the stars by Zeus, placed so that he'd be able to chase the Pleiades forevermore. This does beg the question of whether Zeus was trying to help these ladies, or not.

THE KERES (*kee-res*)

Demons of violent or cruel deaths, the Keres were daughters of Nyx and Erebus, and were agents of both the Fates and the god Moros (the personification of doom). Truth be told, they may have enjoyed their jobs a little *too* much.

Despite their demonic status, their powers were somewhat limited, as they couldn't actually *cause* the deaths that they so craved. Instead, they could only hang around the dying, circling like vultures for an opportunity to swoop in and feast. They would drink the blood of the casualties and, once satisfied, drag the souls from the bodies and deliver them down to the Underworld. Small in stature, they were described as 'dark' creatures, their dresses worn and bloodstained, with sharp teeth and claws that they used to pin down and suck dry their victims. They'd fling the body behind them, then swiftly move on in search of the next. The Keres had great fun during the all-you-can-eat buffet that was the Trojan War, where they showed allegiance to neither side, unlike other deities. When higher-ranking gods were getting themselves involved in the business of mortals (so, always), they would stand over their favourite humans in battle, swatting away the Keres whenever they tried to approach. Zeus alone had the power to send them away from a battle, or rally them to attendance when needed.

There were thousands of them, and some were personifications of certain types of death, such as particular diseases (so there would be one *Ker* for the black plague, another for the common cold, and so on). These demons specifically were known to linger around the towns where sickness and disease were particularly rife. The Keres delighted in the suffering and watched on as people were killed off. They'd often fight amongst themselves when trying to lay claim in towns where the dead and dying were limited.

The Keres were on hand to witness the downfalls from smaller quarrels, plagues, and tragedies, though they of course preferred instances where the stench of death was largest (namely, the battlefields of war).

THE GRAEAE (*grai-aye*)

Also known as the 'Grey Ones' or the 'Grey Witches', the Graeae were three sisters who shared one eye and one tooth between them, taking turns to use each one.

Said to have been born with their signature grey hair, Deino, Enyo, and Pemphredo were the daughters of the sea monsters Ceto and Phorcys, and sisters to the Gorgons. They were each personification of horrible things:

- **Horror** (Enyo)
- **Dread** (Deino)
- **Alarm** (Pemphredo)

The Graeae presented as wrinkled old women with grey-tinged skin. When you consider the fact that they spent most of their time without eyes or teeth, you can start to see why they were largely avoided.

The main myth that involves the Graeae is that of Perseus and his mission to slay Medusa. The ladies were the secret-keepers of the location in which their siblings resided, so Perseus came knocking to find out exactly where that was.

The Graeae refused to give up the whereabouts of the Gorgons, though, especially to some random mortal man, and tried to laugh him out of the door. Perseus would be the one to have the last laugh, though, as when one sister passed their sole eye over to the other, he intercepted the exchange and held the appendage high in the air, out of their reach. He declared that he'd only give it back if they told him what he wanted to know. Scared they'd be left without a single eye between them, they had no choice but to give up the info. Depending on the source, Perseus either respectfully held up his end of the bargain and returned their precious peeper to them, or he gave a whoop of laughter at the Graeae as he tossed it into oblivion.

KAKIA & ARETE
(*kah-kee-a* & *ah-rett*)

As the goddess of vice and moral badness, Kakia was self-indulgent and sly to the very core.

Depicted as a vain, curvaceous woman who wore lots of makeup and favoured revealing clothes, Kakia tried to coerce humans into lives filled with sin, loving nothing more than the instant that one would choose the dark side over goodness. Kakia's opposite, Arete, was the goddess of virtue, excellence, goodness, and valour. Significantly less adorned than her frenemy, Arete is depicted as a fair lady, dressed in a simple white gown with an air of true grace.

The pair are most famously known for their involvement in the life story of Heracles. When he was young, the hero considered his life's direction and what lay ahead of him. Kakia and Arete both appeared to Heracles at a crossroads, in an attempt to persuade him to choose their own path.

Kakia crudely shoved Arete out of the way, declaring that she should be the one to go first. The goddess sauntered up to the young man, who asked for her name. 'Kakia,' she said, 'but my friends call me "happiness" and you surely will, too.'

She told Heracles that, should he choose her path, he'd want for nothing and have riches beyond his wildest dreams. His hands would never grow calloused from hard work, nor his body tired. Heracles nodded respectfully, then turned to Arete, encouraging her to take her turn.

Arete told him that, should he choose *her* path, he would struggle greatly. He'd have to work very hard and would encounter difficulties along the way, but in return would gain courage, wisdom, and discipline. Then, when the time came to reap the rewards of his life, he would enjoy them immensely as he'd know that he had truly earned them. She assured him that if he committed to this life, he would be able to look back on it at the end and know true happiness. Kakia likely blew a raspberry at this, but Heracles knew what was right for him. Despite Arete's path being filled with toil, he knew he'd rather work hard than have everything in life handed to him at the expense of others. He set off down the road with the fairer goddess, leaving the furious Kakia in their dust.

BYBLIS (*bye-bliss*)

When Byblis felt the stirrings of desire for her twin brother, Caunus, she tried her best to squash it down. They had always been close, but now she found it physically painful to be around him without being able to be honest about her feelings. As he grew into a young man, other girls began to take notice of him, and Byblis positively hated it – the idea that Caunus would soon have to take a wife and leave her made her sick with jealousy.

One day, she concluded that she simply couldn't stand it any longer. She wrote down everything she was feeling in a letter and recruited one of the servants to deliver it to Caunus. In the letter, she went to great lengths to give examples of incestuous relationships between the gods, to show him that their love didn't have to be forbidden.

Caunus read the letter with a curiosity that quickly turned into disgust. Without even finishing the love note, he fled their home, wanting to put as much distance as possible between him and his sicko sis.

Byblis was heartbroken, but still held on to hope. She thought if she could just look into her brother's eyes (*shudder*), he wouldn't be able to deny the connection between them. Admittedly, her desire had sent her a bit mad by this point and she certainly wasn't thinking straight, evidenced by her rationalising that it would help her cause to strip down to nothing before leaving on her hunt for Caunus. She searched (again, completely naked) throughout Greece and Asia Minor until eventually collapsing onto the ground, completely worn out by her exertion and grief. She wept bitter tears as she died, and upon seeing her, some local nymphs took pity on her. Empathising, they collected her tears and turned them into a stream.

THE OENOTROPAE
(*ee-no-troh-pee*)

Three princesses of Delos – Spermo, Oeno, and Elais – were the great-granddaughters of the god of wine and general good times, Dionysus.

Their great-grandfather gave them the ability to turn water into wine, grass into wheat, and berries into olives, meaning that nobody around them would ever go hungry (or short of a tipple). Known collectively as the Oenotropae, the ladies were greatly valued in Delos and weren't at all stingy with their gifts.

When the Greeks sailed via Delos on their way to wage war on the Trojans, the Oenotropae showed their support by stocking three of their ships to the absolute brim with provisions to ensure that they'd arrive in Troy well-fed and watered. Agamemnon, arguably the biggest douchebag in all of Ancient Greece, watched this kind act in amazement, and paid the sisters back by . . . abducting them. The trio were bundled into one of the freshly stocked ships and sequestered to the Greek camp, where they were forced to use their gifts to feed the massive army day in, day out, as slaves.

After a few years, the Oenotropae plotted to escape, but their plans were scuppered by their own brother, who was fighting in the Greek army at the time. He shopped them to the commander, who declared that they be put to death for this act of disobedience. As the sisters prepared to face their punishment from the great and powerful Agamemnon, Dionysus deigned to step in, transforming them into white doves. The princesses happily flapped away to freedom.

6

Damsels of Distress

*They might need saving from
time to time, but these ladies
are just as likely to drop
someone else in it*

MEDUSA (*meh-dew-sa*)

The three Gorgon sisters were born to primordial sea gods Ceto and Phorcys. Two of them, Stheno and Euryale, were frightful, winged beasts that invoked fear in anyone who saw them. Medusa, however, was born mortal. More than that, she was charming and very beautiful – her hair in particular was said to be glorious. As a priestess of Athena, she devoted her life to virginhood.

When Poseidon saw Medusa, he immediately decided it was his right to have her. And so, he did, inside a temple dedicated to Athena, no less. Despite not wanting it, asking for it or consenting to it, it was ultimately Medusa who suffered the consequences of the encounter, as Athena transformed her into a vicious beast with writhing snakes for hair, and green-tinged skin. Her mouth constantly gaped, revealing a monstrously long tongue and sharp, gnashing teeth.

Her new face was so hideous, her eyes so piercing, that whoever looked into them was turned instantly to stone. Over time, it's said that the land surrounding her home was overrun with statues of people and animals, transformed by her gaze.

Meanwhile, in Seriphos, King Polydectes was desperately trying to get rid of his pesky potential step-kid, Perseus, so that he could hound his mother, Danaë, in peace. Despite being a king, Polydectes was quite the berk, and Perseus wanted better for his mother. The king came up with a plan – he would send Perseus off on a quest to fetch the head of Medusa. It was genius, he thought, as Perseus was sure to die en route, or at least at the hands of the Gorgons, so he wouldn't be a problem any more. Perseus, however, wasn't the fish out of water that Polydectes assumed he was. For one, he knew enough to draft in some assistance from Athena herself, who was still illogically mad at Medusa for being raped in her sacred space. She roped Hermes into it, too, and Perseus was kitted out good and proper with his winged sandals, the cap of invisibility from Hades, a super powerful sword from Hephaestus, and a shield from Athena. He may have looked ridiculous, but he was ready to rumble.

After some trickery with the Graeae, Perseus eventually landed on the rocky island of Sarpedon and started strategizing on the best way to secure Medusa's head, well aware of what would happen if he locked eyes with the monster before completing his mission. He had the idea to use his shield, which had been polished within an inch of its life, to peer around corners, ensuring that he wouldn't come face to face with her and be turned to stone. When he found Medusa, she was enjoying a snooze with her sisters, and so he used the sword to decapitate her. Easy as that. Medusa was pregnant to Poseidon at the time of her death. Because this is Ancient Greece and there are *no* rules, the winged horse, Pegasus, and the mortal, Chrysoar, sprung from her neck.

Alerted by the commotion, the other Gorgons woke to find their sister's headless body and this random dude covered in blood standing over her. Perseus fled on his winged sandals before Stheno and Euryale could grab him, and the duo mourned Medusa so passionately that even hard-faced Athena was touched, and she modelled the sound of pipe music after the cadence of their grief as homage. Mission accomplished, Perseus took the severed head and proceeded back to Seriphos. As he flew over Libya, the appendage was still leaking, and blood fell to the ground. From it, serpents sprung. To this day, it's said this is why there are so many snakes in Libya.

Absolutely done with King Polydectes and his poxy quests, Perseus stormed into the palace and flashed Medusa's head, which still held its wicked power, turning the monarch into stone. Later, Perseus gifted Medusa's head to Athena, who incorporated an image of it into her own shield. She also collected some blood that was still dripping from it, most of which she gave to Asclepius, god of medicine, who used its power to take life and raise the dead in turn. The remaining two drops she gave to her adopted son, Erichthonius – one drop was a cure-all, the other a deadly poison. Presumably they were adequately labelled to avoid an embarrassing mix-up.

AETHRA (*ee-thra*)

Although best known as mother of Theseus (and OG keeper of Helen), Aethra had quite the life before he came along.

The daughter of King Pittheus, she was once a Troezen princess in love, promised to the young hero Bellerophon. However, before they had the chance to wed, Bellerophon would be exiled for the accidental murder of his brother. Aethra would be left heartbroken and very much alone, her prospects of securing a good husband lessened by her 'damaged goods' status.

Later, King Aegeus of Athens would come to Troezen to seek Pittheus' advice. After many years of trying and failing to produce an heir to the Athenian throne, Aegeus had consulted an oracle in the hopes of turning his luck around. Of course, the oracle was decidedly vague with her words, telling him: 'Do not open the bulging mouth of the wineskin until you have reached home, lest you die of grief.' He had no idea what this meant, so he travelled to his friend Pittheus' kingdom, as he was known to be particularly skilled at interpreting complicated prophecies.

Understand it Pittheus did, but in doing so, saw an opportunity to benefit himself. The prophecy stood as a warning for Aegeus to not get so intoxicated that he'd be unable to make sound decisions while away from home. If he did, he would have an experience so horrible that he'd die of unhappiness. What Pittheus deduced from it was that should Aegeus go against this prophecy and have a child under the influence, that child was sure to grow to be something special. Even if this meant an eventually miserable end for his friend, Pittheus weighed up the pros and cons and decided it was worth him having a slice of the pie – should it be a member of *his* family that Aegeus had a child with, it would create a link between the small city of Troezen and the powerhouse that was Athens. Not to mention, the prospects of his own heir were now extremely slim, after the banishment of his first choice of son-in-law.

As he made a show of deciphering the prophecy, Pittheus offered his old friend some wine. And some more. And some more after that. Eventually, Aegeus was decidedly inebriated, and Pittheus was ready to implement part two of his crafty plan – introducing his friend to his beautiful young daughter, Aethra.

Wits well and truly out of the window, Aegeus slept with the princess that night, and Aethra was impregnated. As she slept, Athena came to her in a dream, telling her to go to an island across the way, pour a libation to the gods, then sleep with Poseidon. As Aegeus snoozed, Aethra scooted across the water to do as the goddess asked, so any child conceived that night could have confused parentage. That being said, it's also possible this didn't happen at all, and was just a rumour created by Pittheus, adding another layer into his plan for domination. After all, it wouldn't hurt to have divine links in his family tree, assumed or otherwise, and Poseidon was particularly worshipped in Troezen.

Despite his longed-for son finally being on the way, Aegeus decided to return to Athens without Aethra. Before leaving, he buried his sandals, shield, and sword under a large rock and told her that when their son came of age, he should retrieve the items, travel to Athens and take his rightful place on the throne.

Aethra gave birth to a baby boy, who she named Theseus, and we know he'd eventually be reunited with his father and thwart

Medea's plan to kill him. While Theseus grew into manhood, Aethra dedicated a temple on the island to Athena, where she introduced the custom of Troezen women offering their girdles to the goddess on their wedding day.

When Helen's brothers came to rescue her from Theseus' clutches, they took Aethra back to Sparta to serve as a slave to their sister. Aethra served this role throughout Helen's teen years, and when the queen ran away with Paris, Aethra went with her. It wasn't until after the war was won and the women of Troy were brought to the Greek camp to be dished out that she crossed paths with Demophon, her grandson, who knew of her. He asked the leader of the army to assist with his grandmother's liberation. Helen, now a sort-of prisoner of the Greeks herself, was more than happy to let her long-serving attendant go.

Aethra returned home finally a free woman, but would end up taking her own life in the end, over her losses.

DANAË (*dan-ay-ee*)

When King Acriseus of Argos consulted an oracle about why he was yet to have an heir, she helpfully told him that any grandson of his would end up killing him. Alarmed, he locked his only daughter, the beautiful Danaë, in a bronze chamber. While suitably furnished for a princess and undeniably comfortable, it lacked any windows or doors (to escape or let lovers in). The one thing it did have was a skylight.

Zeus had already grown fond of the young girl from afar, and wouldn't let something as tedious as a solid bronze wall stand in the way of passion. Transforming into golden rain, he flowed through the skylight to fornicate with Danaë.

Acriseus was petrified of the prophecy coming to fruition, but was unable to simply kill the child, lest he upset the Furies. Instead, he waited for Danaë to give birth, locked mother and babe in a wooden box and threw them into the sea. Expecting their demise, his conscience was somewhat clear. Luckily for Danaë and the baby, Poseidon was on hand to help a brother out, keeping the waters calm and the bounty safe for Zeus. The box washed up on the shores of Seriphos, where it was found by a fisherman and brother of the local king, Dictys. He was a good man, and he helped Danaë raise the child, who she had named Perseus.

As we know, King Polydectes of Seriphos would fancy himself a piece of Danaë. He began pursuing her intensely, showering her with luxurious gifts and compliments. Danaë was completely uninterested in being his queen and made no secret of it to Perseus. When her now grown son asked the king to lay off on the mum-stalking, he sent the budding hero to slay Medusa to get him out of the way.

Head secured, Perseus wooed Princess Andromeda and headed back to Seriphos to be reunited with his mother.

What of the prophecy, you ask? Later, when Perseus was in Larissa competing in some athletics games, he threw a discus particularly hard, accidentally embedding it in the skull of an old man in the audience. This man was his grandfather, Acriseus. Prophecy fulfilled, Danaë was able to return to Argos, and her son took his rightful place on its throne.

HEBE (*hee-bee*)

As the goddess of youth, Hebe had the power to restore mortals back to their prime. Daughter of Zeus and Hera, she was extremely beautiful, with a glowing youthfulness and a kind disposition.

The other gods were enamoured with Hebe from birth. Hera even held a great feast that lasted seven days after she was born to show her off. Baby Hebe was showered with wonderful gifts, and songs were written in her honour.

As she matured, she didn't rest on her goddess status – she was a working girl. Her main job was to serve ambrosia and nectar to the Olympians, but she was known as a bit of a workhorse in general. She's often depicted running baths for her fellow gods, and was an extremely loyal daughter, never straying far from her parents. The gods leaned heavily on Hebe to keep their favourite mortal playthings young and out of the cold clutches of death. Hebe took her divine powers very seriously, though, and had to be persuaded into using them for anything other than their true purpose – keeping her godly family and friends eternally young.

One night, when she was on shift at Ye Ancient Olympian Tavern, she stepped on her regulation flowy Grecian uniform and stumbled. As she fell, her divine breast popped out of her dress and was exposed to the higher-ranking gods. Apollo fired her on the spot, and Hebe fled in shame. This tale was often told as a warning against women being immodest. Ganymede, Zeus' personal cupbearer, was then promoted to server of all.

Now unemployed, Hebe had a lot of free time, which she used to get to know the famous Heracles, after he'd ascended to the heavens as a reward for his heroic labours. It's thought she was the one to accompany him on his journey to Mount Olympus, once he dropped the 'demi' and become a fully fledged god. Hera, ever the enigma, was the one that orchestrated the union between her archenemy and her beloved daughter. Together they had two children, Alexiares and Anicetus, who would grow up to be the gatekeepers of the heavens. With time, Hebe added patron of brides to the list of her responsibilities, and she was also connected with the fertility of the intendeds that prayed to her.

She would use her youth-restoring power as a favour to her beau: when his nephew Iolaus prayed for one more day as a young man so that he might defend Heracles' children in battle, Hebe granted his wish.

PENELOPE (*pen-el-oh-pee*)

When Penelope was born to a Spartan prince, he took one look between her legs and decided she was of no use to him. He promptly picked poor Penelope up by her foot and threw her into the sea. Luckily for Penelope, she was saved by a waddling of ducks and brought back to the shore. Her dad thought this might have been a sign from the gods and decided to let his daughter live. Big of him.

As a young girl, she was married off to Odysseus in exchange for his advice on how to deal with her cousin Helen. They ruled Ithaca quite happily for many years, but when whispers started circulating that the beautiful Helen had been abducted by the Trojans, Penelope couldn't hide her worry. She knew of the oath that her cousin's suitors had taken back in the day, and that it was her good husband's idea in the first place. She hadn't long bore Odysseus a son, named Telemachus, and the idea of losing him to war while raising a newborn and ruling a kingdom for an uncertain amount of time was not one she relished. She begged her husband to come up with a way to avoid going, knowing that if anyone could dream up a scheme, it would be him. As much as Odysseus knew it was his duty to fight, it broke his heart to see his wife so distraught, so he promised to try.

Shortly thereafter the Greek army came calling, heading straight to the palace and declaring to the waiting Penelope that her husband must leave right away. Penelope told the men that, unfortunately, the great Odysseus wouldn't be joining them on this adventure, as he'd gone positively mad. 'See for yourself,' she said, leading them to a nearby field. The soldiers looked in alarm as a stark naked Odysseus, singing a song of absolute gibberish, made his way around the field in a cart being pulled by both an ox and a donkey. Stranger still, he appeared to be throwing handfuls of salt onto the land, making it infertile. Penelope and the soldiers called his name, to no reply. Odysseus didn't even flinch when one of them threw a stone at him. While most of the men solemnly shook their heads, convinced of his madness, one of them, Palamedes, narrowed his eyes. Like everyone, he knew the king of Ithaca was sharp as a blade, and something about this scene didn't ring quite true. Palamedes quickly snatched the infant Telemachus from Penelope's arms, strode over to the middle of the field and laid him down, right in the path of Odysseus' cart. Panicked, Odysseus pulled the reins on the ox and donkey, stopping them before they reached the baby. Palamedes smiled triumphantly, and Odysseus said, 'touché, dick'.

And so, Odysseus sailed for Troy. He hadn't even disappeared over the horizon before hopeful replacement suitors started darkening Penelope's door. The queen, though, was loyal to her husband and uninterested in the men's attentions. As Odysseus' absence went on over a decade, and Penelope totted up a total of 108 hopeful bachelors, she kept finding ways to put off choosing a new beau. Meanwhile, her people were starting to get restless. It seemed clear to them that their king was dead – why else would he still be missing from their kingdom when so many others who fought in the war had made their way home? The longer the queen dragged her feet, the more vulnerable Ithaca became. Young Telemachus was nowhere near ready to rule, after all. Despite her insistence in putting the men off, Penelope suspected Odysseus' interest in enjoying the pleasures of other women had a hand in keeping him away. Although she knew that she was doing the right, honourable thing, both for her marriage and Ithaca, she was becoming increasingly frustrated at her tardy husband and resentful of the situation he had put her in.

Another decade passed, and Penelope's latest attempt to delay things was to tell the men that she simply must finish weaving a burial shroud for her father-in-law, Laertes, but after that she would *definitely* get around to choosing. Every night, though, Penelope would sneak back into her workshop and unpick the weaving of the day, so that she'd never finish. This tactic worked for a while, until she was spotted by her servant, who immediately snitched. The jig was well and truly up.

By now, Odysseus was in fact close to returning home, but had started to worry. Had Penelope stayed faithful to him? (Ironic, considering he'd fathered another child on his travels). To get the lie of the land, he disguised himself as an elderly beggar and made his way to the palace. Here, he found the hopeful admirers tapping their feet in frustration that the queen still hadn't yet made a decision.

Whether Penelope immediately saw through her husband's disguise or not isn't clear, but at that point she announced her decision – she would remarry with whoever was able to string her husband's bow and arrow and shoot through twelve axe-heads. This may well have been another delay tactic, as she knew that only Odysseus had the skills required to do such a thing; or she could have even been setting the stage for his grand entrance.

Either way, the men tried and failed, unable to even string the bow, never mind make the shot. Finally, the beggar man stepped up – he strung the bow easily, shot through the axe-heads, then turned the weapon on his competition, slaying them where they stood.

Penelope, though, was still dubious. She worried that this was all just an illusion by one of the gods, knowing they had form for such trickery. 'If you're my husband,' she said, 'command our servants to move our bed to the other side of our chamber.' Odysseus, having gone through a glow-up transformation from beggar to badass with the help of Athena, laughed out loud. He told Penelope that would be impossible, as he built that bed himself, and knew that one of its legs grew from a live olive tree and was therefore immovable. Satisfied, she fell into his arms, overcome with happiness at being reunited after all this time.

Penelope and Odysseus ruled happily until the end of his days, when a certain illegitimate child came to pay him a visit. We know from Circe's story how Penelope's ends, including how she bags herself a toy boy in the form of her late husband's love child with the enchantress.

ALCYONE (*al-sigh-oh-nee*)

Queen Alcyone and King Ceyx of Trachis were so sure of their love that they'd taken to calling themselves 'Zeus and Hera'. The gods considered this sacrilege to the highest degree, and decided they'd have their revenge.

When Ceyx was called away on business, Alcyone couldn't bear the thought of being separated from him. She specifically dwelled on her fear that, should he die at sea, she'd have no body to bury. As she wept, he stroked her hair and assured her that he'd be home soon.

That night as Ceyx and his crew sailed, Zeus put his plan for retribution into action, sending a great storm to target the ship. As the waves crashed, the crew were thrown around the deck like a bag of marbles. As Ceyx was launched into the open sea, he wished more than anything he'd never left Alcyone. A massive wave dragged the men to the bottom of the ocean and everyone drowned except for the king. As he resurfaced, he clung for dear life to a piece of driftwood and called out to the gods. He begged for survival, but his request fell upon deaf (or likely, selectively ignorant) ears. Instead, he asked that his body find its way back home, so Alcyone would at least have something to bury. Dragged underwater once last time, Ceyx thought of nothing but his wife in his last moments.

Back in Trachis, Hera was growing tired of recieving prayers for a dead man's safety. To put a stop to this, she sent Morpheus, god of dreams, to appear to Alcyone in the form of her husband. When Alcyone saw her love, he was weeping and told her of his death.

Instinctively knowing that the dream's message was true, she informed the servants that they were now without a king. Searching out a spot for a cathartic cry, Alcyone stopped at the beach she'd last saw Ceyx. As she did, though, she saw something bobbing about in the water. Realising immediately that it was the body of her husband, she leapt into the waves and waded towards him. The gods, saddened by Alcyone's display of grief, transformed her into a seabird. With her beak, Alcyone pecked kisses all over Ceyx's body, until he was also transformed. In their new feathered forms, the couple were just as dedicated to each other as they had been as humans.

IO *(eye-oh)*

Io was a princess of Argos, whose river-god father, Inachus, introduced their people to the cult of Hera.

Despite her close links with the goddess of women and marriage, Zeus took an interest in Io, and they had an affair, possibly (probably) against the princess's will. Io was the first mortal woman to tickle the sky god's fancy, though she certainly wouldn't be the last. Zeus was worried that his wife would find out and kill his consort, so he transformed her into a white cow as a disguise.

Naturally, Hera found out anyway, but instead of going in all guns blazing, she decided to take the sneaky approach. Pretending to notice the beautiful heifer grazing, she begged her husband to give it to her as a gift. Zeus, having no logical reason to deny her a simple animal, had to agree lest she sense something was up.

Hera had the hundred-eyed giant, Argus Panoptes, watch over Io the cow. He would then report back if he spotted her husband trying to visit. Zeus knew he couldn't evade the watcher's many eyes, so instead sent in Hermes, who played his panpipe in such a way that Argus fell into a slumber. The messenger god killed the watcher and Zeus seized his opportunity.

Hera got wind that her servant was dead and put two and two together. Furious at being bested, she sent a gadfly to follow Io and sting her behind forevermore. To honour Argus Panpotes, Hera used his eyes to decorate the feathers of a peacock, an animal that was sacred to her.

The now very miserable Io travelled the world trying to escape the darned insect, but it was no use. No matter how far she wandered or how hard she swatted it with her tail, the fly was relentless.

Eventually, Io came across the Titan Prometheus, currently chained up as a punishment from Zeus, who comforted her by revealing that she would return to her human form eventually. What's more, he told her that she was destined to become an ancestress to a prolific hero. Hope restored, Io moseyed on over to Egypt, where she finally regained her human form.

Back in her own skin, Io married the king of Egypt. From her line descended many well-remembered kings and heroes, including Heracles, Cadmus, Perseus, and Minos. It's generally agreed that the hero from Prometheus' prophecy was Heracles.

PSYCHE (*sigh-kee*)

Psyche was the youngest of three daughters to a forgotten king and queen. Kind and astonishingly beautiful, men would compare her to the goddess Aphrodite. Some dared to remark that she was even *more* lovely than the goddess, which naturally had Aphrodite furious.

Instead of punishing the blasphemous men who leered at the young Psyche, Aphrodite focused her revenge on the girl. She called upon her son, Eros, for help. Eros had special golden arrows that struck love and desire into both gods and mortals, and Aphrodite commanded that he use his gifts to make Psyche fall in love with 'the most despicable of all creatures'. Eros set off to fulfil his mother's vague wishes, but upon seeing the princess, felt his own heart swell and knew that he must spare her.

Unbeknownst to Psyche that she'd escaped a frightful fate, the princess got on with her life. Her older sisters, who had always been jealous of her, eventually married kings and left home, but nobody came forward to ask for the hand of Psyche, happy to just admire her from afar.

Worried about his daughter's future, the king consulted the oracle. Pythia revealed that Psyche was destined to marry a being so frightful that even the gods themselves feared it. She advised that the best thing to do would be to dress her in clothes fitting for a funeral and lead her to the tallest rock in the kingdom, on which she would meet her fate.

The king was heartbroken but accepted the word of the oracle, depositing Psyche atop a rock and leaving her with a kiss. Psyche, scared of what was to come, waited. And waited some more. She got so sick of waiting that she eventually jumped off the rock, wanting to cut out the part where she had to meet an unsightly monster before her death. As she fell, though, the god of the west wind, Zephyrus, used his powers to suspend her in the air. Then, he floated her to the home of Eros. With no one around, the princess made herself comfortable in the opulent palace.

Comfortable as she was, Psyche couldn't escape the worry that gnawed at her. She wandered aimlessly around the halls, and when the night descended she finally heard the front gates open. Strangely, though, all the lights in the palace had gone out, and she was unable to see her own hand in front of her face. What she did know was that a man was here. It was Eros, though of course he couldn't have his mother finding out that he'd spared Psyche all those years ago. He told her that they could be together, if she would have him, but she must never look upon his face or learn his name, as the consequences would be dire. That night, they made love in the pitch-black. Psyche was aware that the prophecy had predicted her husband would be a horrific monster, but this stranger certainly didn't *feel* like one. She decided that whatever was happening, she was fully on board.

The couple lived happily for a few weeks in total darkness, but once Psyche's sisters got wind of her apparent death, Eros sensed trouble brewing. He warned Psyche that her sisters planned to visit the rock from which she'd jumped, and he knew she'd be desperate to ease their pain. As mean as they were to her growing up, Psyche possessed a kind-heartedness that her siblings did not. As predicted, as soon as Psyche sensed her sisters mourning, she felt her heartstrings being pulled. Soft Psyche couldn't resist, and chose to go to them, telling them to dry their tears, as she lived! What's more, she was finally loved by a wonderful man (she thought) and happy beyond measure. The sisters, quickly getting over their surprise, requested that Psyche take them to her new abode and show them that she truly was okay. Psyche obliged, asking Zephyrus, who was happy to serve the couple, to carry the three of them back to the palace.

Once there, Psyche gave them the grand tour. They were once again overcome with jealousy. How dare this brat, who sailed through life on her looks, end up in such a magnificent home with a kind, virile man by her side, when they were saddled with balding, overweight old men as husbands, living lives of tedium?

The sisters began to lean on Psyche's doubts, needling that the man of the house was probably playing a terrible joke on her. As much as she tried to fight it, they got into Psyche's psyche.

That night after they made love, Psyche lit an oil lamp and crept into Eros' bedroom. She shone the light over him and found a handsome young man with a gentle face. Breathing a sigh of relief, she silently chastised herself, but as she went to pull away, a drop of hot oil dripped from the lamp and onto his shoulder, waking him. On realising what Psyche had done, Eros fled from the castle and to the home of his mother on Mount Olympus. Aphrodite wasn't there, though – by now, she'd heard about her son's betrayal and was in the process of hunting down the mortal beauty to bestow her own punishment.

Psyche was absolutely devastated. Once she'd had her fill of self-pity, she found that she was actually riled by the whole situation. Though she could never be mad at her darling Eros, she was positively fizzing over the actions of her horrible sisters and decided to take revenge. She travelled to her first sister's kingdom and turned on the waterworks, complaining that the god of love had left her because he was truly infatuated with her *sister* of all people, could she believe it? The sibling was barely able to contain her nasty delight; wasting no time, she fled her own castle to throw herself at Eros. She ran up to the cliff edge where she was last picked up by Zephyrus and dived off – of course, Zephyrus was loyal to Eros and Psyche, so had no qualms about letting the woman fall to her death.

Psyche repeated her devilish plan with her other sister in the exact same way, but when all was said and done, she realised she didn't feel any better, and her heart was still shattered. Around this time, Aphrodite caught up with her. Still annoyed at her son's betrayal and wanting to put an end to this other woman taking the attention, she told Psyche that because of her, Eros was dying (of an oil burn, apparently). In order to make amends and heal him, she must complete four seemingly impossible trials.

Firstly, Aphrodite dumped a massive bag of mixed seeds in front of Psyche and told her to divide them into separate piles before her return. Psyche knew there wasn't enough time but made a start sorting anyway. She was soon joined by an army of ants, who made short work of grouping the seeds. Then, Aphrodite told her to gather the wool of a particularly feisty sheep. Psyche watched the animal storming about its pen, steeling herself for a fight. Before she could enter, a river god popped up from the stream behind her and taught her how to collect the wool that had snagged against the bushes surrounding the pen instead.

Her next task was to bring water from the Underworld into the mortal realm, and since nobody who went to Hades' kingdom was allowed to return, this would surely be the one that would finish her off. It wasn't to be, however, an eagle volunteered to go *for* her.

Lastly, Aphrodite told Psyche to obtain some of the beauty cream belonging to Persephone, queen of the Underworld. As with the other tasks, it appeared that this was going to be somewhat of a breeze, as Persephone appeared before her and gladly handed over a container of the lotion. She did, however, warn the girl that she shouldn't open it, as a divine substance such as this couldn't be looked upon by a mere human. Psyche was finally seeing a light at the end of the tunnel, but she couldn't resist a tiny peek. On being exposed to this, she immediately perished.

Eros, now recovered from his deadly oil burn, swooped down and carried his lover's body to Mount Olympus. He explained the trials and tribulations that Psyche had gone through in the name of love, and begged the gods to bring her back to him. Zeus, who was fond of blaming Eros' influence for his marital affairs and wouldn't like to risk him abandoning his duties, granted his wish but with an extra bonus – he made the mortal woman the goddess of the soul.

ASTERIA (*ass-tee-ree-ya*)

Goddess of falling stars, Asteria was married to fellow Titan Perses, the god of destruction. To him, she gave birth to the legendary enchantress Hecate. It's quite uncommon for goddesses like Asteria to have only one child, but Hecate was a particularly revered addition to the world, so maybe Asteria was one and done.

Because of the respect that her daughter commanded, Asteria didn't need to worry about trivial things like the outcome of the Titanomachy, and once it was won by the Olympians, she was invited to ascend to Mount Olympus, where she could live in great comfort. Being on Olympus, though, came with its own hazards, such as being closer to the ever-wandering gaze of Zeus himself. Despite her best efforts to keep her head down, Asteria caught the chief god's eye, and he began to pursue her. She was absolutely not keen on bedding Zeus in general, or facing the wrath of Hera, so took off at a sprint to avoid him.

Not one to accept 'no' as an answer, Zeus chased her through the sky, causing Asteria ultimately to transform herself into a quail and fall to the earth from the heavens. She landed in the sea, relieved to have finally escaped Zeus' attentions, but his brother, Poseidon, now took up the chase. Exhausted by the first leg of her journey, Asteria transformed herself again, this time into a floating island that would be known as Ortygia, the Greek word for 'quail'.

The island itself was rather barren, and it stayed that way for a long time – it's likely a hard sell for real estate, being a floating island with literally no fixed address. What it did have, though, was an oracle who specialised in the interpretation of dreams, something that Asteria herself had always been associated with.

The she-island would be renamed numerous times, eventually becoming Delos. When the Titaness Leto was forbidden from giving birth on solid ground by Hera, she sought out her sister Asteria's assistance. Asteria was able to give Leto some solace on her untethered shores, and after the birth of her twins, Delos was attached to the sea floor and began to thrive. It would go on to become a sacred place of the four divinities that graced it, as well as a hot spot for maritime trading.

MEGARA (*meg-ah-ra*)

When the young hero Heracles fought alongside King Creon of Thebes, he was rewarded with the hand of the princess, Megara. This is the same Creon that was Antigone and Ismene's uncle, but this story went down before Oedipus would take the throne. She and Herc had many children and lived happily for a little while. Never one to linger in domestic bliss, though, Heracles was called away, leaving his family and Creon's kingdom without protection.

It didn't take long for another man, Lycus, to come sniffing around. Thrilled to hear the city's greatest protector was MIA, he decided he'd quite like the Theban throne. In order to do this, he would have to murder the hero's family, lest they start an uprising against him. Megara and her children took refuge at an altar of Zeus, clinging to his statue for protection, but Lycus just laughed and demanded it be burned down. Megara declared that she wouldn't take the cowards way out, asking only that Lycus allow her to dress herself and her children appropriately for death. He reluctantly agreed, and as Megara attended to them, she told her daughters of the handsome husbands she and their father had hoped to pick out for them, and the cities they would have given to their sons.

However, just in time, Heracles returned home. Lycus barely had time to register the turn of events before Heracles killed him. Chuckling over the puny wannabe-usurper, Heracles immediately got on his knees to give thanks to the gods. As he opened his mind to the divine, however, his arch nemesis, Hera, seized her opportunity to strike Heracles with madness. Getting back to his feet, he looked at his own wife and children, but instead saw the family of Lycus. He was filled with rage over what Lycus had done to his city and brutally killed them all.

Once his family were dead, the madness lifted, and Heracles surveyed the scene. He wanted nothing more than to die himself in that moment, but his cousin Theseus convinced him that it would be selfish of him to not live on and atone. Reluctantly, he agreed and consulted the oracle of Delphi for the best way to make amends, and thus began his famous twelve labours. Of course, Hera was never going to let him have an easy time of it, and was on hand at every turn to ruin his day, as usual.

HIPPODAMIA
(*hip-oh-dam-ee-ya*)

When King Oenomaus of Pisa (son of Ares and the Pleiade Sterope) received the prophecy that his son-in-law would kill him, he immediately put special measures in place. Oenomaus decreed that should anyone wish to take the hand of his daughter, Hippodamia, they would have to beat him in a chariot race first. The king was quite the racer and knew that this wouldn't be an easy feat for potential love interests. In addition, he used the horses that had been given to him by his father, which were destined to always outrun the competition. Sounds a bit like cheating, but go off. As another layer of protection, he made it clear that he would behead anyone who failed. Despite the high stakes, eighteen would-be suitors lined up to race Oenomaus for Hippodamia's hand; each of them lost and ended up dead for their efforts. Fancying himself quite the exterior decorator, Oenomaus impaled the losers' heads on the wooden columns of the palace, as a deterrent to any other hopefuls.

It was looking like Hippodamia would be single forever, and this suited the king just fine. Then came along Pelops, who was under no illusion that he was a better charioteer than the king, but desperately wanted to marry the beautiful princess. What's more, she seemed pretty keen on marrying him, too. With the date of the race in place, Pelops went to the seafront and called on Poseidon, who he'd once taken as a lover. He asked for assistance to win the race, and the god of the sea was only too keen to assist. Waving his trident, Poseidon brought forth a stunning chariot, equipped with winged horses, sure to give Oenomaus' old mares a run for their money.

Hippodamia, meanwhile, was doing some fixing of her own. She was sick of seeing these men chopped down in her name, and she really did like the look of this Pelops character. Once her father was asleep in his chamber, the princess sneaked down to the stables where Myrtius, Oenomaus' racing hand, was checking over the chariot in preparation for tomorrow. She wasn't blind – she knew that this poor sap had always had a bit of a thing for her, and she wanted to use this to her advantage. While it was true that Myrtius had long had a crush on Hippodamia, he knew his abilities as a racer paled in comparison to his employer's, so had never offered himself up. Hippodamia leaned over the man as he worked, twirling her hair around her finger, whispering sweet nothings, and promising not only half the kingdom should Pelops be victorious in the race, but also one night of passion with her. It's hard to say which prize he wanted more, and he readily agreed to help. Myrtius moulded beeswax to look like linchpins from the chariot and swapped them out with the real thing.

When the race began, the spectacular chariot and flying horses quickly gave Pelops and the king an even playing field. Still, though, Oenomaus was gaining on the youth, and Pelops sensed him raise his sword, ready to add another head to the collection. Hippodamia held her breath in the stands, willing the gods to save her fancy man. Suddenly, the king's chariot jerked to the side as one of the beeswax pieces snapped in half. The wheel disconnected, and Myrtius was thrown from the chariot. Oenomaus grabbed at the reins to try and haul himself up, but the panicked horses ran in every direction until the king was thoroughly tangled, and was dragged to his death.

Pelops, victorious, jumped from his chariot and swept Hippodamia into an embrace. From behind him, though, Myrtius emerged from the wreckage, bloody but expectant. He headed straight for Hippodamia, eager to claim his prize. Pelops, having no idea of the agreement, mistook the scene for the racing hand forcing himself on his new bride. He seized Myrtius by the scruff of the neck, dragged him to the edge of a nearby cliff and kicked him from the top.

As Myrtius lay dying on the rocks, he called out to curse the couple and their descendants. Considering Pelops' family were *already* cursed because of the transgressions of his father, Tantalus, this would worsen the plague of bad luck on the family tree that lasted for five generations, with a barrage of betrayal, murder, revenge, and general nastiness, only ending with the trial and acquittal of Orestes.

With her father dead, Hippodamia and Pelops would ascend to the throne of Pisa and have fourteen children, including Thyestes, father of Pelopia. Pelops would go on to erect a temple in remembrance of the eighteen men who'd lost their lives in the quest for the hand of Hippodamia, and start the basis of the Olympic games by establishing a chariot race to honour his father-in-law's memory, and his own victory.

HYPSIPYLE (*hip-sip-pile*)

Queen Hypsipyle of Lemnos was the granddaughter of Dionysus and Ariadne.

Remember way back in Aphrodite's story, when she cursed the women of Lemnos to stink to the high heavens and murder their husbands? Well, Hypsipyle was ruling over these fetid females when the madness struck, and she managed fight it long enough to warn her father, Thoas, to flee.

When the Argonauts washed up on their shores and Aphrodite deigned to let the women mate with them (and thus repopulate the island), it was Jason himself that coupled with their queen. As the women discussed the terms of the copulation agreement amongst themselves, they decided to tell a softer story of how Lemnos came to be a female-only dwelling. Instead of sharing the gory details of the massacre that occurred, they said that when the men had returned from a raid one day, they had taken a stand and denied them and their concubines access to the island. The Argonauts had no reason to doubt the tale.

Instead of treating the mating like a means to an end, the women encouraged the crew to stick around, and that they did, staying for at least two years. Hypsipyle bore a set of twins to Jason and, while they grew in her stomach, the hero made big promises to the queen. He vowed to stay in Lemnos, to raise their boys together and that they'd rule as the royal couple. In fact, they did formally marry during his time on the island and lived happily in the palace for a spell. Hypsipyle gave birth to twins Euneus and Thoas, the latter she'd named after her father.

Jason was all talk and no trousers, though, as he knew he'd have to depart to get the Golden Fleece eventually. As he stood on the shore, ready to board the ship, Hypsipyle handed him their baby boys and asked that he always remember her fondly. She gifted him a beautiful, royal purple robe that was woven by the Graces themselves, and he told her that his heart was forever hers.

Time passed and Lemnos was restored to a bustling isle once more. The queen heard stories of Jason over the years, but didn't find them particularly comforting. She learned that he'd taken Medea as a lover, and later a wife. Though she tried to reason that the witch had tricked him into loving her, she knew deep down that he'd forgotten all about her. As revenge, she prayed to the gods that Medea would be cursed to lose her children and husband . . . wish granted, then?

Rumours would eventually come to Lemnos that their queen had helped her father escape the massacre of the Lemnian men, and when the women found out they were furious. They'd lost their husbands and sons; to learn that their monarch had found a way to hold back the madness but had only used it to save her own was unforgivable. They turned on Hypsipyle, ready to kill her in retribution, but she was able to flee before they did her any harm.

Her salvation didn't last long as she was quickly picked up by barbaric pirates. There's not much known about her time with the swashbucklers, but we do know it ended with her being sold to King Lycurgus of Nemea. After some time, Hypsipyle was tasked with being the wet nurse to his young son, Opheltes. Unfortunately, she wasn't very good at her new job, and the child was killed by a snake while under her care. It seemed that the fallen monarch would finally meet her death, as the queen of Nemea demanded that Hypsipyle pay for her son's life with her own. At the last minute, though, the queen was approached by the seer Amphiaraus. He told the queen that it wasn't the slave's fault; it was the prince's destiny to die by that snake. Begrudgingly, she allowed Hypsipyle to live. Elaborate funeral games (a sporting event to honour someone who had passed, usually royalty) would be held to celebrate the short life of Opheltes. Around the same time, two young men arrived on Nemea looking for shelter.

These men were Hypsipyle's sons, Thoas and Euneus, who had been raised by the musician and Argonaut Orpheus. Orpheus had told the boys all about their mother and father, but of course they had no way of reuniting with her, since she was currently off-radar. Both boys took part in the funeral games, winning in their chosen field. As they announced the winners, the names of their parents were read out to the cheering crowds as was customary, and Hypsipyle couldn't believe her ears. After all this time, fate had brought her beloved boys back to her. They were equally overjoyed to find her safe and well. The story says that they then returned to Lemnos, where they surely received a frosty reception from the womenfolk.

BRISEIS (*bris-ay-us*)

Briseis was a princess of Lyrnessus, and was thought to have been very sweet and pretty.

When Achilles and his soldiers rocked up to Troy, ready for war, they quickly realised it wouldn't be easy to penetrate the great city. Jacked up on excitement and restless for a fight, they instead turned their attention to pillaging the neighbouring towns and cities. Lyrnessus was an ally of Troy, so it wasn't long before the Greeks landed on their shores with plundering on the mind. Achilles was at the helm, and he personally killed the king, along with all three of Briseis' brothers. He decided to take the young woman as his prize and concubine, and they left for the next battle.

Briseis, stripped of her nobility and all ties to her home, was terrified of what her future held. As time passed, though, she was surprised to discover that her captor was actually kind to her. She also developed a close friendship with Achilles' right-hand man and lover, Patroclus, who revealed to her that Achilles was planning to make her his lawful wife after the war. Despite the devastation that Achilles had brought to her life, Briseis began to look forward to the day she would become his bride (or perhaps she had a touch of Stockholm Syndrome).

Elsewhere, the Trojan town of Chryse had been taken over by Agamemnon, in much the same way that Achilles had taken

Lyrnessus. As a reward for his efforts, Agamemnon had taken for himself the young Chryseis, daughter of the priest, Chryses.

Chryseis' father tried desperately to bargain with the soldier, offering to buy his daughter back, but the powerful Agamemnon had no need for such promises or riches, and refused. The priest begged the god Apollo to intervene, who obliged by sending a plague through the Greek camp. Agamemnon went to the seer, Calchas, who advised that the outbreak wouldn't be reined in unless they relinquished Chryseis back to her family.

Agamemnon had no choice, but was very sore at having lost his 'prize' and decided that the only way to make himself feel better was to have Achilles' favourite concubine instead. He ordered that Briseis be taken to his tent immediately, and in a show of true sulkiness, Achilles refused to fight and retired to his own camp. Along with Patroclus, all of the Myrmidon's put down their weapons in solidarity.

Briseis was heartbroken – just when it looked like she might finally gain back some happiness, it was ripped away from her.

With their best fighter missing in action, the Greeks quickly lost their advantage. When the Trojans finally decided the time was right to attack with their full chest, the frenzy of the real war began. It was becoming increasingly likely that the Greeks would fall and, though he tried to deny it, Agamemnon couldn't really get away from the fact that it was pretty much all his fault. Let's not forget that the commander had 'sacrificed' his own daughter, Iphigenia, in support of this war. He went to Achilles and told him that he could have Briseis back. He also promised that, in the time that Briseis had been with him, he hadn't had sex with her.

Achilles wasn't finished brooding, though, and refused the offer of his apparent future wife's return. He did, however, allow Patroclus and the rest of his army to return to the fight. Patroclus donned

Achilles armour in an attempt to intimidate the opposition and set off once again to fight. It wasn't long before the prince, Hector, killed him. Only then did Achilles return to the battlefield, in order to exact revenge. In the midst of his raging grief for Patroclus, it seemed Briseis was the last thing on his mind.

Achilles and Agamemnon kissed and made up, and the latter said he'd honour his promise to return Briseis if he desired to have her. Achilles said, 'meh, sure'. When Briseis heard the news, she was overjoyed, much preferring to be owned by Achilles than the cruel and bullying Agamemnon. She ran to his tent but was met with the dead body of her confidant and friend, Patroclus. She grieved for him deeply, and when Achilles allowed him to be buried, it was Briseis who tended to his body, preparing him for his passage to the Underworld. Achilles would die soon after, at the hands of Paris, and the broken-hearted Briseis did the same for him.

Unfortunately, nothing is known of Briseis' fate after the death of her lover and master, but she likely died in the storm – sent by Athena to punish Ajax for raping Cassandra in her sacred place – that swallowed up a good portion of the returning Greeks.

PHYLLIS (*fill-iss*)

A Thracian princess, Phyllis married hero and king of Athens, Demophon, after he washed up on her shores on his way home from the Trojan War.

The ink on the marriage certificate wasn't even dry, though, before Demophon had to return home to help his kingdom. As he prepared to leave, Phyllis gave him a box, telling him to only open it if he was sure that he'd be unable to return to her.

After some time, Phyllis became convinced that Demophon wasn't coming back. Initially she thought that he'd died on his travels, but quickly moved to the idea that he just wasn't that into her.

With each day that passed, Phyllis began to feel more and more foolish for falling in love with the suspected scoundrel. With the responsibility of the Thracian throne on her shoulders, she couldn't help but feel that she'd let her people down, failing to secure a good king. She felt used and violated by Demophon, but also stupid for giving away her hand, the only thing she had to offer for the prosperity of Thrace. To make matters worse, word had spread that Phyllis was 'damaged goods', making it harder to find a good enough replacement for Demophon. It was all well and good having a dowry that equalled a literal kingdom, but it wasn't appealing for a man to marry a woman who had already been with another. Naturally, roles reversed, the men in these scenarios did not experience the same anxieties.

Broken-hearted, Phyllis ran into the nearby woods and hanged herself amongst the trees. As she died, she cried out that her death sat squarely on her delayed husband's shoulders. Where Phyllis' body was buried, an almond tree sprouted.

When Demophon eventually did return to Thrace, he learned of her death and went straight to visit her resting place. He touched the tree, and flowers bloomed beneath his fingers.

In another version of Phyllis' tale, Demophon had no intention of returning to his bride from the moment he set sail. Knowing this to be the case, he opened the mysterious box as soon as he was back in Athens. What it contained was so shocking that he attempted to flee, (we don't know what this is, use your imagination) but in doing so spooked his horse, who bucked him off and caused him to fall on his sword and die.

SAPPHO (*saff-oh*)

Unusual for these lores, Sappho was actually a verifiably real woman, though the mythology behind her story here is fiction. Sappho was a renowned poet of Lesbos, and the leader of a cult of Aphrodite and the Muses. The followers of this cult were mainly young women, who Sappho expressed her love for in her poetry. The ladies lived together with Sappho during their coming of age, and when they were considered grown, they were married off. Sappho would compose their wedding songs for the big day. As much as she loved her ladies, it would be a man that would bring about her demise.

Phaon was an aged and supposedly 'unattractive' boatman with a kind heart. When a crooked old beggar woman asked him for a ride, he was happy to oblige. Luckily for him, the old crone was actually the goddess Aphrodite in disguise. When she tried to pay him, he wouldn't accept it. As a reward for his kindness, Aphrodite gifted Phaon a bottle of lotion. When he rubbed the lotion on his skin later that night, the old man found that his wrinkles disappeared. He eagerly rubbed it into his whole body and was transformed, not just back to his youth, but into someone more classically handsome.

Phaon decided to scrap the ferrying game in favour of enjoying his newfound attractiveness and went on a bit of a boinking spree across Lesbos and beyond. One of the first women he tangled with was Sappho, who showed him a thing or two about lovemaking. Despite her sexual ferocity, though, Phaon simply couldn't commit himself to just one person, especially after a lifetime of being ignored by beautiful women. He left Sappho and carried on his merry journey of bedhopping.

After he'd left, Sappho was driven to distraction with yearning for him. No longer taken with the beauties who used to enchant her, Sappho couldn't even write her poetry. Every night, she'd dream of her lovemaking with Phaon and wake devastated by his absence. Unwilling to carry on living without either her passion for words or her beautiful Phaon, Sappho threw herself into the sea.

Aside from her great talent, not much is known about the real Sappho, which may be due to the attempted erasure of lesbian and bisexual women of ancient times. Her talent earned her the moniker 'the tenth Muse', and one of her very limited surviving pieces is her poem, *Ode to Aphrodite*. The words 'sapphic' and 'lesbian' derive from her name and home, and it's suggested that the whole introduction of the Phaon myth comes from people trying to attach her to a man in general, instead of the women she's widely believed to have enjoyed, to make her more 'palatable'.

MYRINA (*Mi-rin-a*)

When the beautiful maiden Myrina was kidnapped from her home by raiders, they stashed her in a cave they used to hide their spoils. After some time, she managed to escape and returned to her home, praising the gods for keeping her safe and giving her back her freedom. She felt particularly indebted to Aphrodite, so from then on decided to dedicate her life to the goddess's cult, eventually becoming a priestess.

One day, when Myrina was out in town, she recognised one of her kidnappers in the crowd. She marched straight up to the fiend and dragged him into the middle of the courtyard. The man, not so brave without his cronies, confessed to his crimes in front of the whole township and gave Myrina the names of his associates. Amongst these townsfolk was a man who had previously been in love with Myrina before she was abducted – he made his way through the throng and vowed that he would track down and kill the whole group in honour of the maiden. Myrina graciously accepted the stranger's offer, and went back to priestess-ing.

Off he went, returning sometime later with all the names neatly ticked off, and sniffing around for a reward. The town had a meeting (of which Myrina likely wasn't even invited to) and decided that the prize for this noble act of revenge would be the hand of Myrina. Of course, as a priestess she'd sworn a vow of chastity, but there was a man who wanted something from her, so why should that matter? Myrina had no choice but to go with the man, and Aphrodite was so disappointed in her for breaking her promise that she transformed her into a myrtle tree, which would from then on be a sacred symbol of the goddess.

SEMELE (*sem-eh-lee*)

Semele was a priestess of Zeus who attracted the lustful eye of her favoured god.

He'd first seen Semele when she was sacrificing a bull in his honour; he had appeared to her in a semi-mortal form, but told her the truth about who he was. Semele was absolutely in awe, tripping over herself to please the god. Zeus may well have been the 'hump and dump' type usually, but something about Semele touched him deeply, and he promised to return to her regularly to check in (and presumably get a little *somethin' somethin'*). Later, Semele was delighted to discover that she was pregnant to Zeus.

Naturally, Hera had been spying on their union and was racking her brains to come up with a way to make the priestess pay. She took on the form of Semele's nurse and went to her in the middle of her pregnancy, using her wily ways to trick the young woman into telling her who the father of her child was. The 'nurse' snorted in Semele's face, saying that she was sure that's what they all say, but how could Semele know for sure? Semele's resolve started to wobble, and Hera continued to sow the seeds of doubt in her mind. She told Semele that she should ask her lover to swear an oath on the river Styx to grant her any wish she desired, and when he did, she should ask him to show her his true form. After all, she was sure that's the form Zeus took when he was with his wife – you know, HIS WIFE . . . EVER HEARD OF HER?!

Semele agreed this was a good idea, so the next time Zeus visited her she asked him to take the oath. Zeus laughed as he did so, telling her he'd always give her whatever she wanted. The laughter soon disappeared though, when Semele revealed her terms. Zeus begged her to reconsider, wasn't there anything else he could do to prove his divinity to her? But no, Hera had well and truly got in the mortal's head and she wouldn't be swayed.

With tears in his eyes, Zeus changed into his full godly glory and Semele was completely incinerated at the divine sight. Zeus managed to save the child from her womb, sewing it into his leg and allowing it to grow there until it was ready to be born. This baby would be Dionysus, the god of wine.

7

Brutish Babes
*The girlies who just wake up
and choose violence*

STYX (*sticks*)

The Oceanids, born from water gods Oceanus and Tethys, were beautiful sea nymphs. Thought to be three thousand in number, the eldest was Styx, whose name meant 'hateful' and was the personification of the horror of death. She gave her name to the river that created the boundary between earth and the Underworld. While Styx was considered the main entrance, there were actually five rivers in total – Lethe (forgetfulness), Acheron (woe), Phlegethon (fire), and Cocytus (lamentation) – that all flowed into her. Souls of the dead would be ferried along the river as they said goodbye to the mortal realm.

Styx married her fellow Titan (and cousin), Pallas, who represented battle and warcraft. With him, she had the personifications: Kratos (strength), Bia (force), Zelos (rivalry), and Nike (victory).

When Zeus called all the gods to Olympus to ask them where their allegiance would lie in the coming Titanomachy, Styx was one of the very few Titans who chose to support Zeus, siding against her own people (Oceanids were considered second generation Titans, due to their parentage). She would become a staunch ally of the Olympian king and the first on the scene once the fighting began, calling on her offspring to support him in the fight, too.

When asking the gods to pick a side, Zeus promised those who chose him that they'd be allowed to keep any domain or special roles they had before the war. If they had nothing, they'd receive a reward. To Styx, Zeus decreed that her waters would be used to seal an oath taken by the gods. Those who broke it would suffer severe consequences: for an entire year, they would completely lose their senses, able to do nothing but lie in a trance. During this time, they could only drink from the river Styx, going without their much-loved ambrosia and nectar. After they had served their sentence, they'd be banned from Olympus for a further nine years. Despite the gods having *literally* all the time in the world, the fate of breaking an oath on the river Styx was taken very seriously, and the water itself had unmatched power - it was here that Achilles gained his own invincibility (save for that pesky heel).

Her children were also compensated for their efforts, becoming constant companions of Zeus from then on, as well as receiving cushy pads on Mount Olympus. Because of this alliance, the Oceanids would benefit, too, being allowed to generally continue their existence as they were, rather than being shut up in Tartarus with the other Titans.

METIS (*met-ees*)

A Titan and an Oceanid, Metis was the personification of good counsel, wisdom and cunning.

Rhea, mother of Zeus, once came calling for her assistance in taking down her ghastly husband. They agreed that Metis would mentor Zeus, teaching him how to be a great leader and fulfil his destiny of becoming king of the gods. During his coaching, Zeus couldn't help but fall hard for the brilliant Titaness, and Metis is thought to have been his first (but certainly not his last) real love. She rebuffed him initially, telling him to concentrate on the pressing matters at hand, and to forget his silly little crush.

Zeus did get his head down, but he couldn't resist flirting with his teacher, and by the time his tutelage had come to an end, Metis found herself quite smitten with the charismatic god. With her part of the agreement complete (and having provided the magical potion that made Cronus vom up his children), she felt quite within her rights to take her protégé to bed.

By now, Zeus had heard of a prophecy that said any daughter of Metis would grow up to be wiser than her mother, and any son more powerful than his father, but Zeus was Zeus, and even as a teen he operated on a strict 'act now, think later' regime. Their night of passion was everything he dreamed it would be, and as they lay together, spent, they got to some pillow talk. They found themselves in a transformation-off, each trying to outdo the other with the forms they could morph into. Zeus, now extremely wise thanks to Metis, saw an opportunity to protect himself from the prophecy. He bet her that she couldn't turn into a fly, which of course she did. As fly-Metis turned around to gloat, Zeus quickly opened his mouth and gobbled her up. Swallowing as a method of birth control is something of a family tradition at this point. Unfortunately for Zeus, Metis was already pregnant by the time she found herself in her new stomached abode, and the daughter she was growing would turn out to be very impressive indeed. Before the babe would find a way out of her father, Metis crafted her armour, a shield, and a spear.

After this, Metis was thought to always live inside of Zeus, counselling him from within his own mind.

ATHENA (*ath-ee-na*)

Daughter of Zeus and Metis, Athena was the legendary Olympian goddess of wisdom, war, and handicrafts.

As the daughter of the Olympian king, it's obvious that Athena would be powerful, but even he wasn't prepared for quite how much. We know he couldn't resist sleeping with Metis despite the prophecy, but when he consumed his lover he thought that'd be the end of it. Little did he know, Metis was thoroughly enjoying her maternity leave in his stomach and, when she was ready, simply gave birth to Athena inside of him.

Between swallowing his baby mama and meeting their child, Zeus had continued to seduce and bed a multitude of other goddesses, eventually 'settling down' with Hera, in the loosest sense of the phrase. Complaining of a terrible headache one evening, he called upon Hephaestus, who gave him his own unusual brand of pain relief – an axe to the forehead.

Hephaestus struck Zeus right between the eyes, and from the gash sprung Athena, fully grown and clad in complete armour. She let out a spectacular war cry that shook the world and terrified all of the gods. All, that is, except Zeus, who was delighted he'd produced such a fine, fiery offspring. Athena took off her helmet, and the other gods were relieved to see she was only a female, nothing to worry about, surely. Prophecy forgotten, Athena quickly became her father's favourite child.

Later, Hephaestus would attempt to rape Athena when she visited his forge to request some weapons. The god had other things on his mind, leering clumsily at the goddess. She fought him off, but he, shall we say, *arrived early* on her leg. Disgusted, she wiped the offending globule off with a piece of wool and dropped it to the earth. As the earth was Gaia, this impregnated her, and she went on to give birth to a boy named Erichthonious. Athena took the child under her wing, and he'd go on to be an important founding hero of Athens (after causing the madness of Herse and Aglaurus.) She had a real soft spot for the Greek heroes, and was somewhat of a mentor to the likes of Heracles and Odysseus. The divine weren't able to present to mortals in their true form (as we saw in Semele's tale), as the sight would be so awesome that their tiny minds would combust and they'd die, so Athena had to get crafty to be seen by her favourites, taking on various disguises.

Although we know Ares as the god of war, he and Athena are thought to be different manifestations of it. Athena is associated with the intellectual and strategic components of war, whereas Ares loved the physical act of the fight, rejoicing in the bloodlust. It was clear to see what rallied a soldier by which divinity they would honour pre-battle.

Athena is sometimes known as Athena Pallas, which comes from her adopting the name in honour of her bestie. A daughter of the merman Triton, Pallas and the Olympian were very close, and the pair were thought to be almost matched in terms of strength and vigour. Once, though, while they engaged in a friendly sparring match, Athena accidentally killed Pallas. It's possible this was down to Zeus, who was watching the faux fight, worrying that his daughter would be shamefully bested by a nymph. To avoid this, he *may* have distracted Pallas who was then unable to dodge the jab from Athena. Athena grieved her friend greatly, crafting a wooden statue (a palladium) in her image. This palladium would end up in Troy in time, where a prophecy said that, as long as the statue stayed within the city, it could never fall. *Spoiler alert, it was stolen, and it did.*

During the Trojan War, Athena fought on the side of the Greeks, which may not come as a surprise after the Trojan prince Paris chose Aphrodite as the most beautiful during his judgement. In battle, she assisted heavily with hero Diomedes' strategies (he was another one of her faves).

In time, she came to blows with Ares, who was fighting for the opposition. She was able to deflect his strikes with her shield, and when she threw a boulder at him, he went down like a sack of potatoes. When Aphrodite arrived to rescue her injured lover, Athena pierced her with her spear.

At some point, Athena and Poseidon argued over who would be the patron of Athens, one of Greece's most prosperous cities. To tip the scales in their favour, they both offered the Athenians a gift. Poseidon struck a boulder with his mighty trident – from the crack flowed salty water that enabled travel for trade deals. For Athena's present, she gave the first olive tree which provided food, wood, and oil, and the Athenian's declared this the winning contribution.

The fiercest female in all of Greek mythology, Athena certainly wasn't scared of going head-to-head with her fellow Olympians, and is remembered for her wisdom and passion, as well as her penchant for warfare, which typically wasn't something associated with women back then, godly or not.

ATALANTA (*at-a-lan-ta*)

Born a princess of Arcadia, Atalanta was abandoned by her father, King Iasus, who was rooting for a male heir. As a daughter was no good to him, Iasus left her in the woods, assuming she'd die from exposure, or be gobbled up by a wild animal.

Luckily, a bear that had recently lost her cubs to hunters found baby Atalanta and took care of her until the same hunters returned and claimed her as their own.

Atalanta quickly became the best hunter amongst her surrogate family, eclipsing the men with her talent. At some point, she visited an oracle who prophesised that any marriage of hers would end in disaster – this was fine, however, as she had no interest in love. Atalanta committed herself to the goddess Artemis, choosing to live a simple, solitary life in the wilderness as a virgin. Spending her days hunting and honing her skills, she was happy to build friendships and alliances with those she encountered, but never anything more. That's not to say that men didn't try and have her, regardless. Once, while Atalanta was out hunting, two centaurs tried to rape her. Atalanta swiftly killed them with her bow and arrow.

Atalanta was desperate to join the Argonauts, who were initially hesitant to let a feeble female taint their mighty crew, but eventually looked outside of their misogynistic box and allowed it. Naturally, she totally smashed it and won the respect of most of the men in the process.

Later, when King Meleager of Calydon upset Artemis and she sent the Calydonian Boar to the city, Atalanta and the crew were called in to help kill it. Initially, many of the men withdrew from the hunt refusing to fight alongside a woman, but Meleager told them to get a grip. Atalanta was the first of them to draw blood from the animal. Meleager landed the final blow, and he insisted on gifting Atalanta the beast's head and hide. We know that drama ensued when Meleager's uncles took the hide, claiming it dishonourable for a woman to receive such a prize, and it resulted in the king's death (as well as his mother's, Althea).

When Atalanta participated in an athletics competition, she impressed her estranged father so much that he allowed her to come home. Because daddy issues can plague even the most badass of babes, Atalanta jumped at the chance to be in her father's good graces and returned to Arcadia. Barely having the chance to unpack her bags, Iasus decided that he must marry her off. Atalanta agreed, on the condition that the successful suitor had to beat her in a race, and that anyone who failed would be killed. To even the playing field, Atalanta agreed to run in full armour, while the men could run naked and unrestricted. She expected to buy herself some time at least. And that she did – many men tried to best her, but the bodies quickly piled up.

That is, until a fellow comrade of the boar hunt, Hippomenes, came along. He'd fallen madly in love with the incredible heroine during their time together, but wasn't naive enough to think he could defeat her. Instead, he prayed to Aphrodite for help. As we know, Aphrodite doesn't appreciate anyone who spurns love and sex in favour of a virginal lifestyle, so she was only too happy to lend a divine hand. She provided Hippomenes with three golden apples (fresh from the garden of the Hesperides) and advice on how to use them to win the contest.

The race began, and Atalanta took the lead. Seeing his chances getting slimmer with each passing second, Hippomenes followed Aphrodite's instructions and threw one of the golden apples into Atalanta's path. Atalanta bent down to retrieve and admire it, knowing that she had plenty of time to catch up with her positively average opponent. She did so easily, but Hippomenes threw another apple and the same happened again. By the time he threw the third, he'd gained enough of an advantage to win the race. Backed into a corner by her own conditions, Atalanta had no choice but to marry.

As warned by the prophecy, though, their marriage was destined to be short. Too concerned with enjoying his new wife, Hippomenes completely forgot to make his promised sacrifice to Aphrodite to show thanks for her aid. She didn't take this too well, and while the couple were out hunting one day, she struck them with a passion so fierce that they couldn't control themselves. The newlyweds stole into a nearby temple of Zeus and made love, after which they were transformed into lions. This was a particularly sick burn at the time, as it was believed that lions could only mate with leopards rather than each other.

CYRENE (*sy-ree-nee*)

Daughter of King Hypseus of the Lapiths and the Naiad Childanope, Cyrene was a brilliant huntress. So good that Athena herself gifted her two hunting dogs and asked if she'd join her inner circle of followers. Although honoured, Cyrene rejected the offer, telling Athena that she wished to experience love and marriage one day, which wouldn't be acceptable as a devotee of hers. Surprisingly, the goddess took no offence and let Cyrene go on her way.

One day, a lion attacked Cyrene's fathers' sheep, and she didn't think twice about wrestling with it to save them. Apollo was watching, and upon seeing her strangling the beast with her bare hands, he immediately fell in love with her spunk and knew instantly that he wanted to make her his.

Apollo brought Cyrene, along with her loyal dogs, to North Africa, to a spot of land that was rich and healthy, and made her its queen. In honour of her, he named the spot Cyrene. The pair enjoyed a wonderful romance, and together they had two sons. Hearing of the queen's fairness, strength and kindness, people flocked to Cyrene to make it their home. Of course, Apollo was honoured greatly there, with their best temple being dedicated to him.

Life was pretty sweet for a while, but as her children flew the nest, her devoted pooches passed on, and her lover's visits became few and far between, Cyrene found herself growing increasingly bored and lonely. She decided to visit her childhood home and catch up with her father, who she hadn't seen since leaving with Apollo many years prior.

By this point, though, Hypseus had passed away, and the kingdom she remembered was a million miles away from what stood before her. Cyrene wandered through the countryside, thinking wistfully of old times. Here, she bumped into the god of war, Ares. In a sour mood, Cyrene was rather hostile towards the Olympian, and the pair engaged in battle. Rage suddenly transformed into passion, and the pair began a love affair that spanned a few months.

On her return to Cyrene, she was surprised to find Apollo waiting for her. Although aware of her tryst with his fellow Olympian, he was overjoyed to reunite with her. Eventually, he transformed her into a Naiad like her mother, who were said to have lived for almost ten thousand years.

HECATE (*heck-a-tee*)

Hecate was a Titaness and may well have been the very first witch. She was the primordial goddess of magic, who was said to be so great that she had access to powers in all realms – the heavens, the earth, and the Underworld. As one of the oldest gods, she had immense authority and influence. Hecate could bestow brilliant gifts on those who were loyal to her, but would withhold just as much from those she felt disrespected by.

Hecate was well and truly a dog person, often followed by a pack. It's thought that one of the dogs was actually Queen Hecuba, which Hecate likely had a hand in transforming. The other dogs in the gang were manifestations of the lost souls who followed her. She was also often accompanied by a polecat, who could have been either Gale, a fellow witch who Hecate transformed as punishment for her poor hygiene and bad attitude, or Galanthis, a midwife punished by the goddess Hera for assisting with Heracles' birth. If the latter, Hecate felt sorry for the animal and looked after her as a domesticated pet.

As the chief goddess of magic and spells, she did tend to sway more to the dark side of the craft with a particular interest in necromancy and creatures of the night. As a virgin goddess, there're no records of her consorting with any gods or mortals, so it seems she was so powerful that the male gods *actually* respected her decision for once, lest they be turned into toads or something.

Hecate was particularly attentive to those who followed her cult of magic, and because of this she was held in high regard by her fellow gods, especially Zeus. After the Olympians won the Titanomachy (in which Hecate sided with the victors), she was one of the very few Titans to retain her post-war status. In fact, Zeus would even go on to gift her the Lampades, who were nymphs of the Underworld.

Hecate was often depicted as having three bodies that stood with their backs to one another. Able to see from all directions, she was considered goddess of crossroads and entrances. Figures of her in this form were often left in doorways, as they were thought to protect the home from evil spirits.

HIPPOLYTA (& THE AMAZONS)
(*hip-oll-uh-tah* & *the ah-mah-zons*)

The Amazons were a race of warrior women, famed for their skills in warfare. They lived on their own island, thought to be located to the south of the Black Sea, called Themiscyra.

They were all thought to be descendants of the god of war, Ares, and they worshipped the hunting goddess, Artemis. The Amazons were particularly skilled in riding and hunting, and some sources say that they used to burn off their right breast to aid their handling of a bow and arrow.

With their taste for combat and adventure as strong as any man, the Amazons would often leave their island for military expeditions, completing raids and erecting temples for their favourite deities. Some cynics deduced that the Amazons were not women at all, but a particular race of men who wore long clothing, grew their hair and shaved their beards, because it was so unthinkable that a group of women could be so bloodthirsty and powerful. *Eye-roll.*

The Amazon queen, Hippolyta, inherited the throne from her mother. She had been gifted a magical belt from her father, known as 'the girdle of Hippolyta', which was thought to bestow superhuman strength. On top of this, it signified her supremacy amongst the

Amazons, and was to be passed down to whoever succeeded her. Retrieving this girdle was one of Heracles' twelve labours, mainly because it appeared to be an impossible task. The Amazons were proud people who didn't think much of men, only allowing them into their vicinity to mate and keep their lineage alive. They even murdered any children born male, so the general consensus was that they weren't going to take too kindly to Herc sailing in and taking their gear.

Anyway, Heracles pulled up on Themiscyra with a strong army, ready to secure the belt. Hippolyta was adamant that she'd meet the visitor and when he introduced himself, the queen was so enchanted with the hero that she just . . . gave him what he wanted.

It appeared Heracles could class this one as a done deal, but Hera was watching in the wings, keen to stir up some trouble, as always. She transformed herself into an Amazon and frantically ran around the island, shouting to the tribe that their queen was being abducted. The women attacked the ship, and a bloody battle ensued. During the struggle, Hippolyta was killed, either by Heracles himself, or accidentally by her sister, Penthesilea, who would take on the role of queen after her death.

ANTIOPE (*an-tie-oh-pee*)

Many Amazons fell during the bloody battle that ensued when Heracles came to secure Hippolyta's girdle. Antiope, however, lived and was abducted by Heracles' fellow soldier, Theseus (yes, him again). Some accounts say that the pair fell in love, and that Antiope left her home to be with him willingly, but when we consider the timescales of the men arriving, the battle that followed, and the death of Hippolyta, it seems more likely that she was taken by force. That, and the fact that it's almost *always* abduction with this lot. Regardless of how she left, Antiope and Theseus appeared to be smitten, and she had no desire to return to Themiscyra. She bore him a son, named Hippolytus in honour of her late sister.

The story of Antiope splits off into two versions from here. In one, the Amazons sail to Attica to rescue her and bring home the girdle. They were defeated by Theseus and his army, and Antiope was terribly wounded in the fight by her own husband and died from her injuries. With no Antiope to rescue, and with the girdle being nowhere near Athens anyway, the Amazons had no choice but to return home. This would go on to be known as the Attic War.

In the other – arguably juicier – version of the tale, after Antiope and Theseus have their son, he gets itchy feet. When he's offered the Cretan princess Phaedra, it seems to him a logical upgrade – not only would their match mean allies in high places, but she also wasn't bad on the eyes, either. And so, Theseus shamelessly abandoned

Antiope and their son, booting them out of the palace and moving in this new babe.

Understandably miffed, Antiope sent word to the Amazons, asking them to stand with her in revenge. Always game for a bit of justified combat, the ladies made the journey to join her.

On the day of Theseus and Phaedra's wedding, the Amazon women lay in wait until the whole party were secured in the great hall, then they attacked. Unfortunately for them, a large portion of the wedding guests were the great fighters they'd already lost to on Themiscyra, and they overpowered the women once more. Again, in this tale, Theseus is the one to mortally wound Antiope. Fellow Amazon and friend Molpaida couldn't bear the thought of Antiope dying at the hands of this scoundrel, so took it upon herself to slay her to spare the shame.

THE CADMEAN VIXEN
(cad-mee-an vix-en)

A dog who never failed to catch its prey was a massive asset for any hunter, and word of the good boy called Laelaps spread throughout Greece quickly.

Somewhere between Procris returning to her husband and him accidentally killing her, Thebes was being plagued by the Cadmean Vixen, a massive fox named simply because Cadmea was the citadel of Thebes. The sight of the beast was alarming in itself, but the citizens quickly realised this wasn't your average fox – for one, she seemed to particularly enjoy the taste of children and, no matter what they did, nobody could catch her. Even when their best hunters banded together to set their top traps and throw their shiniest, pointiest spears, the fox simply dodged and dashed away. It got to the point where the king at the time decreed that they must leave a child as an offering every thirty days to appease the animal.

This upsetting sacrifice went on for a while, until Amphitryon (stepfather-to-be to Heracles) came along. He was hoping for a purification from the king as well as to ask for help building an army. King Creon (the brother of Jocasta and father of Megara – this dude certainly gets around in these myths) said he'd love to help, but his full attentions were currently taken up with this whole vixen business. Amphitryon asked whether favours could be exchanged if he sorted this fox problem, and Creon agreed.

Amphitryon tried the usual methods to capture and kill the beast (his own hunting skills were nothing to sniff at), but he was unsuccessful. Then he had an idea – he'd heard of a mythical dog by the name of Laelaps that always caught its target. Amphitryon quickly travelled to the home of Cephalus and Procris and asked for a lend, promising to share the spoils of the eventual war he was going to wage. All agreed, and back to Thebes he went.

Amphitryon wasted no time releasing Laelaps, who tracked the vixen quickly. He took chase, and on the pair ran, and ran . . . then ran some more. The spectators, excited to see the show at first, started to yawn and eventually left for bed. The next morning, the orange and brown streak that was the fox and the hound continued to loop around town. Zeus had been watching, too, and although it entertained him for a while, he also found himself rather bored. He put both animals into the sky as Canis Minor (the Cadmean Vixen) and Canis Major (Laelaps), where the constellations still chase each other to this day.

Procris, meanwhile, was like, 'where TF is my dog?'

ECHIDNA (*eck-id-na*)

Echidna was the daughter of sea gods Phorcys and Ceto. She's typically depicted with the top half of a beautiful woman, and the bottom half of a beastly snake, but since her main passion in life was eating people, some say it's more likely that these forms were swapped.

Known as 'mother of all monsters', from her unions with the fearsome beast Typhon, she birthed most of the best-known creatures of Greek mythology, including:

- **Cerberus**, the giant, three-headed dog that guarded the entrance of the Underworld, and made sure no living mortals passed through.
- **The Lernaean Hydra**, a massive water snake that grew two more heads for every one that was chopped off. Hera raised the creature in the hopes that it would grow to kill Heracles.
- **The Gorgon sisters**, including Medusa of the stony stare.
- **The Caucasian Eagle**, a bird that continuously ate the liver of the Titan Prometheus after he gave mortals fire.
- **The Chimera**, a fire-breathing monster with a lion's head, a goat's body, and a snake's tail.
- **The Sphinx**, the woman/lion/eagle/snake that loved a good riddle and hated a bad Theban, from Jocasta's story.

- **The Nemean Lion**, a ferocious jungle cat whose golden fur was resistant to mortal weapons and terrorised the citizens of Nemea.
- **Ladon**, the dragon that guarded the garden of the Hesperides.

Echidna lived alone, in the cave that she was born in, located deep beneath the earth. She only emerged to either snatch up some mortal-shaped munchies, or mate with Typhon and produce the next nightmarish beast.

When the couple decided they'd had enough of the gods shunning them (and their irritating demi-god children insisting on slaying their own offspring), they attacked the Olympians. Typhon would be killed by Zeus, who flattened him under Mount Etna. In an apparent show of fairness, Zeus allowed Echidna and her children to live, so that they could keep getting in the face of up-and-coming mortals, who levelled up to hero status once they defeated any of Echidna's offspring.

Echidna was immortal, but immortality doesn't necessarily mean invincible, and just like her baby-daddy, she could be killed. When Hera (who seemed to have forgotten that Echidna provided her with the Hydra) got sick of the she-monster and her brutal babies killing anyone who dared pass by their lairs, she sent her trusty servant Argus Panoptes, who killed her in her sleep.

ARTEMIS (*art-em-iss*)

We've come across Artemis a few times already, as the goddess of the hunt is widely intertwined with many of the Greek myths. She's the daughter of the Titaness Leto and Zeus, and twin sister to Apollo, god of music and prophecy.

As a consort of Zeus, Artemis' mother faced the wrath of Hera like so many others. Leto's specific punishment was that she would be forbidden to give birth anywhere on solid ground. When her contractions started, Leto crossed her legs and searched desperately for a place to get down to birthing. This was difficult, considering nobody was keen to help the mother-to-be, as they didn't want their home to become somewhere reviled by Hera. Eventually, she came across the island of Delos (formerly Ortygia, formerly still, Asteria), which was floating so, technically, wasn't breaking Hera's rule. Here, she gave birth to Artemis. When Hera got wind that she'd been outsmarted, she went to her daughter, Eileithyia, the goddess of childbirth, and forbade her to assist Leto in the delivery of the second child. This delayed the arrival of Apollo by nine days, but he had to come out some time. At just over a week old, Artemis assisted Leto in birthing her own twin.

Artemis and Apollo were very protective of their mother, and anyone who dared disrespect her got the full extent of their wrath. When Tityus, one of the Giants, tried to rape her, they shot and killed him with an arrow. When the mortal woman Niobe boasted that she'd birthed more children than Leto, Apollo slaughtered all seven of her sons to protect his mother's honour. Clearly, Niobe didn't know when to shut up: as she wept over the bodies of her children, she shouted to the heavens that even in her misery, she was *still* better than Leto; her grief was more powerful than any happiness the goddess could ever feel. As Niobe's seven daughters ran to comfort her, Artemis shot the lot of them. Niobe had finally learned to zip it, but her husband killed himself over the horror. As she lamented, Artemis turned Niobe to stone.

Artemis was particularly proud of her virgin status, having taken the oath at a very young age. What's more, she made the oath directly to her father, so it was also a sacred promise to him.

Many men would try to have her, but none would succeed, and most wouldn't live to tell the tale. She didn't particularly care much for circumstances, either; when the mortal hunter, Actaeon, accidentally glimpsed her naked body while she was bathing in a spring, Artemis cursed him on the spot, telling him that he was hereby forbidden to speak a single word, or he'd face her wrath. Actaeon nodded fervently, but when his hunting party shouted to him, he instinctively returned their call, and she transformed him into a stag. The panicked Stagtaeon bolted, and it wasn't long before his own hunting dogs picked up on his scent. They ripped their master to shreds. The mortal was a descendant of Cadmus and Harmonia, so maybe he had the cursed necklace to thank for that one.

Artemis' resolve to stay single wavered only once, and in order to accept this, we have to acknowledge that two versions of one person's story exist. The Orion in this story of Artemis appears to be a good guy, and it's certainly more romantic to believe this version. In the story of the Pleiades, though, he's quite the opposite. Maybe for the sake of the magic of mythology, we can pretend this Orion and the Pleiades-pest are two separate people.

It's said that Artemis grew particularly fond of Orion, who was a long-time hunting companion of hers, and the couple were engaged to be married. After announcing the upcoming nuptials to her brother, he tried desperately to change her mind. Apollo knew how much her vow of virginity meant to her. Assuming she was temporarily blinded by the D, he told her she'd live to regret the marriage if she went through with it. She wouldn't be swayed, so Apollo took matters into his own hands. He dared Orion to swim out to a particular point on the horizon, then wagered that Artemis would never be able to hit the supposed animal in the water that was so far away. Artemis, sure of her skill, aimed, shot, and killed Orion. Mourning for her would-be husband, she turned him into the constellation by the same name.

As one of the primary goddesses of childbirth (despite shunning the act that is a precursor to pregnancy), women in labour would often call on Artemis to help them through the pain.

OMPHALE (*om-full-ee*)

When Heracles was sentenced to serve the queen of Lydia as a slave, he certainly wasn't prepared for Omphale.

The original ruler of Lydia, King Tmolus, was killed by a bull years prior, and after his death, his wife, Omphale, continued to reign alone. This certainly wasn't common practice in Ancient Greece, but Omphale was a great and beloved leader, so even though the mountain town was primitive and thought to have been rather uncivilised, they had great respect for their queen.

For strapping young Heracles, to serve a woman would have been considered shameful in itself, but Omphale added insult to injury by forcing the hero to dress in typically 'feminine' clothing and gave him 'shameful' tasks to do such as holding her weaving baskets as she worked with friends. As Heracles had been assigned something of a uniform by his master, he didn't have a need for his usual garb, so Omphale thought she'd put it to good use donning his famous lion's skin and carrying his club around the palace for good measure.

For his part, Heracles didn't seem to mind the humiliation too much. The duo got on so well, in fact, that Omphale insisted that he be released from his sentence early, and married him instead. Throughout their (albeit short) marriage, they continued to rebuff the typical gender roles of the times.

At some point, the couple travelled to take part in a festival in Dionysus' honour. The dominant Omphale had piqued the interest of the god of the wild, Pan, who decided to try his luck with her. One night, spotting her bedclothes through an opening in the tent, he quietly sneaked inside, slipped under the covers, and snuggled in – imagine his surprise when the burly Heracles turned over to face him. Pan fell out of the bed, completely naked, and scrambled to get away. The couple laughed heartily at the foolish god.

Together, Omphale and Heracles had two sons, Agelaus and Tyrsenus, but eventually parted ways.

THE MAENADS (*mee-nads*)

The female followers of Dionysus, as a collective, were called the Maenads, and they were the most significant of the god's entourage.

After Dionysus invented wine, it really took the world by storm. Where some were anxious and fearful of the strange feelings the drink brought forward in them, most were keen to embrace it, whether that meant drinking it, selling it, or using it in medicine.

To be a worshipper of Dionysus meant embracing this exciting new elixir and everything that came with it – the amplified feelings of happiness, the dulling of sadness, and the inexplicable need to get on your feet and dance. The Maenads, whose name translates to 'raving ones', loved drinking, dancing, and working themselves up into a frenzy in the name of worship. Their outfits of choice were animal skins, and they'd carry ivy-choked sticks topped with acorns, sometimes with snakes around their necks.

The Maenads were rather feared by non-followers, as their version of praising their lord looked significantly different to what most people were used to seeing. Although most of their practices happened far away from the eyes of others, usually in the mountains, it was rumoured to involve human sacrifice, and despite the distance, terrifying sounds could often be heard all the way in the towns when they were practising.

The cult contained a mixture of ladies – lots of them were women who'd decided to leave the shackles of their expected paths of wifedom and motherhood, but not everyone was there of their own free will, and it wasn't uncommon for the god to punish women by forcing them into becoming Maenads.

When Dionysus brought his worship to Boeotia, he faced resistance from the daughters of King Minyas of Orchomenus: Alcathoe, Leucippe, and Arsippe. A priest of Orchomenus ordered a festival for the budding god, excusing everyone from their daily tasks so they could partake. Most people seemed more than willing to participate, dressing in animal skins and thoroughly enjoying the merry drinking and crazy parties involved. A handful of people didn't feel the pull, though, and this included the princesses and the king. The priest warned the citizens that their absence would incur punishment from the gods, but the royal house didn't listen. Instead, they stayed in the palace, judging their unruly subjects and telling stories to pass the time.

When Dionysus heard that the family didn't RSVP to the festivities, he transformed himself into a woman and visited the palace himself. Once there, Dionysus asked the sisters to let down their hair and worship this new, interesting, and undoubtedly handsome god.

However, the girls wouldn't be peer-pressured into partying, and told the disguised god to get lost. As the princesses returned to their seats, they were suddenly battered by the sound of banging drums and the sickly-sweet smell of perfumes. Around them, the walls sprouted ivy that spread rapidly around their furniture. The candles and hearth's fires intensified so that there were no dark corners to hide in, and Dionysus appeared. He started shapeshifting into various animals, and at the frightening sight, the three sisters went completely insane. In their new state, they wanted nothing more than to devote their entire lives to this groovy god, embracing the status of Maenads. Wanting to impress him with an offering, they squabbled over who would have the honour of making the sacrifice. This privilege would fall to Leucippe. So, the ladies sneaked up on her son, Hippasus, and ripped him to pieces in the name of devotion. After, they went to the mountains to frolic, murder, and cause general mayhem for a while. Eventually, the messenger god Hermes transformed them into bats.

The Maenads were believed to have been given super-strength from the god (figures, as it's not just anyone who can tear a person's limbs clean off their body, even with the help of their girlfriends). Dionysus was often referred to by the haters as the 'feminine god', and it's true that the women in his retinue added to this reputation, but the Maenads could send even the most battle-hardened soldier running once they got going.

These 'wild women', as they were dubbed, were used as cautionary tales of what would become of the female population without the guidance of men, warning them to be good girls and stay in their lane. On the other hand, it showed women the possibility of living a life *without* men, where they could put their pleasure and enjoyment first – well, second to Dionysus', of course.

AURA (*or-a*)

The personification of the gentle breeze, Aura was a close friend of Artemis and had quite the similar skillset. Not concerning herself with small game such as rabbits or birds, Aura preferred to hunt bigger beasts and wrestle them with her bare hands. Because of her 'airy' nature, she was thought to be as fast as the wind.

Like the famed huntress, Aura also held her virginity proudly. One morning, Aura awoke in a foul temper. Fellow deity and husband of Psyche, Eros, had taken it upon himself to plague her with sensual dreams to test her resolve. Attempting to shake off her bad mood, she spent the morning hunting with Artemis. Being a rather hot day, the ladies decided to take a quick dip in a stream to cool off.

As they stripped, the still prickly Aura passed comment on Artemis' body. Remarking the differences between her own breasts and the fellow goddesses, she noted how hers were small and pert like that of a man's, but Artemis' were voluptuous and bouncy, much more appealing to the opposite sex. Aura wondered aloud if, as Artemis possessed such typically 'appealing' appendages, the goddess was as resolute with the rejection of sex as she claimed. Instead of calling out her friend for being so rude, Artemis went to Nemesis, goddess of divine retribution, and asked her to do her thing.

Knowing of Eros' vested interest in Aura and her virginity, Nemesis called upon him for assistance. Eros shot Dionysus with one of his lust-evoking golden arrows. Dionysus, completely mad with desire but knowing there was no way Aura would willingly sleep with him, spiked her wine, and took her in her sleep.

When Aura awoke from her drug-induced slumber, she could tell that she was no longer a virgin, but didn't know who was responsible. In her rage, Aura went on a killing spree, slaughtering any man who dared to cross her path. Later, when she found out she was pregnant, she tried to kill herself, but was unsuccessful.

After nine long months of resentment, Aura gave birth to twin boys, who she took to the mountains and tried to tempt a lioness into eating. The animal declined, so Aura threw both babes into the air, and as they hit the ground, she swallowed one of them whole. Artemis managed to grab the remaining boy and ship him away to safety, and Aura was transformed into a spring by Zeus.

DAPHNE (*daff-nee*)

The Naiad Daphne was the first love of the god Apollo, though it wasn't exactly a meet-cute. In a particularly arrogant mood one day, Apollo was needling at Eros, questioning why he always used his powerful bow in the pursuit of love, but never in war. Eros, thinking he'd show the brazen god exactly how powerful he could be, shot Apollo with one of his golden arrows, making him fall madly in love with Daphne. To exacerbate his fellow deity's plight, he used one of his lead arrows (that repelled passion) to shoot Daphne.

Daphne, who was extremely beautiful, was resolute in her decision to remain a virgin, and had already shunned countless would-be wooers in favour of chastity. She was loved by Apollo's sister, Artemis, who had given her the ability to always shoot straight. Apollo knew that Eros' lead arrow would make Daphne double-down on her rejection of him, so he sat back for a while and observed, looking for the best way to approach his beloved.

Soon, another hopeful bachelor entered the picture. Prince of Pisa and brother of Hippodamia, Leucippus was in awe of this magnificent nymph, but knew that he didn't stand a chance. Instead of respecting Daphne's wishes, Leucippus dressed as a woman and tried to infiltrate her inner circle of gal-pals. Sure enough, it didn't take long until the disguised Leucippus was invited on the gang's next hunt.

Apollo, impressed but insanely jealous, thought it was about time he stepped in. Using his powers, he planted the thought into Daphne's head that she was so hot and bothered, she simply *must* cool off with a dip. She suggested that her group join her, and the ladies agreed. Everyone stripped off their clothes and slipped into a nearby stream, with only Leucippus abstaining. Smelling a rat, the women rounded on their new supposed girlfriend and began ripping away Leucippus' clothes. With the reveal, the group were furious, clubbing together to kill the imposter.

By now, Apollo had decided that he'd done enough waiting – no longer willing to take the softly-softly approach, he began chasing the nymph. The chase went on for a while, and eventually Daphne called desperately to Gaia to remove her beauty, as it had caused her nothing but problems. Hearing her wish, Gaia transformed her into a laurel tree. As Apollo caught the end of her transformation, he reached out and felt Daphne's beating heart underneath the bark. He declared that he'd use her leaves to make crowns for heroes and would build palaces with her saplings.

ATË (*ah-tee*)

We can all say we've been influenced by the goddess Atë at some point: she is the embodiment of mischief, delusion, and rash action. She was the personification of reckless impulse and could execute her powers over both mortals and the gods.

A daughter of Eris (strife and discord, bringer of the golden apple and instigator of the Trojan War), she and her siblings were all personifications of the world's worst horrors, like starvation, pain, fighting, and murder. As much as she could wield her own powers, she was highly desired amongst the other gods to carry out their own wills, too. She was roped in when Hera wanted to delay the birth of Heracles, as the queen of the skies used her to make Zeus swear the oath that a boy born on that day would be a king amongst men. When Zeus heard of Atë's involvement in this trickery, he was enraged. He rounded on the goddess, grabbing her by her hair and hurling her down to earth. As she fell, he shouted that she was no longer welcome on Mount Olympus.

As she hit the ground, Atë was furious – she may have sometimes enjoyed the power that she had over others, but even if she didn't, who was she to refuse the queen of the heavens? Zeus had punished her for exacting another's wishes, and for that *he* would pay. Knowing that the king had a soft spot for mortals, Atë focused her full efforts on wreaking havoc in their realm, leaving a trail of devastation and destruction wherever she went. Zeus, as predicted, was alarmed at the effect Atë was having on the world, so sent his daughters, known as the Litae, after her. They were the personification of prayers, so in effect the opposite of Atë's reckless impulse. The goddess alone was quicker and more cunning than them, though, since the Litae were old crones. They were never able to catch up to Atë, so instead, they did their best to clean up the messes that she left behind.

Although the Litae could bestow great things on mortals, they weren't to be crossed, as they could always nudge Atë to turn her attentions in a particular direction.

PENTHESILEA
(*pen-thess-ill-ay-uh*)

Penthesilea was the queen of the Amazons during the time of the Trojan War. The warrior women might not have concerned themselves with the war at all, if it weren't for their monarch. Back when Heracles attacked the Amazons, it's possible that Penthesilea was the one to strike down the previous queen (and her sister), Hippolyta, by accident. Devastated by this, the new queen went to Troy to ask King Priam to purify her of the terrible sin. He agreed, but only on the condition that she and her people side with them should war ever come.

The Amazons didn't actually get involved in the battle until quite late, but when it became apparent that the Greeks were going to win, they thought it time to step in to defend their allies. Twelve of their best warriors arrived on the shores of Troy, led by Penthesilea. The women of Troy were awed to see the Amazons fight – they'd spent their lives being told to be quiet, look pretty, bear children, and leave the warfare to the menfolk. Watching these amazing women going toe to toe with soldiers and giving as good as they got was so inspiring that a few of them even made to join the fight, too. A priestess of Athena called Theano stepped in to discourage her sisters, stating it would be ultimately pointless and perhaps even detrimental to the cause; their inexperience would get in the way of the real soldiers.

Penthesilea spent her fist day in combat on the battlefield, getting the lie of the land and establishing herself as the brilliant warrior that she was. Then, she challenged Achilles.

Achilles fought with everything he had but couldn't help feeling a stirring of both respect and attraction as the blows landed on both sides. The demi-god got the upper hand and fatally stabbed the Amazon queen, but as she fell to the ground, he immediately felt that he'd made a terrible mistake. As the lifeblood drained out of Penthesilea, Achilles began to weep over her body.

Another soldier, the vulgar and dull-witted Thersites, had the gall to mock Achilles' tears. Quite promptly and rightly, Achilles told him that boys cry too and slew him where he stood. Still, the demi-god was pretty torn up, even taking a brief break from fighting to travel to Lesbos, where he was purified for killing her. Funnily enough, he didn't feel the need to atone for Thersites.

CAENIS (*ke-nees*)

When the mortal girl Caenis was raped by Poseidon, he declared that, as a 'reward' (for suffering from his abuse), he would grant her one wish. The devastated Caenis wished that she'd be transformed into a man, and that, in her new form, she be given impenetrable skin, to protect her from being attacked again. Wish granted, Caenis became Caenus.

Free from the shackles of womanhood, Caenus absolutely loved his new life as the favoured sex and found he had quite the affinity for typical 'manly' past times, like hunting and combat. He even took part in the Calydonian Boar hunt, alongside some of Greece's strongest fighters, including our girl Atalanta. Though he's not particularly remembered in any mythology of his own, other great heroes made nods to his strength and valour.

At the wedding of his friends Pirithous and Hippodamia (not the one who married Pelops), a fight broke out when a group of intoxicated centaurs began trying to carry off the women, including the bride. Caenus got stuck in, protecting the wedding party alongside the likes of Theseus (who you'll remember would go on to team up with the groom to abduct Helen and Persephone). The centaurs were familiar with Caenus and his story, and one of them began to mock him loudly, declaring that Caenus would never be a truly great fighter. Caenus laughed heartily and invited the centaur to have a go if he thought he was hard enough.

Caenus barely broke a sweat as the centaur unleashed his full brutality on him, but barely left so much as a scratch. Eventually, he got bored and killed the gloating beast. The other centaurs had been watching, and they were very embarrassed that one of their own had been bested. They came up with a plan amongst themselves and attacked. Half of them tackled Caenus and wrestled him to the floor, and the other half began piling heavy tree trunks on top of him. Eventually, the weight of the trees was so great that Caenus eventually sank through the ground, all the way down to the Underworld. In death (because if he'd managed to enter the Underworld, he was considered dead), the Fates transformed him back into a woman.

NICAEA (*ny-see-ya*)

A nymph and gifted huntress, Nicaea was a loyal follower of the goddess Artemis.

As with most of this goddess's devotees, Nicaea had vowed to preserve her virginity for all of her life, dedicating herself to the hunt only. In a trend that's getting old by this point, though, the men around her didn't care about her wishes. Eros, likely on the instruction of his mother Aphrodite, shot a young shepherd by the name of Hymnus with one of his golden arrows, making him fall in love with Nicaea.

In a childish attempt to make her notice him, Hymnus stole her hunting gear and ran away, shaking them in the air as he did so. When the nymph followed and found him harbouring her belongings, he dramatically declared that if she truly wasn't interested in his love, he'd rather be dead, and she may as well be the one to kill him. Nicaea said, 'sure!' and shot an arrow into his heart.

When Aphrodite and Eros learned of Hymnus' death, they didn't consider the blood to be on their hands, and instead wanted to punish Nicaea. Eros' next shot went to Dionysus, and he immediately dropped what he was doing in an attempt to woo her. He showered Nicaea with lavish gifts and sweet words, but his godly standing didn't give him any more pull than the shepherd. Realising he wasn't getting anywhere, Dionysus waited until Nicaea bent to drink from a stream, then he transformed the water into wine. Nicaea swallowed a considerable amount of the vino and found herself extremely drunk. She settled down under a tree to sleep it off, and Dionysus raped her.

When she woke up, hungover and heartbroken at being defiled, she knew who was responsible and burned for revenge. Try as she might, though, she never could find Dionysus who, having got what he wanted from her, had quickly forgotten his devotion to the nymph. When Nicaea found out that she was pregnant to the god, she tried to end her own life, but wasn't successful.

This story is very similar to that of the goddess Aura's, but we know that they are different women, as Aura herself offered her condolences to the unhappy Nicaea, relating to what she'd been through.

Dionysus would later name a city after the nymph, because that makes up for everything, right?

PHEME (*fee-mee*)

Goddess of fame and renown, Pheme would greatly reward those in her good books, but to cross her would prove foolish. Her wrath could bring on the most scandalous rumours.

She was a notorious gossip and loved the thrill of finding out about the private lives of both gods and mortals alike. She also couldn't keep a secret if her divine life depended on it. She would start spreading the word of what she had heard with a whisper at first, but every time she passed it on, her voice would get just that little bit louder. This eventually resulted in her bellowing people's deepest, darkest transgressions for the whole world to hear.

Her fellow deities had a bit of a love-hate thing going on with Pheme – most of them had been burned by her at some point or another, but they couldn't help but call on her when *they* needed some dirt dished. When Queen Hera was getting pissed off about Heracles gaining so much fame, she sent the goddess to Deianira to whisper in her ear that he'd been having an affair with Iole. *Scandalous*.

She wasn't all bad, though. Pheme could also use her particular skillset when you wanted some *good* news spreading – she wasn't fussy about what she shared, so long as it was interesting, and was known to be an excellent communicator when she set her mind to it.

The goddess lived in a bronze mansion with one hundred windows, located between the heavens and earth, where she would spend her time listening intently for a scrap of drama to delight in. Because of the material that her home was built from, even the smallest whisper couldn't escape her as the sound would reverberate through the walls and reach her waiting ears.

CHARYBDIS (*ka-rib-dis*)

Before she was a monster that struck fear into the heart of any sailor worth his sea salt, Charybdis was a beautiful water nymph. The daughter of Poseidon and Gaia, Charybdis was fiercely loyal to her father, and had no qualms supporting him in his occasional grasp for power against his brother Zeus. One such time, Charybdis was gobbling up entire islands with apparently no reasoning other than to piss her uncle off. As revenge for the nymph stealing so much of his land, Zeus shot a thunderbolt at her that dragged her to the bottom of the ocean. Charybdis soon discovered the bolt had done more than give her a headache – she had been transformed into a hideous monstrosity. What's more, she suddenly had an unquenchable thirst for seawater. When she tried to flee in shame, she realised Zeus had chained her to the seabed.

From then on, Charybdis would emerge from the depths three times a day and swallow a stomach-full of saltwater. Then, she'd let out an almighty burp, creating a massive whirlpool that dragged many a sailor to their doom.

Now living under a rock on one side of a narrow channel, Charybdis got to know her neighbour and fellow sea monster, Scylla (love rival of Circe), who resided on the other side. Charybdis and Scylla were mentioned in many a famous myth, including a run-in with Jason and his Argonauts. Jason received assistance from Hera, though, who asked that Thetis rally her Nereids to guide his ship to safety. Another such sailor who almost fell into their clutches was the hero Odysseus.

On his way back home to Ithaca, Odysseus and his men tried to give Charybdis a wide berth (as per the advice of Circe), and in doing so ended up running into Scylla, who made a significant dint in their numbers. As Odysseus passed again later on a raft, Charybdis started guzzling, attempting to swallow both man and vessel whole. Odysseus clung on tight to nearby overgrowth, and when she burped, Charydbis accidentally released his raft, and he was able to paddle furiously to safety.

Some think Charybdis isn't a sea monster at all and just a naturally occurring whirlpool, but what fun is that?

From the tale of the neighbouring sea monsters, the idiom 'to be between Scylla and Charybdis' would evolve over time until it became the more popular phrase we know now: 'stuck between a rock and a hard place'.

LIMOS (*lee-mos*)

As the goddess of starvation, hunger, and famine, Limos wasn't ever going to be the first person on the guest list at a party.

Depicted with coarse, short hair, sunken cheeks, withered, hanging breasts, and skin so thin that you could see her insides through it, Limos is considered the polar opposite to the harvest goddess, Demeter. It's said that she and Demeter could never meet, or the consequences would be dire. That being said, Demeter could call on Limos when she needed to, asking her to inflict her hunger onto certain mortals that had offended the Olympian. She'd have to send a messenger, of course, so their paths didn't cross.

Limos was able to invoke a desperate hunger in her victims by wrapping herself around them, clutching them tight, and breathing deeply into their mouths. Her rotting breath would spread throughout their entire body, filling it with a cold, dreading hunger. From then on, the victim would find that, no matter how much they ate, their hunger was never sated.

Limos was the daughter of Eris and is sometimes considered to be male depending on which account we are looking to. She was believed to have stood guard at the entrance of the Underworld as departed souls passed on through, along with her siblings, who were personifications of things like pain, lies, ruin, and lawlessness.

When she wasn't looking threatening in the Underworld, she could be found at home, which was a frozen wasteland, where the soil was so infertile that not a single thing could grow. Fitting.

8

Not-So-Dutiful Daughters

*Far from being daddies' girls,
they really don't care what
their parents say*

MYRRHA (*mee-ra*)

When Myrrha's mother, Queen Cenchreis of Cyprus, openly bragged of her daughter's beauty, she brought on the wrath of Aphrodite.

The goddess cursed Myrrha with a burning desire for none other than her own father, King Cinyras. Despite her incestuous yearning being all consuming, Myrrha fought greatly between her lust and shame. Her internal struggle disturbed her so much that she tried to commit suicide. She was found in time by her nurse who was able to save her. While being patched up, Myrrha confessed her suffering and begged for help. Initially, the nurse tried to aid her resistance, but it quickly became clear that the taboo crush was too deep, so she had to change tack. Instead, she agreed to help Myrrha seduce her father, on the condition that she would never again try to kill herself.

During a festival to honour the goddess Demeter, women of Cyprus were not to be touched by men for nine nights. Myrrha's own mother was participating in the festival, so together with the nurse, the young princess hatched a plan. The nurse told Cinyras that someone was in love with him, giving a fake name to protect Myrrha's identity. As the poor king was looking at nine whole nights without the love of a woman, he was more than eager to agree to an affair. The 'mysterious stranger' had one condition – their lovemaking could only take place in total darkness. *Nothing suspicious about that,* Cinyras thought, signing on the metaphorical dotted line. This steamy and gross affair went on for several nights, but eventually Cinyras decided he must gaze upon the woman giving him his jollies, so he sneaked a lamp to their meeting place. Upon seeing his own daughter, Cinyras was so disgusted that he immediately tried to kill her.

Myrrha managed to escape, but quickly discovered a rather devastating souvenir of their escapades – she was pregnant. She spent the next nine months wandering aimlessly through Arabia, worrying about the fate of the unborn child. Ultimately done with living but fearful of death, she begged the gods to help her. Sympathising, they transformed her into a myrrh tree. They couldn't alleviate her sadness though, and tears flowed from the tree as drops of myrrh. A few days after her transformation, a wild boar passed Myrrha and pierced her trunk with his tusk – from this tear, the tree-woman's child was uncovered. Naiads rushed to protect the newborn, and it would soon be collected by Aphrodite. He was none other than Adonis.

ARACHNE (*ah-rack-nee*)

Arachne was the daughter of a Lydian shepherd and a mother who died during childbirth. Her father couldn't have been prouder of her, especially of the weaving skills she showed from a young age. Arachne was able to create beautiful and intricate tapestries as if her fingers were made solely for the act, and she wasn't particularly humble about it.

She boasted openly of her skill, telling anyone who would listen that she was a better weaver than Athena, the goddess of handicrafts herself. What's more, she refused to even acknowledge that her gift came in part from the influence of the goddess. Of course, Athena wasn't going to take this blasphemy lying down. She appeared to Arachne as a crooked old woman and scolded her for being so immodest, telling her that she should beg for forgiveness from the Olympian. Arachne laughed in her face, stating that if Athena thought herself better, then she should come to earth and challenge her!

Enraged at the gall of this puny human, Athena dropped her disguise, appearing to Arachne as a truer version of herself. Arachne was mortified and immediately fell to her knees, spewing apologies and begging Athena for forgiveness. The goddess didn't want to hear it. She told the girl to get on her feet and put her money where her mouth was. Arachne tried to shake off her terror as girl and goddess threw themselves into a fierce weaving competition. In an assumed attempt to reprimand Arachne further through her art, Athena chose to depict humans being punished for their hubris. Also speaking pointedly through her own tapestry, Arachne spun scenes in which the gods wrongfully abused mortals, including depicting the chase of Canace by Poseidon.

When they were both finished, Athena looked upon Arachne's masterpiece and was filled with a godly rage – not only was the subject matter a sassy jibe, but the needlework was undoubtedly better. She snatched the tapestry from her opponent's hands and ripped it to shreds. Taking the bits of material, she whacked Arachne continuously over the head with them. The mortal woman was filled with shame and scared senseless by the incensed goddess, running to a nearby tree and hanging herself to escape her wrath.

As Athena considered Arachne's lifeless body, she thought, *yeah, maybe that was a bit harsh*, and brought the girl back to life by transforming her into the very first spider. It's not clear whether Arachne was particularly pleased by her new form, but Athena decided that at least she'd be free to weave for the rest of her days.

AGAVE & AUTONOË
(*a-gay-vee* & *aw-ton-oh-nee*)

Remember the story of Semele, who was basically fried when Hera made Zeus appear to her in his true form? Well, she had three sisters – Agave, Autonoë and Ino. They were all members of the royal family of Thebes, with Agave being queen mother to the current king, Peritheus. Unlike the shy and trusting priestess Semele, these three sisters were greedy, caring only for power and riches. We've already heard the fate of Ino, the hater-stepmother-turned-sea-goddess.

When Semele died, Zeus was able to save the unborn child in her belly by sewing the babe into his own thigh until they were ready to be born. When the child was fully formed and detached from his father's leg, Zeus entrusted his care to some nymphs. This child grew up to be Dionysus, god of wine, fertility, religious ecstasy, and insanity. Once he was grown and established, the nymphs would become the first Maenads. Dionysus was very unhappy with the people of Thebes – Semele's own father, King Cadmus, spread the word that his daughter was murdered by Zeus after lying about having relations with him. With this in mind, there could *be* no child with the god, therefore no reason to acknowledge Dionysus' existence or respect and worship him.

Once he came of age, Dionysus arrived in Thebes ready to clear the name of his poor mother and punish the Thebans that denied his existence. By now, Peritheus had inherited the throne from Cadmus, who ruled with the same stock line as his gramps (aka, *Dionysus who??*) The god cursed Peritheus' mother and his aunt Autonoë with madness in retribution, turning them into Maenads.

When Peritheus heard reports of his mother and auntie acting strange, he claimed to be too busy to investigate, thinking, *meh, women be crazy*. What he did manage to do was order the arrest of the weird stranger claiming to be the cause. The outlaw was taken into custody, where Peritheus bound his arms and legs in chains. However, when he stepped back to admire his handiwork, he was surprised to see he'd actually chained up a bull. Frustrated, he stabbed at Dionysus over and over again, but the blade was met with thin air. Peritheus stomped away, still unwilling to accept he was dicing with the divine.

Meanwhile, the noble ladies of Thebes were causing absolute havoc in the throes of their madness, ripping cows' heads off and whatnot. Stories of them continued to reach the palace, and despite himself, Peritheus found his interest piqued. A cowherd arrived to tell the king about the women, how he'd witnessed them pierce rocks so that milk, honey, and wine flowed freely. Peritheus couldn't believe it, the idea that mere women could yield such power was wild to him. He had to see it.

Dionysus offered to help, and Peritheus accepted. He led his captor to the fields where the women were hanging out and guided him up into a nearby tree so that he could see properly. Once in situ, the king grumbled that the women looked fine – they were currently sitting around peacefully, mending their torn robes and making flower garlands for one another. Dionysus nodded his head in agreement and gave a whistle, alerting the women to their whereabouts. Their demeanour changed in the blink of an eye, as they stood and focused on the trespasser. Their mouths began to froth, their eyes rolled back in their heads, and they menacingly approached the tree that their king was perched upon. They began pelting stones at him, but he was too high to do any real damage. Peritheus was delighted that he was getting to experience the true horror of their sickness from this safe distance. His satisfaction soon wavered, though, as Agave and Autonoë began shaking his tree, eventually uprooting it enough to drag him down to earth. As Peritheus fell to the ground, he cried out to his mother to recognise him and forgive his errors, but his pleas fell on deaf ears as he was torn limb from limb by their bare hands. Agave was the one to decapitate him.

The two ladies returned to the city, telling anyone who'd listen the tale of how they'd just fought a lion. Agave, who was brandishing her son's head to the horrified onlookers, couldn't understand why everyone was being so hysterical over a dead lion. She called to Cadmus to look at what she'd accomplished, shouting that they simply must hang the head in the palace as a trophy. Her father couldn't bear the sight. Assuming that he was being unreasonably squeamish, she instead called out for her son, who she was sure would appreciate it more.

Cadmus, now older and wiser than he'd been at the time of his first daughter's passing, pulled Agave aside and revealed the situation as it really was. In her hands, the lion's head transformed into that of her son. With the madness lifted, the women were able to see what they had done. Cadmus decreed that their family had been harshly but rightly punished for their slight of the god.

Dionysus would later ascend to Olympian status, and the people of Thebes wouldn't dare disrespect him again.

DEMETER & PERSEPHONE
(de-meet-er & per-seff-oh-nee)

Demeter was an Olympian goddess, in charge of agriculture and the grain.

Compared to the other deities, she didn't have many rendezvous of the lustful variety, but she *did* have a special relationship with Iasion, a mortal. She fell for him hard during the wedding of Cadmus and Harmonia, and the pair had a truly deep connection. In fact, Iasion was the only human that Demeter felt comfortable being her full self around. Unfortunately for both of them, her big bro Zeus got wind of the affair and thought it inappropriate for such an important goddess to be having relations with a mere mortal (see: irony), so he struck and killed Iasion with a thunderbolt.

It'll come as no surprise to learn that Zeus thought himself a much more fitting match for Demeter. She refused his advances though, so he raped her. From this horrendous act, Demeter birthed her favourite daughter, Persephone. From the moment she was born, mother and daughter were pretty much inseparable. Persephone grew to be a beautiful, sweet young girl who was devoted to her mother. Knowing from personal experience how awful men could be, Demeter wanted nothing more for her daughter than a life of chastity.

One day, as Persephone picked flowers in a meadow with her nymph friends, the ground opened up beside her and she was snatched by Hades, ruler of the Underworld. Unbeknownst to Persephone or

Demeter, Hades had been watching the young woman and had fallen completely in love with her. He'd even requested Zeus' permission for his daughter's hand in marriage, though obviously didn't extend the same courtesy to Demeter. Zeus thought it was a great idea, though he was well aware of the close bond between mother and daughter, and warned Hades that he might have some issues. This is possibly why he chose his method of abduction – it all happened so fast that none of the nymphs could even tell Demeter what had happened. She was simply there one second and gone the next.

After her daughter's snatching, Demeter was inconsolable – she scoured the earth for Persephone but couldn't find a single trace. She was completely defeated, spending all her time mourning and neglecting her godly duties – crops began to wither, and nothing new would grow. Her good friend and confidante, the witch Hecate, saw her suffering and suggested she go to Helios – as the god of the sun, surely he would have seen what happened to her precious daughter that day. Demeter followed her advice, and Helios was finally able to give her the truth – her daughter had been abducted by Hades, who wanted her as his bride. Helios tried to reason with Demeter that Persephone's future as queen may be a good thing. Even he was aware of how devoted Hades was to his new beau, but Demeter wouldn't hear it. She ran straight to Zeus, telling him that she knew where their daughter was and wanted to know what he was going to do about it. Zeus had to come clean at this point and admit that he knew everything; what's more, that he'd given the abductor permission to take her in the first place.

Demeter couldn't believe what she was hearing – her sweet, beloved daughter had been taken against her will and was going to become queen of . . . *dead people?!* Demeter's legacy, after all, was fertile and living things, so this really had to sting. She stewed over what to do next, finally deciding that if nobody would help her retrieve

Persephone, she was going to retire her position. She transformed herself into an old woman and went down to earth to live life as though she were mortal.

Living amongst humans suited Demeter just fine. It wasn't long before she secured lodgings in the palace of Eleusis, where King Celeus and Queen Metanira hired her to be a nurse to their young sons. Although still heartbroken at the loss of her daughter, she took to the role like a duck to water. One day, the queen would be caught spying on the nanny. Demeter was furious at being snooped on, so she angrily quit her post and revealed her true identity. She instructed the people of Eleusis to build her a great shrine and taught them how to properly honour her there. Divine status restored, Demeter kicked back in luxury, but continued her constant grieving for many years.

By this point, earth was truly suffering from the actions (or lack thereof) of their harvest goddess – the land was barren, and humans were starting to die of starvation. Finally, this caught the attention of Zeus, who was particularly fond of his human playthings and was worried about their chances of survival. He sent each of the gods to Demeter's earthly abode, who were to offer her presents along with their pleas for her to get back to work. Demeter held her ground – gifts and prayers were of no use to her, all she wanted was her daughter back where she belonged. At last, Zeus accepted what he must do. He called on Hermes to travel to the Underworld and bring Persephone home to the heavens.

While all of this had been going on, Persephone was actually getting quite comfortable with her new life, enjoying the moody goth vibes of the Underworld palace that Hades had spent so many millennia perfecting. Although not the most romantic of starts, her relationship with the god of the dead had blossomed, and, unexpectedly, he really was quite the doting partner. Not to congratulate a man for abducting women and doing the absolute least, but despite Hades' dark demeanour and spooky job, he was actually a pretty nice guy, at least if you compare him to his brothers. It's said that by the time Hermes came to fetch Persephone, she didn't really want to go. On top of this, she had eaten six pomegranate seeds during her stay, and a very specific, very helpful rule said that anyone who consumed the food of the Underworld would not be able to leave. It's entirely possible of course that Persephone knew of this rule and gobbled up those seeds of her own accord. Both Hades and Demeter looked to Zeus for what would happen next. *Cue *gulp* from the big man.*

So, it was decided that Persephone's time would be split – because of the number of pomegranate seeds she had consumed, she would spend six months of every year above ground with her mother, and the remaining six with Hades, cooperatively ruling the Underworld. When the young queen travelled between the two realms, it was her mother's friend Hecate who accompanied her, along with the Lampades that she'd grown up with. During the time Demeter and her daughter were reunited, earth would thrive, but when they were apart, the land would once again become inhospitable. With this tale comes the creation of the seasons we have now – spring and summer mark Persephone's time on earth; autumn and winter are when she's down below. Before the abduction, there was only thought to have been three seasons (hence why there were only three Horae).

Hades and Persephone never had any children, but the consensus is that they lived quite happily as king and queen. Hades was always faithful to Persephone once they were married – something there's not much record of amongst his other godly friends and foes. As queen, she had quite a bit of influence over her territory, too, unlike her heavenly counterpart, Hera, who was more of a bystander next to her ruling husband.

Despite Demeter not being exactly thrilled with her new son-in-law, she wouldn't allow others to demean their relationship – when Hades' ex, Minthe, bragged that she was more beautiful than the new queen of the dead, Demeter trampled all over her and transformed her into a mint plant.

THEMIS (*th-eh-miss*)

A Titan goddess, Themis lives on to this day as Lady Justice, her image residing over judicial processes the world over. The personification of law and order, she is depicted holding a pair of scales for balance, and with a blindfold over her eyes to show impartiality. Back in the day, though, she was part of the uprising to overthrow her father, Uranus, when he got too big for his boots.

Saying that, when the time of the Titanomachy came around, Themis actually sided with the Olympians and was a lover of Zeus' for a bit. It's thought that Themis helped Zeus harness his powers and advised him on how to conduct his affairs (in life, not love). She would bear him many children, including the Fates and Horae. She was a seer, and some think that she may have created the oracle herself (though it's more popularly believed to be the work of Gaia).

She was a great help to the gods when it came to her prophecies. For example, she warned Zeus and Poseidon not to marry the goddess Thetis because she saw that she would bear a child that would grow up to be greater than its father (Achilles certainly was quite the man, but Peleus was happy enough coming second to him).

When Aphrodite came to Themis for advice on her son Eros, she admitted that she was worried he would stay a child forever, as he didn't seem to be growing at all. Themis prophesised that the reason for his stunted growth was loneliness, and she encouraged Aphrodite to give him a sibling. She did, in Anteros, the god of requited love, and the brothers grew heartily together.

She was also tasked with calling all the gods to Olympus to confer with Zeus when he needed a group vote on something, and she helped to raise Apollo, nursing him with the food of the gods so he could grow up big and strong.

Themis was highly logical and very fair – when Zeus' sacred birthplace, the Diktaean Cave, was raided by a motley crew for its divine honey, he was ready to thunderbolt the lot of them into next year. Themis, along with the Fates, reasoned with Zeus that should anyone die within the confines of his cave, it would be disrespectful to him. Zeus had to agree, instead transforming the group into various birds.

THISBE (*thiz-bee*)

In Babylon, there were two grand connected homes that housed families which were bitter rivals, their feud spanning generations. Despite the hatred that both households felt for each other, they still thought it apt to live in such close proximity, apparently. On one side lived Thisbe, the young daughter. In the other, a boy of around the same age, called Pyramus.

Through a crack in their interconnecting walls, the teenagers whispered sweet nothings to each other, dreaming of a life they'd never be able to have, for their families would never allow such a union. Eventually, the pair decided that they'd had enough of their families standing in the way of their true love, so they agreed that they would run away together and get married. They each made their preparations, planning to meet up under a nearby mulberry tree at the tomb of a Babylonian king.

Thisbe arrived first but found herself face to face with a lioness, whose jaws were soaked in ox blood from a recent kill. The animal's nose twitched at the thought of Thisbe as desert and she let out a low growl, calling the young woman into action. Thisbe fled the scene, accidentally dropping her veil in her urgency. The disappointed lioness sniffed at the garment and gave it a little nibble, smearing the ox blood onto it. When Pyramus arrived a few minutes later, the lioness was gone, but he was faced with the bloody veil and, more importantly, the absence of his love. Assuming Thisbe dead and blaming himself for luring her out there in the first place, he fell on his sword, joining her in death (or so he thought).

Thisbe returned a little while later, conscious of her tardiness and eager to tell Pyramus of her close encounter with the wild animal. Instead, she found his corpse, his flowing blood staining the white fruit of the mulberry tree, still clutching her veil. She took his sword and stabbed herself, looking into his eyes as she welcomed death. The gods, touched by their star-crossed love, permanently changed the white mulberry fruit to a deep red in their honour.

The feuding families rushed to the sight of the tragedy, where they were finally able to put their differences aside. Thisbe and Pyramus' ashes were mixed together and kept in one urn, so that finally they could be together.

CHIONE (*kai-own-nee*)

Daedalion, the brother-in-law of Alcyone, was a warmonger at heart. There was one thing he loved more than a bloody battle, though, and that was his daughter Chione.

Chione was ludicrously beautiful and is said to have had at least a thousand men desperate to make her their wife. However, her father wouldn't see her paired off with just anyone, and many potential suitors were considered and quickly discarded, ultimately not measuring up. Her magnetic pull wasn't limited to just mere mortals, either, and two gods in particular were enamoured with her.

Hermes had no interest in a traditional wooing of the beauty, instead walking straight up to Chione and touching her face with his wand, causing her to fall asleep. Then, he had his way with her without her knowledge. The same night, Apollo appeared to Chione as an old woman, and the pair slept together. There's limited information as to just how he seduced her in this form, but if that's what Chione was into, who are we to judge? As a result of her twice-godly relations, Chione found that she was pregnant by both of them. To Hermes, she gave birth to Autolycus, a renowned trickster, and to Apollo she had Philammon, a legendary musician.

By now, Chione was feeling pretty smug about being the object of so many mortal and divine affections, and she started to brag about it. She singled out the goddess Artemis in particular, boasting of how she must be so much more beautiful than even her, to attract so much attention. Despite having no interest in men, divine or otherwise, Artemis was thoroughly vexed by this hubristic statement, and thought she would teach Chione a lesson. Using her bow, she shot an arrow straight through the princess's wagging tongue. Artemis, proud but unsurprised by her clean shot, suspected Chione wouldn't go bad-mouthing her again.

Actually, Chione wouldn't do much of anything again, as she died of blood loss from the wound. At her funeral, Deadalion was so distraught that he tried to throw himself onto her funeral pyre no less than four times. Each time, though, he was restrained by others. In the end, he took a run and jump off Mount Parnassus. He still wouldn't be put to rest, though, as Apollo was watching and, feeling sympathy for the man, transformed him into a hawk.

LEUCIPPUS (*loo-sih-puss*)

When the mortal woman Galatea was pregnant, her husband, Lamprus, told her that he'd only acknowledge the child if she birthed him a son (and therefore an heir).

Lamprus was off on his travels when Galatea went into labour, and of course she had a baby girl. The new mother was torn – she loved her daughter immediately and fiercely, but worried greatly about her chances in the world as a girl. She also feared what her husband might do once he discovered that she had not given him the heir he'd hoped for. And so, Galatea gave the baby the typically masculine name of Leucippus and just . . . pretended. When Lamprus returned, she rejoiced with him that they now had a son to carry on their family name. Happy days – Lamprus was none the wiser.

Things went okay for a while, but soon enough puberty hit the young Leucippus like a truck. As her curves were uncovered and her breasts began to swell, it became increasingly hard for the pair of them to hide Leucippus' true identity from Lamprus. In desperation, Galatea went to a temple of the goddess Leto and prayed for her help and guidance. Prayers heard, Leto transformed Leucippus into a young man.

In later years, a festival would be established in both Leto and Leucippus' honour in Phaistos, Crete, where the family were thought to have lived. Every year, the residents would come together to feast and celebrate the transformation of Leucippus, as well as holding an initiation ceremony for their boys growing into men. During the rites, the youths would put on women's clothing and make an oath of citizenship to the community's *agela*, a place where they'd then go to live from the age of seventeen up until they got married. After the pledge, they'd shed their attire in a nod to the transition of Leucippus.

ANTIOPE & DIRCE
(an-tie-oh-pee & dir-see)

A different Antiope from the Amazonian queen, this one was a young woman of Boeotia, who was extremely beautiful and had great respect for her father. The usual tale: Zeus saw her beauty and decided that, as king of the heavens, he had a right to it. He transformed into a satyr (a nature spirit with the ears, legs, and tail of a horse) and raped her. Of course, because godly sperm was the most potent of all, Antiope became pregnant to her attacker. Terrified of what her father's reaction would be, she fled Boeotia and married the king of Sicyon, Epopeus. The newlyweds consummated their marriage quickly, and she got pregnant once again (while still in the early stages of her first pregnancy with Zeus). Antiope seemed to be settling in nicely to her new life in Sicyon, with Epopeus either unaware that one of the children she was carrying wasn't his, or otherwise happy to raise it as if it were, when her uncle, Lycus, came for her (this isn't the Lycus who was killed by Heracles in Megara's story, but he was just as much of a dick).

Lycus insisted that Antiope must return home on the order of her father. She told her uncle that she was happy where she was, and although she missed her father terribly, she would not go back. Lycus couldn't have that, so he grabbed Antiope by the scruff of her neck and dragged her the whole way home. On the journey, Antiope went into labour and gave birth to twins, Zethus and Amphion, the latter being the child of Zeus. Unsure of her fate, but expecting it wouldn't be good, Antiope abandoned the children, happy that they'd at least escape the cruelties of her family. The boys were picked up and raised by a shepherd. You'd be forgiven for thinking all of the herdsman in Ancient Greece were adoptive fathers at this point.

Before they arrived back at the palace, Lycus revealed that his brother, the king, had already killed himself due to the 'shame' Antiope had brought on their family by being a victim of Zeus' desire. Lycus was now ruling the kingdom, a titbit that he'd helpfully left out back in Sicyon. Rather than leave Antiope to her new life, Lycus wanted his niece close enough to taunt her. His wife and the current queen of the city, Dirce, had always hated Antiope, so the new king gave her the pleasure of dishing out Antiope's punishment. Dirce forced Antiope to be her slave for many years. Eventually, though, she managed to slip out of the kingdom and free herself of her tyrannical family. She ran as far as she could manage but eventually needed to rest. Knocking on the nearest door, she was invited into the home of two young men and their father, a local shepherd. The youths invited her to stay a while, and since she had nowhere to go anyway, Antiope agreed.

Sometime later, news reached the evil queen of Antiope's location, and she sent word to the shepherd's sons to hold her. They obeyed, as who were they to go against the monarchy. Sneaking up on Antiope, they bound her arms and legs, making her a prisoner once again. While the boys waited on Dirce, their father arrived home to the shocking scene. His sons explained the situation, while Antiope pleaded her case from the corner, and the shepherd had the good sense to put two and two together and figure out who this woman was. He revealed to the youths that he was not their real father, and that he'd actually adopted them after finding them abandoned in the wilderness. He knew, now, that the woman they had tied up in their living room was their birth mother. Antiope, dumbfounded, recounted to her sons how she thought she was doing the right thing for them, and that they'd have likely met quite a horrific end had she kept them with her. As everyone digested this turn of events, Dirce arrived at the house and found her niece exactly how she'd ordered – at her mercy. Or so she thought.

Happy to demand the violence, but unwilling to get her own hands dirty, Dirce commanded Zethus and Amphion to tie the prisoner to the horns of a wild bull and provoke it. What Dirce didn't expect was for the men to turn on her. They overpowered the queen and tied her to the bull instead. The ruthless Dirce was dragged to her death.

Rid of her tormenter and reunited with her sons, things seemed to be finally looking up for Antiope, but any relief or happiness she felt didn't last very long. Before her death, Dirce was a loyal follower of the god Dionysus, and he was super annoyed to lose her worship. To avenge her, he drove Antiope mad. In the grips of this affliction, Antiope aimlessly wandered around Greece for years, until she bumped into an abdicated king of Corinth, who was able to cure her of her mania and went on to marry her. Finally, the poor Antiope would have some years of peace before dying with her husband and being buried in the same grave as him.

LEUCOTHOE & CLYTIE
(*loo-coe-thow* & *klai-tee*)

Of Helios' various consorts, there was one particular lady who flipped his sunny world on its axis.

When he revealed the affair between Aphrodite and Ares to her husband, Hephaestus, the goddess of love wanted revenge. Aphrodite cursed Helios to fall madly in love with a young Babylonian princess named Leucothoe. He was so enamoured with the girl, that he made the winter days longer, just so he had more time to gaze upon her lovely face from afar. His other WAGS noticed the cold shoulder they were getting from Helios, and felt uneasy – when you've held the attention of the sun, it's hard to go back to living in the shadows. Clytie, an Oceanid, was particularly troubled by his absence.

Eventually, Helios grew tired of just looking, and decided it was time to make his move. He disguised himself as Leucothoe's mother and went to her chambers. Once inside, he dismissed her attendants and revealed himself to the princess. Leucothoe, for what it's worth, seemed happy enough with this surprising turn of events and basked in his glow for a little while.

Clytie, watching the affair unfold, was filled with jealousy, and felt she'd do just about anything to rid her lover of this absurd little crush of his. She went to Leucothoe's father, King Orchamus, and told him what his daughter had been up to. Angry that Leucothoe had dared show such promiscuousness, Orchamus buried her alive.

By the time Helios found out what had happened, it was too late. He tried desperately to revive her by shining his rays onto her skin, but she could not be brought back. Instead, he transformed her into a frankincense tree, so that she could thrive above ground and once again bathe in his light. As an added touch, he sprinkled the ground around her with sweet nectar.

Elsewhere, Clytie readied herself for their reunion. Now that she'd got rid of that drab princess, she assumed things would quickly go back to normal. In fact, she thought she'd now cemented herself as the favourite of all his consorts, after showing him such devotion. On the contrary, Helios now absolutely despised the Oceanid. Devastated, Clytie shed her clothes and sat for nine days without food or water, staring lovingly at him as he travelled across the sky. He never once returned her gaze.

Ultimately, Clytie turned into a heliotrope – a flower whose head always turns towards the sun.

THE DANAÏDES
(*dan-ay-uh-dees*)

Descendants of the ex-cow/lover of Zeus, Io, princes Danaus and Aegyptus were given land by their father when he passed. Danaus was gifted Libya, while Aegyptus took Egypt.

Both brothers would go on to father fifty children. Danaus had all daughters, known as the Danaïdes, and Aegyptus all sons, who didn't get a cool collective name. Where Danaus was happy enough with his lot in life, Aegyptus was desperate to extend his reign. He pressured his brother into setting his daughters up with their cousins, which would effectively give him control of Libya.

Danaus, aware of his brother's lust for power, wasn't keen. To avoid this fate, he prayed to Athena, who helped him to build the first ever ship, and the family sailed to Argos. At the palace, Danaus begged the king, Pelasgus, to hide and protect them. Pelasgus wasn't particularly eager to bring on the wrath of another kingdom, but his people urged their monarch to help the hapless brood.

Aegyptus and his sons were hot on their heels. Arriving in Argos, they demanded that the king hand Danaus and his daughters over, or they'd have no choice but to wage war on the protecting city. Just when it looked like all was lost, Danaus had an idea.

He told the Danaïdes that they were to go through with the weddings, but when they went to bed with their new husbands on the night of the nuptials, they were to kill them. As a macabre wedding gift, Danaus gave each daughter a knife to stash in their respective boudoirs. He asked that they each bring their husband's head to him the next day as proof of a job well done.

Danaus threw a lavish wedding for the combining families, making sure that Aegyptus and his sons got nice and drunk. That night, the fifty couples broke off to enjoy their first night of wedded bliss. As the husbands tried to get down to business, the wives whipped out their blades and slaughtered them. All of them, that is, except for Hypermnestra.

Danaus' eldest daughter had been particularly worried in the run-up. Not only was she expected to commit murder, but she also risked losing her virginity in the process. Hypermnestra blurted out to her husband, Lynceus, that she didn't want to go through with consummating their marriage. Much to the princess' surprise, Lynceus understood. Instead, they talked and, as the night crept on, found that they really did like each other. By morning, Hypermnestra was completely in love.

There was no way she could kill Lynceus. Instead, she admitted her father's gruesome plan, and urged him to flee the city. Lynceus heeded her warnings, escaping to a neighbouring town and lighting a beacon so Hypermnestra knew that he'd made it safely.

In the throne room, each of her sisters happily carried along with them a hacked-off head, but she was at the end of the queue empty-handed. Danaus was furious and demanded that she stand trial in front of the people of Argos.

The citizens once again took a logical approach – forty-nine out of fifty heads ain't bad, after all. What's more, Aphrodite herself appeared at the trial and testified in the young woman's defence, stating that true love should never be punished. Hypermnestra was acquitted of her crimes. Or, her absence of crimes. Whatever.

As for her sisters, they may have avoided their fate, but now Danaus had landed himself in the sticky situation of having fifty unwed offspring with a history of groom-decapitation.

Danaus decided to make his daughters a bit more appealing by announcing that they'd require no bridal gifts. With the promise of a significant amount of money saved, there were suddenly *too many* eligible bachelors tripping over themselves to marry the sisters. To make it fair, Danaus declared that the potential suitors would compete in a footrace. The winner of the race would get first pick of the daughters, the second would choose next, and so on. This way, all but two of them found husbands.

The first unmatched sister was, of course, Hypermnestra, who still pined for Lynceus. The second was Amymone, who had stumbled across a sleeping satyr some days before whilst collecting water from a stream. When the satyr awoke, he immediately tried to attack her, but Poseidon was nearby and heard Amymone's screams. Intervening, he took her as his consort.

Hypermnestra waited for Lynceus but suspected his fear of her father kept him away. The young woman begged Danaus to send word that there would be no acts of vengeance from his end, and Lynceus returned. The pair lived happily as husband and wife, producing a strong line of kings that would go on to rule Argos.

Despite being purified for their atrocities, once each of the Danaïdes (bar Hypermnestra) died, they would be punished for their crimes in the Underworld, having to constantly wash away their sins, but using a bucket with a permanent leak.

LAODAMIA (*lo-dame-ee-ya*)

Daughter of the wicked Astydameia and her husband Acastus, Laodamia would be given in marriage to Protesilaus, a well-respected Greek soldier.

Protesilaus was one of the many potential suitors of Helen of Sparta back in the day, so when the Trojan War broke out, he was duty-bound to join the fight. He and Laodamia had only just been married by this point, so it was a particularly wretched goodbye at the docks for them.

Protesilaus and his men, the Phylaceans, were the first to arrive in Troy and immediately got down to combat. They were not aware, however, of a prophecy that stated whoever was the first to step on Trojan soil would be the first to die from the Greek fleet. Protesilaus planted the first foot and, though he got four kills under his belt first, was indeed the opening fatality on their side.

When word got to Laodamia, she was inconsolable with grief. The gods, taking pity on the newlyweds, decided to allow Protesilaus to return from the Underworld to his wife, but only for three hours. Hermes was tasked with helping the soldier make the journey, and when Laodamia saw him approaching their home she was stunned but elated, assuming there had been some terrible misunderstanding and that he had come home to her, alive and well. Protesilaus explained the situation, and the pair were able to enjoy a few more precious hours together. When he was called back to his new home with Hades, though, Laodamia's grief returned tenfold.

In an effort to pacify her pain, Laodamia secretly had a bronze statue commissioned of her late husband, which she hid in her bedroom. Once stationed, she would ignore her day-to-day duties and spend all her time talking to the statue, pretending it was the real Protesilaus.

Soon after, one of the servants passed by her bedroom; sneaking a peek through a crack in the door, they saw Laodamia kissing and caressing her bronzed beau. They immediately assumed that she had taken a lover. The servant told Laodamia's father, who stormed into her bedroom to catch her in the act. When he saw his grieving daughter, Acastus was pained – it upset him to see Laodamia in such a state, but he couldn't allow this charade to continue, so ordered the servants to take the statue away and melt it down.

Laodamia wasn't willing to let go, though, and as the bronze liquified on the fire, she threw herself into the blaze to join her love in death.

SCYLLA OF MEGARA (*silla*)

When King Minos invaded Nisus' kingdom of Megara, he knew the odds were stacked against him. King Nisus had a lock of purple hair (punky) which gave him and the city he ruled over invincibility.

Luckily for Minos, Nisus' daughter, Scylla (*not* the nymph turned sea monster), saw the opposing king while hiding on top of the city walls and fell madly in love. Family ties be damned, Scylla knew she would do everything in her power to give Minos what he desired, so she sneaked up behind her father and secretly lopped the lock off. Then, she crept out of the palace, headed into the enemy camp, and handed it over to Minos, bracing herself for his thanks and returned devotion. Minos looked at the hair, then at the hopeful princess and curled his lip. He was absolutely disgusted by Scylla's act of betrayal against her own family and kingdom. Breaking her heart, he told her in no uncertain terms he would never endanger the people of Crete by bringing such a disgrace home as their queen. Scylla of course was devastated, even more so when Minos attacked the city and slaughtered her father.

As Minos and his soldiers returned to their ships to sail for home, Scylla jumped into the sea and tried to cling on to his vessel. Just then, an osprey appeared and began assaulting her, breaking the skin of her hands with its beak. The bird was actually Nisus, who had been transformed by the gods. As Scylla lost her grip on Minos' ship, she was also transformed into a bird, and the father-daughter duo would spend the rest of their lives relentlessly pecking at one another.

HERMIONE (*her-my-own-ee*)

As the only daughter of Helen and Menelaus, Hermione had quite the bumpy childhood.

The princess of Sparta was only nine years old when Paris and Helen bolted, and she was shipped off to her uncle Agamemnon's palace while her dad went to retrieve his wife. She'd be raised by Clytemnestra alongside her cousins Electra and Orestes – there was an arrangement for Hermione and Orestes to marry when they both came of age.

As we know, Orestes would be taken away from Mycenae for his own protection during the Trojan War, and it appears that absence very much made the heart grow fonder for Hermione. When the war was finally over, Hermione was looking forward to her nuptials tremendously.

When Helen returned to Sparta, she didn't even recognise her daughter. Then, Menelaus threw a curveball at her – he'd actually promised Hermione's hand to his fellow warrior, Neoptolemus. As the fallen hero Achilles' only son, it made sense that Menelaus would want to keep him on side, previous betrothal or not. Hermione was devastated, but it was done – she would leave as soon as possible for Pthia, where her husband-to-be was currently residing.

Hermione decided that she'd try to make the best of it – look at what the pursuit of 'true love' did for her mother, after all. Plus,

Orestes was too busy to marry her right now anyway, as he was repenting for the murder of his mother and Hermione's aunt, Clytemnestra.

Once the wedding was out of the way, though, Neoptolemus went straight back to his very public affair with the former princess of Troy, Andromache, who he'd taken as a slave after the war. Considering what a doting wife Andromache was to Hector, it's unlikely she was a particularly enthusiastic participant of this affair, but she was a slave, so didn't really have a say in the matter.

One day, years into their marriage, Neoptolemus was away in Delphi on business when who should show up but Hermione's ex-fiancé, Orestes. He sought Hermione out at the palace to reveal that he'd killed the king for stealing his sweetheart, and he was here to claim her once again. Hermione was thrilled, stopping only to give Andromache the finger before they boarded the ship back to Mycenae.

Hermione and Orestes were wed quickly and she was able to give him a son, Tisamenus.

CHARICLEA (*ca-ri-clay-a*)

After a decade of unsuccessfully trying to conceive a child, Queen Persinna of Aetheopia was over the moon to find out she was finally pregnant. When she went into labour, though, she gave birth to a white baby girl, even though she and her husband, Hydaspes, were both black. The reason for this was a case of maternal impressioning – during the conception, Persinna had found her gaze wandering over to a portrait of the princess Andromeda (wife of Perseus), from which her family descended. Andromeda was (and still is) almost always depicted as a white woman in art, despite the fact that as an Aetheopian queen, she would very likely have been black.

Persinna had never been unfaithful to her husband, but she knew exactly how this may have looked. Before Hydaspes returned, she bundled the babe up in a basket and ordered for it to be abandoned somewhere far away from the palace. Inside the child's blanket, Persinna tucked up a note explaining who she was, as well as a ring and a necklace that belonged to their family.

The baby would quickly be found and given to a Pythian priest called Charicles, who adopted her and named her Chariclea. The pair lived in Delphi, and though Charicles harboured the dream that she would grow up to marry his nephew, the girl decided to become a priestess of Artemis, meaning she would never take a husband.

Things ticked along for a while, until one day a group of Thessalians arrived for a festival. The leader of the party was a man called Theagenes, and as soon as Chariclea set eyes on him, she forgot every word of her vows. Theagenes felt the same about the young priestess, and they made a plan to escape their responsibilities and be together as husband and wife.

Under the cover of night, the lovers fled Delphi on a ship, but it wouldn't be smooth sailing. You could fill a twelve-book epic (and they did) with the trials and tribulations the couple faced over the next few years, from being captured several times, to their forced separation, and even some necromancy for good measure. Wherever they went, men were positively tripping over themselves to marry or at least bed the beautiful Chariclea, but she used her quick wit every time to thwart them, saving hers and her fiancé's skin by posing as his sister. Together they uncovered the truth of her heritage, but they didn't have time to even digest the news before they were captured once again.

This time, the couple wound up as prisoners for the Aetheopian king. Hydaspes planned to sacrifice the youths to appease the gods, and his people were super buzzed to witness it. As the captives were brought out to face the music, Chariclea cried out to the royal couple that she was their daughter and she could prove it. The king found the story quite fantastical and hard to believe at first, but when his wife hesitantly admitted what she did all those years ago, he had their servants bring down the portrait of Andromeda for a test. Indeed, the resemblance between Chariclea and Andromeda was undeniable. Next, Chariclea whipped out the ring and necklace that she had been abandoned with. (The servants wondered why she hadn't done that before they hefted that massive artwork down the palace steps, but they kept that musing to themselves.) Persinna's and Hydaspes' eyes brimmed with tears as they embraced their long-lost daughter at last.

'Anyway,' said the king, 'this has been lovely, truly it has. Now if you can just assume the position, we'll get to the killing.'

The citizens were expecting a sacrifice, after all, and what kind of king would he be if he didn't give the people what they wanted? Chariclea's and Theagenes' mouths hung open, but before they could plead for their lives, the courtyard was filled with commotion. The people of the kingdom were sure their princess returning to them was a miracle sent from the gods, and they wouldn't allow their king to kill her in front of them now. Hydaspes, reading the room, was like, 'ha ha, just kidding. I guess.'

Just as everything looked to be working out, Chariclea's adopted father Charicles arrived at the palace. He'd been looking everywhere for his daughter since that Thessalian scoundrel 'abducted' her. He couldn't quite believe his eyes when he saw Theagenes standing there, bold as brass, at the court of the king. The elderly man geared up to take a swing at the much bigger, much stronger youth, but before he could release the full force of his rage, Chariclea pulled her old dad into a hug and explained everything. The king and queen expressed their gratitude to Charicles, saying that they owed him big time for raising their daughter so well. With such a close call being thankfully avoided, the people of Aethiopia decided to banish the ritual of human sacrifices forever, replacing them with animal sacrifices.

With everything sorted out, there was nothing left to do but for the princess to marry her beloved Theagenes.

Further Reading

Madeline Miller
- Circe
- The Song of Achilles
- Galatea

Claire North
- Ithaca
- The House of Odysseus

Jennifer Saint
- Ariadne
- Elektra
- Atalanta

Susan Stokes-Chapman
- Pandora

NON-FICTION

More deets on the gods, goddesses and mortals.

Liv Albert
- Greek Mythology: The Gods, Goddesses & Heroes Handbook

Stephen Fry
- Mythos: The Greek Myths Retold
- Troy: Our Greatest Story Retold
- Heroes: Mortals & Monsters, Quests & Adventures

Natalie Haynes
- Divine Might: Goddesses In Greek Myth
- Pandora's Jar: Women in the Greek Myths

<u>CLASSICS</u>

These OG's are some of the foundation of everything we know about the myths today.

Aeschylus
- The Complete Plays

Aristophanes
- The Birds and Other Plays
- Lysistrata and Other Plays

Euripides
- Medea & Other Plays
- Electra & Other Plays
- The Baccae & Other Plays

Heliodorus of Emesa
- Aethiopica

Hesiod
- The Complete Works of Hesiod (Works & Days, The Theogony, The Catalogues of Women and EOIAE, The Shield of Heracles & Others)

Homer
- The Iliad
- The Odyssey

Ovid
- Heroides
- The Metamorphoses

Sappho
- Ode to Aphrodite: The Poems & Fragments of Sappho

Sophocles
- The Three Theban Plays (Antigone, Odedipus the King, Oedipus at Colonus)

<u>PODCASTS</u>

Something for your earholes to enjoy . . .

- DeMythifying (DeMythifying)
- Let's Talk About Myths, Baby! (Liv Albert/ iHeartPodcasts)
- Mythology (Spotify Studios)
- Natalie Haynes Stands Up for the Classics (BBC Radio 4)
- The Ancients (History Hit)

Acknowledgements

This book has been a constant in my life for years now, either as an idea, an ongoing project or an actual, real *thing* that I now have to put out into the world and hope people like. Though I've spent countless hours discussing and arguing with myself over *Bad Girls*, there are a lot of people that, without their support and insight, this book would never have been.

My daughter Bella, who by taking up residence within me gave me time to write, but also a whole new reason to put it out there. This is for you and because of you.

My husband Andy, who was always on hand to listen to me whinge, help me work out timelines, and selflessly watch the football of a night instead of our shows while I worked. Thank you for always supporting and loving me.

The Bad Girls from my own life - my mam, who always blindly believed I'd do something great despite having no evidence to back it up. Norma, for being mam #2. My hype girls, Joanna, Michael and Naomi, for always being there to bounce ideas and vibes off. My brother Adam (aka Specky) for fulfilling the true job of a younger sibling, namely knowing how 'techy' things work and making me look better for it.

Special mention to my firstborn son, King the staffy, for being my constant writing companion and providing the soothing tones of his snoring throughout.

To the Viney agency, especially my agent Amberley Lowis, who was the first person in the biz to believe in *Bad Girls*. You truly saw my mad ramblings and said "I'll take it!".

To the whole team at HarperNorth, who are doing fantastic things for Northern writers, particularly Megan Jones, who is truly the most patient gal I know - thank you for taking a chance on me, and for being as excited about this book as I am. Thanks to Laura Brett for creating the coolest front cover I could have ever hoped for.

Lastly, thank you to the women leading the resurgence of mythological storytelling through a female lens. Long may it last, because I'm certainly not finished talking about it yet!